Trends in Modern Banking

Prof. S. S. Prasada Rao
Dr. R. Radhika

BSP **BS Publications**
A unit of **BSP Books Pvt. Ltd.**
4-4-309/316, Giriraj Lane, Sultan Bazar,
Hyderabad - 500 095.
Phone : 040 - 23445605, 23445688

Disclaimer

The Publisher and Organisers do not claim any responsibility for the accuracy of the data, statements made, and opinions expressed by authors. The authors are solely responsible for the contents published in the paper.

Published by

BSP **BS Publications**
A unit of **BSP Books Pvt. Ltd.**
4-4-309/316, Giriraj Lane, Sultan Bazar,
Hyderabad - 500 095
Phone : 040 - 23445605, 23445688
e-mail : info@bspbooks.net

ISBN: 978-93-5230-129-4 (HB)

Preface

National Conference on Contemporary Issues on Banking and Finance conducted on 20th November at the HBS campus evinced enormous interest from industry, academicians and media persons alike.

It also received active participation and support from researchers and students from across the country. The conference was inaugurated by prominent personages from the industry and academia. The Chief Guest for the conference was **Sri. P.V. Krishna Rao**, General Secretary, Indian Bank Employees Union AP and Guest of Honor was **Mr. Meher Pradeep,** Vice President, BNP Paribas Employees Federation.

The National conference invited papers and participation from across the country and the response was humungous. The papers were received from researchers, students and academicians from Ahmedabad, Goa, Noida and many other places. After a thorough screening process, papers that met the quality standards were shortlisted for publication and selected authors were invited to present at the conference.

Most of the papers presented by the authors focused on the influence and impact of technology adoption on the delivery of banking and allied financial services. These included in-depth papers on specific current practices and upcoming technological trends like the following: Problem & Prospects of E-Banking In India, A Study of Channel Innovations & their Impact in Indian Banking, The Role of Cryptographic Algorithms in The Banking Industry, Problems & Prospects of Mobile Banking in India, A Study on Indian Public Sector Banks regarding Linkage b/w ATMs, credit & debit cards & Employee Productivity, etc.

Overall, the conference was a success in terms of the response received from various quarters as well as from the ensuing participation. Students and participants were very appreciative of the learning derived and for getting a much more comprehensive understanding of the inner workings of the banking industry. They also displayed enthusiasm for directly interacting with the leading professionals in the industry and understanding the opportunities and challenges.

It is felt that publishing the Conference Proceedings will immensely benefit all the banking industry stake holders, namely, aspiring professionals, students and the incumbents in the industry to keep themselves abreast of the developments. We are confident that this effort of bringing out selected papers as an edited volume will be well received and utilized by the banking fraternity.

Prof. S. S. Prasada Rao

Dr.R. Radhika

Contents

Trends in Modern Banking

EVOLUTION OF INDIAN BANKING INDUSTRY AND ITS PRESENT STATUS

Globally, Banking evolved with the moneylenders accepting deposits and issuing receipts in their place. Money lending activity in India could be traced back to the Vedic period, *i.e.*, 2000 to 1400 BC. The existence of professional banking in India could be traced to the 500 BC. *Kautilya's Arthashastra*, dating back to 400 BC contained references to creditors, lenders and lending rates. Banking was fairly varied and catered to the credit needs of the trade, commerce, agriculture as well as individuals in the economy. Mr. W.E. Preston, member, Royal Commission on Indian Currency and Finance set up in 1926, observed "....it may be accepted that a system of banking that was eminently suited to India's then requirements was in force in that country many centuries before the science of banking became an accomplished fact in England." An extensive network of Indian banking houses existed in the country connecting all cities/towns that were of commercial importance. They had their own inland bills of exchange or *hundis* which were the major forms of transactions between Indian bankers and their trans-regional connections. Banking practices in force in India were vastly different from the European counterparts. The dishonoring of *hundis* was a rare occurrence. In fact, the classic '*Arthashastra*' also had norms for banks going into liquidation. If anyone became bankrupt, debts owed to the State had priority over other creditors.

I must say that history beckons us to not to mimic the western banking structure and practices blindly but to have an innovative banking structure for serving a billion of our country men and women.

In reality we lost our traditional institutions of banking and their practices during British rule, as the beginning of commercial banking of western variety of joint stock banking was brought to India by the English Agency houses of Calcutta and Bombay (now Kolkata and Mumbai). The first bank of a joint stock variety was Bank of Bombay, established in 1720 in Bombay. This was followed by Bank of Hindustan in Calcutta, which was established in 1770 by an agency house.

The first Indian owned bank was the Allahabad Bank set up in Allahabad in 1865, the second, Punjab National Bank was set up in 1895 in Lahore, and the third, Bank of India was set up in 1906 in Mumbai. All these banks were founded under private ownership. The *Swadeshi* Movement of 1906 provided a great impetus to joint stock banks of Indian ownership and many more Indian commercial banks such as Central Bank of India, Bank of Baroda, Canara Bank, Indian Bank, and Bank of Mysore were established between 1906 and 1913. By the end of December 1913, the total number of reporting commercial banks in the country reached 56 comprising 3 Presidency banks, 18 Class 'A' banks (with capital of greater than Rs.5 lakh), 23 Class 'B' banks (with capital of Rs.1 lakh to 5 lakh) and 12 exchange banks.

The World War I and subsequent great depression had an impact on the Indian banking industry with the number of banks failing rising sharply due to their loans going bad. Most of the small banks were local in character and had low capital base. As a result, they were not resilient enough. Apart from the global factors, one of the major reasons for failures of small banks was fraudulent manipulation by directors and managers and inter-connected lending. Also, several banks that failed had combined trading functions with banking functions. Partly, in order to address the problem of bank failure, the Reserve Bank was set up in 1935. In fact, central banks in several other countries, including the US, were also set up to address the problem of bank failure. However, the Reserve Bank had a limited control over banks and lack of an appropriate regulatory framework posed a problem of effective regulation of small banks. By the end of this phase, the country's financial requirements were still catered to, in a large measure, by the unorganised sector. The focus of the banking sector was on urban areas and the requirements of agriculture and the rural sector were neglected. Although the co-operative credit movement had a very encouraging beginning, it did not spread as expected despite Government patronage.

THE HISTORY OF INDIAN BANKING CAN BE DIVIDED INTO THREE MAIN PHASES.

Phase I (1786-1969)-Initial phase of banking in India when many small banks were set up.

Phase II (1969- 1991) - Nationalization, regularization and growth.

Phase III (1991 onwards) - Liberalization and its aftermath.

The banking scenario that prevailed in the early independence phase faced three main issues.

First, bank failures had raised the concerns regarding the soundness and stability of the banking system.

Second, there was large concentration of resources from deposits mobilisation in a few hands of business families or groups. Banks raised funds and on-lent them largely to their controlling entities.

Third, agriculture was neglected in sofar as bank credit was concerned. In order to address the issue of bank failures, the Banking Companies Act (renamed as Banking Regulation Act in March 1966) was enacted in 1949 empowering the Reserve Bank to regulate and supervise the banking sector. Banks continued to fail even after the Independence and the enactment of the Banking Companies Act, although the number of banks that failed declined.

It was, therefore, felt that it would be better to wind up insolvent banks. The Reserve Bank, therefore, was granted powers in the early 1960s for consolidation, compulsory amalgamation and liquidation of small banks. Although some banks had amalgamated before 1960s, the number of banks amalgamating rose sharply between 1960 and 1966. Several other small banks otherwise also ceased to function. The Reserve Bank was fairly successful in improving the safety and soundness of the banking sector as several weak banks (most of which were non-scheduled) were weeded out through amalgamations/liquidations.

The deposit insurance was also introduced, which increased the trust of the depositors in the banking system and encouraged deposit mobilisation. In early years of banking in India there were thus several instances which suggest that the small and weak banks struggled to survive. Even in recent years, it is several small banks that have merged with the large banks.

Another feature that emerges from the evolution of banking till the end of this phase was that despite the existence of small banks, a large segment of the population remained outside the banking system. In other words, the existence of small banks did not necessarily promote financial inclusion.

On the eve of independence, the banking system was concentrated primarily in the urban and metropolitan areas. Efforts, therefore, were made to spread banking to rural and unbanked areas, especially through the State Bank of India and through the branch licensing policy. The number of bank branches rose significantly between 1951 and 1967, as a result of which the average population per branch fell from 1,36,000 in 1951 to 65,000 in 1969. However, the pattern of bank branches in rural and urban areas remained broadly the same.

Although the Indian banking system had made considerable progress in the 1950s and the 1960s, the benefits of this did not percolate down to the general public in terms of access to credit. This was primarily due to the nexus between banks and industrial houses that cornered bulk of bank credit, leaving very little for agriculture and small industries. Efforts, therefore, were made to increase the flow of credit to agriculture.

However, the share of agriculture in total bank credit remained broadly at the same level between 1951 and 1967. In this period, various objectives such as enhancing the deposit rates, while keeping the cost of credit for productive activities at a reasonably low level led to a complex structure of interest rates and other micro controls.

The second phase after independence (1967 to 1991-92) was characterised by several social controls over the banking sector. The major issue faced at the beginning of this phase was the strong nexus between banks and industry, as a result of which agriculture was ignored. The focus in this phase was, thus, to break the nexus and improve the flow of credit to agriculture. The main instruments used for this purpose were nationalisation of major banks in the country and priority sector lending.

These initiatives had a positive impact in terms of spread of the bank-branch network across the country, which in turn, accelerated the process of resource mobilisation. As a result of rapid branch expansion witnessed from 1969, the average population per bank office, which was 65,000 at the time of nationalisation, declined to 14,000 by end-December 1990. Large branch expansion also resulted in increase in deposits and credit of the banking system, especially in rural areas. The share of credit to agriculture in total bank credit increased from 2.2 per cent in 1967 to 15.8 per cent in June 1989.

However, these achievements extracted a price in terms of health of banking institutions. Banks did not pay adequate attention to their profitability, asset quality and soundness. The increase in credit to the priority sector led to the reduction of credit to the other sectors. Attempts were, therefore, made to bring some financial discipline in respect of credit to the corporate sector. However, norms stipulated for the purpose were found to be too rigid. On the other hand, in order to meet the priority sector targets, credit appraisal standards were lowered. The high statutory pre-emptions eroded the profitability of the banking sector. Lack of enough competition resulted in decline in productivity and efficiency of the system.

At the end of this phase, banks were saddled with large non-performing assets. Banks' capital position turned weak and they lacked the profit motive. During this period, the deposit and lending rate structure became very complex. By the early 1980s, the banking sector had transformed from a largely private owned system to the one dominated by the public sector.

In the mid-1980s, some efforts were made to liberalize and improve the profitability, health and soundness of the banking sector. This phase also saw some diversification in banking activities.

The most significant phase in the evolution of banking was the phase of financial sector reforms that began in 1991-92, which had two sub-phases (1991-92 to 1997-98; and 1998-99 and beyond).

The main issues faced in the first sub-phase (1991-92 to 1997-98) was the weak health of the banking sector, low profitability, weak capital base and lack of adequate competition. The reforms in the initial phase, thus, focused on strengthening the commercial banking sector by applying prudential norms, providing operational flexibility and functional autonomy and strengthening the supervisory practices.

To infuse competition in the banking sector, several measures were initiated such as allowing the entry of private banks into the system. A major achievement of this phase was significant improvement in the profitability of the banking sector. Some improvement was also observed in the asset quality, capital position and competitive conditions, although there was still a significant scope for further improvement. However, banks in this phase developed risk aversion as a result of which credit expansions slowed down in general and to the agriculture in particular.

The focus in the second sub-phase (1998-99 and beyond) was on further strengthening of the prudential norms in line with the international best practices, improving credit delivery, strengthening corporate governance practices, promoting financial inclusion, strengthening the urban co-operative banking sector and improving the customer service. While strengthening the prudential norms, it was necessary to ensure that risk aversion, which had surfaced in the previous sub-phase, did not aggravate.

Focused attention, therefore, was paid to put in place appropriate institutional measures to enable banks to recover their NPLs. The impact of these measures was encouraging as banks were able to bring down their non-performing assets sharply. This was the most important achievement of this phase. As the asset quality began to improve, banks also started expanding their credit portfolio. Capital position of banks also improved significantly. Competition intensified during this phase as was reflected in the narrowing down of margins. Despite this, however, banks slightly improved their profitability among others, due to increased volumes and improvement in asset quality.

Two concerns arose with regard to corporate governance practices followed by banks. These related to concentrated ownership and quality of management that controlled the banks. The corporate governance practices were, therefore, strengthened.

Another major achievement in this phase was the sharp increase in the flow of credit to the agriculture and SME sectors. With a view to bringing a larger segment of excluded population within the banking fold, banks were advised to introduce a facility of 'no frills' account. About 13 million `no frills' accounts were opened in a short span of two years.

With the reforms in Phase III the Indian banking sector, as it stands today, is mature in supply, product range and reach, with banks having clean, strong and transparent balance sheets. The major growth drivers are increase in retail credit demand, proliferation of ATMs and debit-cards, decreasing NPAs due to Securitization, improved macroeconomic conditions, diversification, interest rate spreads, and regulatory and policy changes (e.g., amendments to the Banking Regulation Act).

Certain trends like growing competition, product innovation and branding, focus on strengthening risk management systems, emphasis on technology have emerged in the recent past. In addition, the impact of the Basel II norms is going to be expensive for Indian banks, with the need for additional capital requirement and costly database creation and maintenance processes. Larger banks would have a relative advantage with the incorporation of the norms.

The major challenges faced by banks today are as to how to cope with competitive forces and strengthen their balance sheet. Today, banks are groaning with burden of NPA's. It is rightly felt that these contaminated debts, if not recovered, will eat into the very vitals of the banks. Another major anxiety before the banking industry is the high transaction cost of carrying Non Performing Assets in their books.

The resolution of the NPA problem requires greater accountability on the part of the corporate, greater disclosure in the case of defaults, an efficient credit information sharing system and an appropriate legal framework pertaining to the banking system so that court procedures can be streamlined and actual recoveries made within an acceptable time frame. The banking industry cannot afford to sustain itself with such high levels of NPA's thus, "lend, but lent for a purpose and with a purpose ought to be the slogan for salvation."

The Indian banks are subject to tremendous pressures to perform as otherwise their very survival would be at stake. Information technology (IT) plays an important role in the banking sector as it would not only ensure smooth passage of interrelated transactions over the electric medium but will also facilitate complex financial product innovation and product development. The application of IT and e-banking is becoming the order of the day with the banking system heading towards virtual banking.

As an extreme case of e-banking World Wide Banking (WWB) on the pattern of World Wide Web (WWW) can be visualized. That means all banks would be interlinked and individual bank identity, as far as the customer is concerned, does not exist. There is no need to have large number of physical bank branches, extension counters. There is no need of person-to-person physical interaction or dealings. Customers would be able to do all their banking operations sitting in their offices or homes and operating through internet. This would be the case of banking reaching the customers.

Banking landscape is changing very fast. Many new players with different muscle powers will enter the market. The Reserve Bank in its bid to move towards the best international banking practices will further sharpen the prudential norms and strengthen its supervisor mechanism. There will be more transparency and disclosures. In the days to come, banks are expected to play a very useful role in the economic development and the emerging market will provide ample business opportunities to harness. Human Resources Management is assuming to be of greater importance. As banking in India will become more and more knowledge supported, human capital will emerge as the finest assets of the banking system. Ultimately banking is people and not just figures.

India's banking sector has made rapid strides in reforming and aligning itself to the new competitive business environment. Indian banking industry is the midst of an IT revolution. Technological infrastructure has become an indispensable part of the reforms process in the banking system, with the gradual development of sophisticated instruments and innovations in market practices.

Despite significant progress made by banking industry as a whole, still we are hampered by inadequate coverage of the banking and financial sectors. I will explain you further. We are having 157 domestic banks operating in the country [comprising 26 Public Sector Banks, 7 New Private Sector Banks, 13 Old Private Sector Banks, 43 Foreign Banks, 4 Local Area Banks (LABs), and 64 RRBs], just about 40 per cent of the adults had formal bank accounts. Deepening the engagement of formal banking for low income households and providing access to the unbanked would require increasingly innovative approaches (including channels, products, interface, etc.).

In order to address the above issues, Nachiket Mor committee was set up in 2013, to look into the issues relating to financial inclusion and Comprehensive Financial Services for Small Businesses and Low-Income Households. The committee came up with two broad designs for the banking system in the country - the Horizontally Differentiated Banking System (HDBS) and the Vertically Differentiated Banking System (VDBS) based on the functional building blocks of payments, deposits and credit.

In a HDBS design, the basic design element remains a full-service bank that combines all three building blocks of payments, deposits, and credit but is differentiated primarily on the dimension of size or geography or sectoral focus. In a VDBS design, the full-service bank is replaced by banks that specialise in one or more of the building blocks of payments, deposits, and credit. Among others, the Committee suggested licensing of Payments Bank and Small Finance Banks.

PAYMENT BANKS

Payment system has been proving to be the arena where new ideas, products and services have been successfully introduced. Starting from the Real Time Gross Settlement System (RTGS), the National Electronic Funds Transfer (NEFT) system, the Pre and Post Paid Instruments, the card present and absent transactions, the different types of e-wallets and to the mobile banking products, we have been experiencing a payment revolution in our country.

The objective of setting up of payments banks will be to further financial inclusion; the strategies will be by providing (i) small savings accounts and (ii) payments/remittance services to migrant labour workforce, low income households, small businesses, other unorganised sector entities and other users. The scope of the activities permitted for the Payment Banks included:

(a) Acceptance of demand deposits. Payments bank will initially be restricted to holding a maximum balance of Rs. 100,000 per individual customer

(b) Issuance of ATM/debit cards

(c) Payments and remittance services through various channels

(d) BC of another bank and

(e) Distribution of non-risk sharing simple financial products like mutual fund units and insurance products, etc.

As you can see, the scope has been carefully crafted to sub-serve the primary objective of furthering financial inclusion. It is also being insisted that the Payment Bank should be a fully networked and technology driven institution. Though it is very early to comment on the success of payment banks, we can be safely bet that the Payment Banks will further revolutionise the payment arena.

SMALL FINANCE BANKS

A parallel major disruptive innovative change for inclusive growth will be the advent of Small Finance Banks. Smaller banks have greater access to local information, greater commitment to local prosperity, differences in costs and risk management, and competition policy could explain the specific influence of such type of banks on local economic development. In developing countries where economic development is hampered by insufficient and inadequate access to financial services in rural areas, small banks could improve financing opportunities to small and medium size enterprises and encourage entrepreneurship.

Thank you friends, for your patient hearing about the evolution and present status of Indian Baking Industry. Now we will focus on the future of banking industry and try to visualize the vital aspects which will play major role in shaping up banks of tomorrow.

We can broadly categorize the future of banking industry depends on 6 main pillars.

REGULATION & CAPITAL

You are well aware that, RBI is the main regulator of Indian Banks and FIs. RBI uses the following tools to regulate banking business in this country.

- Licensing
- Prescribing capital requirements
- Monitoring governance
- Setting prudential regulations to ensure solvency and liquidity of the banks
- Prescribing lending to certain priority sectors of the economy

I have already touched upon the new vistas opened by RBI in introducing Payment banks and Small Finance banks to bring in new methods in speeding up financial inclusion and payment systems.

Another major area in regulation of banks is prescribing capital requirements for banks. Here RBI the regulator, follows the code of BCSBI, popularly known as basel norms. We have already travelled from Basel I to Basel II and at present our banks are in the midst of implementation of Basel III norms.

Basel III framework was basically the response of the global banking regulators to deal with the factors, more specifically those relating to the banking system that led to the global economic crisis or the great recession. In the advanced economies, there was a huge fiscal cost for protecting the financial system, which those governments did not want a repeat of. The framework therefore sought to increase the capital and improve the quality thereof to enhance the loss absorption capacity and resilience of the banks, brought in a leverage ratio to contain balance sheet expansion in relation to capital, introduced measures to ensure sound liquidity risk management framework in the form of liquidity coverage ratio (LCR) and net stable funding ratio (NSFR), modified provisioning norms and of course enhanced disclosure requirements.

In India, Basel III capital regulation has been implemented from April 1, 2013 in phases and it will be fully implemented as on March 31, 2019. Further, we have also introduced Basel III Liquidity Coverage Ratio (LCR) to be implemented by banks in India from January 1, 2015 with full implementation being effective from January 1, 2019.

Let us ponder over the challenges posed in implementing Basel III norms and the changes it will bring in. Any change, big or small, of whatever nature brings with it challenges. The issue one must look at is whether the challenges are as onerous as one would think them to be and whether the challenges are worth facing up to.

The first element in this debate was whether we needed Basel III at all for a country like India. On this, Dr. Subba Rao, the then Governor of RBI[1] made an interesting point and I quote him:

"One view, although not explicitly spelt out in that form, is that India need not adopt Basel III, or should adopt only a diluted version of it, so as to balance the benefits against the putative costs. To buttress this view, it is argued that Basel III is designed as a corrective for advanced economy banks which had gone astray, often times taking advantage of regulatory gaps and regulatory looseness, and that Indian banks which remained sound through the crisis should not be burdened with the 'onerous' obligations of Basel III.

The Reserve Bank does not agree with this view. Our position is that India should transit to Basel III because of several reasons. By far the most important reason is that as India integrates with the rest of the world, as increasingly Indian banks go abroad and foreign banks come on to our shores, we cannot afford to have a regulatory deviation from global standards. Any deviation will hurt us both by way of perception and also in actual practice.

The 'perception' of a lower standard regulatory regime will put Indian banks at a disadvantage in global competition, especially because the implementation of Basel III is subject to a "peer group" review whose findings will be in the public domain.

Deviation from Basel III will also hurt us in actual practice. We have to recognize that Basel III provides for improved risk management systems in banks. It is important that Indian banks have the cushion afforded by these risk management systems to withstand shocks from external systems, especially as they deepen their links with the global financial system going forward."

To sum up, adoption of Basel norms are very crucial though requirement of capital from PSBs is huge and major share should be met by Government of India.

TECHNOLOGY & INNOVATION

Technology was identified by banks as a crucial element in their strategy to improve productivity and render efficient customer service. The computerisation of bank operations in a big way began in the early 1990s following the agreement between the Indian Banks' Association (IBA) and employees. Over the years, the use of technology increased significantly.

These early steps slowly improved to total computerization of banking operations especially on the advent of new private sector banks. PSBs who were lagged behind in adopting new technologies slowly but steadily progressed in technology arena.

Now time has come for moving further in technology wave and new digital India. The rush to move into digital banking is very visible across all major banks in India.

Retail banks across the globe have adopted digital technologies — be it internet banking or mobile/smartphone banking — to improve operational efficiency and the ability to manage customers. In parts of Asia with a significant millennial demographic, banks have successfully managed to motivate their customers to go digital. For example, in countries like South Korea, Singapore, Australia and Hong Kong, over 90% of banking customers are digital and interact with their banks via digital channels. Nations like Malaysia, Thailand and Indonesia are beginning to catch up with digital adoption rates of 30-40%.

With digital banking penetration of just 15-18 per cent, India still has a lot of ground to cover. However, the fact that India has the highest internet user base after the US and China, and very high mobile phone penetration also represents an upside for banks.

Digital technologies present a huge opportunity for Indian banks to not just deepen customer relationships, but also expand their customer base. Banks are able to understand their customers better, online. They have greater insight into spend patterns, investment records, mortgage payments and so much more about their customers' lifestyles. Overlay broader browsing behaviours, and banks can create a close-to-perfect personal of the user to effectively cross-sell more banking products. Hyper-personalisation is no longer an abstract technology — it is already feeding customised promotional offers. While devising and implementing digital banking strategies, banks must look at operational and cost efficiencies as well as the speed and convenience of services.

Digital banking is also turning out to be a very effective tool to increase customer base. A case in point is the jan dhan yojana. Launched last year with the goal of opening a bank account for every household for greater financial inclusion, it has resulted in a whopping 125 million new bank accounts. In order to unearth the wealth at the bottom of the pyramid, banks should look at tapping this vast number of account holders and interacting with them in simple and cost-effective ways.

The low penetration of digital banking in India is largely owing to cultural and trust issues. While India is still a largely cash-based economy, more important is the trust factor. There is an inherent suspicion or lack of comfort in going digital and interacting with a 'virtual' bank. Many customers are still more comfortable walking down to their neighborhood banks and find security in having a physical entity safeguard their savings. This is a significant barrier.

A contrast of sorts is presented by the e-commerce industry in India, which has transformed the retail industry and growing at an impressive 30-40 per cent every year. Customers no longer hesitate to shop online, armed as they are with multiple payment options. Key among them is cash on delivery, which accounts for around 75 per cent of online transactions in India and has helped e-commerce players build consumer trust. Banks also need to think innovatively about ways in which to win new customers and build relationships.

CUSTOMER SERVICE

Retail banks today are under pressure to improve their quality of service, while also reducing costs to remain competitive in an extremely volatile and uncertain market. Improving customer service is imperative for banks in the current market and economic scenario, where product and price no longer provide a clear competitive edge. Distribution channels play a key role in delivering an enhanced customer experience as customer interactions begin and end with channels.

Banking customers are increasingly expecting more convenience, accessibility, personalization, and reliability across the distribution channel network. Banks need to deliver these features by leveraging innovative technologies and solutions for a seamless and personalized experience. There is a clear demand for banks to invest in their channel networks to make them more customer-centric and user-friendly, while in the process improving the channel efficiencies for better return on investment and increased profitability.

These changes have led to the emergence of five key trends across retail banking channels

- Increased online market presence using advanced technology platforms such as Web 2.0 and social networks.
- Investment in enterprise mobile financial service solutions to drive innovation and reduce costs.
- Increased push towards web-based activities to put the online channel on an equal footing with branch networks.
- More emphasis on seamless multi-channel integration to better serve clients and gain competitive edge.
- Increased spending on customer analytics tools to improve customer relationships.

While banks will have to overcome the above challenges, Web 2.0 technologies can help firms realize the full potential of their online platforms by creating new possibilities for enhanced communication with their clients. For example, banks can start blogs or forums to discuss new products or services with clients, or participate in social networks to increase transparency and foster customer loyalty. Web 2.0 can also help banks reduce their overall channel costs by opening up significant opportunities to sell complex products and services through the online channel, resulting in faster turn around and much lower operational costs.

RISK MANAGEMENT

Risk is inevitable in the banking business and hence, a sound risk management framework is the touchstone of an efficient bank. The risk management effectively aims at balancing the Risk-Return Trade-off which is “maximizing return for a given risk” and “minimizing risk for a given return”. The responsibility of setting a risk appetite for the bank as a whole is that of the Board and the Top Management. In practice, however, we seldom see the articulation of an objective risk appetite statement by the PSBs. If you haven’t set out a risk limit for each type of risk that the bank runs and an aggregate risk appetite for the bank as a whole, how do you measure and monitor risk? We must understand that risk management is integral to the success of the bank and hence, the Top Management should strive to put in place an efficient risk management framework keeping in view the changing market dynamics and the regulatory prescriptions.

ASSET QUALITY

Though on the whole, the banking system has remained resilient, asset quality has seen sustained pressure due to continued economic slowdown. The levels of gross non-performing advances (GNPAs) and net NPAs (NNPAs) for the system have been elevated. As on March 15, while the GNPAs have increased to 4.45% for the system as a whole, the NNPAs have also climbed up to 2.36%. When seen in isolation, the NPA ratios do not appear very distressing; however, if we add the portfolio of restructured assets to the GNPA numbers, this rises alarmingly. Stressed Assets Ratio (Gross NPA+ Restructured Standard Advances to Gross Advances) for the system as a whole stood at 10.9% as at the end of March 2015. The level of distress is not uniform across the bank groups and is more pronounced in respect of public sector banks. The Gross NPAs for PSBs as on March 2015 stood at 5.17% while the stressed assets ratio stood at 13.2%, which is nearly 230 bps more than that for the system.

It is pertinent here to also note the observations made in the Global Financial Stability Report released by IMF recently. Referring to the high levels of corporate leverage, the report highlights that 36.9% of India's total debt is at risk, which is among the highest in the emerging economies while India's banks have only 7.9% loss absorbing buffer, which is among the lowest. While these numbers might need an independent validation, regardless of that, it underscores the relative riskiness of the asset portfolio of the Indian banks.

In addition to present steps which are in vogue to improve the system's ability to deal with corporate and financial institution distress i.e. a) formation of Joint Lenders' Forum (JLF), b) Corrective Action Plan (CAP), c) 'Refinancing of Project Loans', d) 'Sale of NPAs by Banks' the main legal and technical hurdles in reducing the delay in early resolution to be focused upon. Otherwise, many smaller and midsized banks will face enormous stress on their profitability as well as continuity.

HUMAN RESOURCES

HR management is an important function for banks covering the whole gamut of areas such as recruitment, role mapping, training, skill set identification, building up of HR data base, and performance assessment. It is very important for this function to be taken up as a specialised area and given its due importance rather than as just a routine operational work to be done.

HR is going to be at the forefront of change in the years to come and it should be understood that banks having clear HR policies with awareness of employee engagement and development will gain a vital competitive edge in a tough market environment in the years ahead.

The HR function world over has undergone many developments/evolution over the years, particularly from its administrative beginnings to a strategic orientation as is seen today. However, it is a fact that in a majority of the banks in India even today, the HR function is at best a supplementary function which is not given its due importance in the banking hierarchy.

There is a need for change in the mind set to underscore the fact that to drive your efficiency, as well as the topline and bottomline in your balance sheets, you need skilled resources. Such skill resource base is not possible if you do not have a structured approach to the entire gamut of HR management.

HR is an essential element of corporate strategy and is invariably linked to the performance of banks as well.

TRAINING METHODOLOGIES AND INTERVENTIONS

With a fast changing environment, skills and qualifications acquired could fast become redundant if there is no on-going updation. While it needs no emphasis that the initiative should also come from the employees themselves to keep abreast of the developments, it is also the duty of the organisation to equip their employees by providing a minimum training support at periodical intervals. Apart from taking away the monotony of their daily work, and expanding their horizons and knowledge levels, it can also change employee attitude and behaviour, thereby contributing to the organisational performance.

Studies have shown that training and effectiveness programs have a positive impact on employee performance.

We need to combine the training programmes with certification which will improve training efficiency and will offer quality assurance. This will also ensure that training efforts are taken seriously by the recipients.

The next set relates to the steps needed to be taken on a system-wide basis to drive capacity building. We need to look beyond an individual institution's perspective and consider various measures on a system-wide basis to support and drive capacity building. The success of these measures would hinge on coordination and collaboration of all relevant stakeholders.

Public sector banks have been witnessing increasing number of younger officers at top levels of hierarchy over the last few years. Some of them have risen rapidly to senior positions over a short period of time. While this can bring fresh perspectives on various issues, it is also a fact that given the strategic importance of leadership at the top, it is important to understand the training requirements of top management & fulfill the same.

Banking sector plays a very important role in the economic growth of the country and our banking system has to ensure that its capacity to deliver has to continuously evolve and adapt to the developments in above vital areas. Banks have to make conscious and structured effects in bringing innovation so that they can reach new horizons which ultimately results in serving more than a billion people in a sustainable manner and lead our country in a secure path.

Quote from Mahatma Gandhi "Poverty is the worst form of crime" Let us eradicate the poverty in India by strengthening our banks with innovation and empowerment.

Sri. P.V. Krishna Rao,
General Secretary, Indian Bank Employees Union AP

Problems and Prospects of E-Banking in India

Radha Raghuramapatruni
Associate Professor in Economics & International Business
GITAM School of International Business, GITAM University.

ABSTRACT

Now-a-days banking is known as innovative banking. Developments in information technology have given a rise to innovations in the product & service designing and their supply in the banking sector and finance industries, customer services and satisfaction are their centre point of all the efforts. One of the most important areas of banking where Information Technology has a positive influence on the substitutes for traditional funds movement services. With the advent of online banking, electronic funds transfer and other similar products & services for funds transfer within quick time which was impossible a few years ago. India is still in the early stages of E Banking growth and development. Competition and changes in technology and lifestyle in the last 10 years have changed the face of Banking. E Banking is likely to bring a host opportunities as well as unprecedented risks to the fundamental nature of Banking in India. The concept of scope of E Banking is still evolving several initiatives taken by Government of India as well as Country's Central Bank, the Reserve Bank of India have facilitated the development of E-Banking in India. In this context the paper aims to present the E-Banking challenges and opportunities in India.

INTRODUCTION

The Banking sector in India has experienced a rapid transformation. Just about a decade back this sector was limited to the nationalized and co-operative banks. Then came the multi-national banks, but these were confined to serving an elite few. One could regard the past as the 'medieval ages' in the banking industry, wherein every branch of the same bank acted as an independent information silo, and multi-channel banking (ATMs, Net banking, tele-banking, etc) was almost non-existent. The first major reason for this transformation is because of the improved security and encryption methods developed on the Internet. The second reason is that banks do not want to lose a potential market share to banks that are quick to offer their services on the Internet. Competition and changes in technology and lifestyle in the last 10 years have changed the face of Banking. E-banking has emerged as a next big thing in the banking industry, which has brought about host of new opportunities to the banking industry. In this context the paper discusses the problems and prospects related to the banking industry in India.

REVIEW OF LITERATURE

Raghavan (2006) opined that at present, over 85% of the finished payment transactions are electronic and traditional way of doing banking at the branch level has relatively little importance to electronic banking users. Many banks, including PSU banks, would have online ATMs, phone banking, virtual banking, e-banking, Internet banking, etc., by 2020. Mohan (2006) remarked that Indian banking is at the threshold of a paradigm shift and a significant development has been achieved by banks in offering a variety of new and innovative e-banking services to customers today, which was not thought of before. However, public sector banks have not been able to harness the benefits of computerization. Kamakodi et al (2008) found that a wide gap exists in human service in Indian banking while technology based services are exceeding expectations. Uppal and Chawla (2009) found that the customers of public sector, private sector and foreign banks in Ludhiana district of Punjab are interested in e-banking services, but at the same time are facing problems like inadequate knowledge, poor network, lack of infrastructure, unsuitable location, misuse of ATM cards and difficulty to open an account. Indian customers' perception in the context of e-banking has been examined by Reeti Agarwal et al (2009) and found that people in the age group of 31-45 years using e-banking most frequently. Respondents opined that using e-banking for balance inquiry to be the most useful, closely followed by inter-account transfer of funds and they found e-banking least useful for lodging complaints. Slow transaction speed was found to be the most frequent problem faced, closely followed by non-availability of the server while using e-banking. Sharma (2009) opined that the trend towards electronic delivery of banking products and services is occurring partly as a result of consumer demand, and partly because of the increasing competitive environment in the global context. Kumar and Sinha (2009) cited various instances of hacking and phishing attacks reported throughout India. They remarked that cyber crimes prove that e-banking has several loopholes that can be easily exploited and users need to be extra cautious while making online transactions. Srinivas (2009) discussed various e-banking channels and suggested security tips for customers which include changing password frequently, abstaining from revealing PIN either via mails or phone, avoiding cyber cafes for net banking etc. In a study conducted by Mohammed and Shariq (2011) in the city of Lucknow, U.P to examine the adoption of e-banking channels, particularly ATM, it was found that ATM was the most adopted technology by banks. Shukla (2011) stated that E-banking offers a higher level of convenience for managing one's finances even from one's bedroom. However, it continues to present challenges to the financial security and personal privacy. Customers are advised not to share personal information like PIN numbers, passwords etc with anyone, including employees of the bank; change ATM PIN and online login and transaction passwords on a regular basis; ensure that the logged in session is properly signed out. Mishra (2011) provided useful tips to ensure safety of IB transactions. IB users are advised not to reply to any mail, phone call or letter, asking for the IB information like login id or password, and not to click on any link provided in any mail, claiming to be the link for the bank's website are the important tips, among others.

EVOLUTION OF MODERN BANKING

The evolution of modern banking technology began with the use of Advanced Ledger Posting Machines (ALPM) in the 1980s. The Reserve bank of India which is a regulatory central body under whom various public sector banks, financial institutions, NBFCs etc work in India had then advised all banks to go in for massive computerization at the branch level. Two options were put forth i.e., either to automate the front office or back office. Many banks opted for automating the front office ALPM in the first phase. Banks like State Bank of India, which is a public sector commercial bank, concentrated on the back office automation at the branch level. The Rangarajan committee report of 1985 ensured that banks had to get computerized. The second wave of development called for Total Bank Automation (TBA) in late 1980s. This automated both the front-end and back-end operations within the same branch. TBA comprised of total automation of a particular branch with its own database. In the third wave, the new private sector banks entered the field. These banks opted for a different model of having a single centralized database instead of having multiple databases for all their branches. This was possible due to the availability of good network infrastructure. In the beginning of the 1990s, leased line costs were coming down. The Dot was expanding its capacity and new technologies were being implemented. Earlier, banks were not confident of running the whole operation through a single data center. However, when a couple of private sector banks implemented it efficiently, other banks began to show an interest, and they also began consolidating their databases into a single database. Banks followed up on this move by choosing suitable application software that would support centralized operations. The fourth wave started with the evolution of the ATM delivery channel. This was the first stage of empowerment of the customer for his own transactions. The second stage was the Suvidha experiment in Bangalore city of India. This showed the power of technology and how the reach can be increased phenomenally at a great pace. Seeing these, all the banks started revamping their retail delivery channels. Their core focus became the number of customers they can service at lower cost. The main channels for these were channels such as Internet Banking and mobile banking. After this came alliances for payment through various gateways. The third important development happening now is the real-time gross settlement system of the RBI. Once this is in place, transactions between banks can be done through the settlement system, online, electronically. So the collections will become very fast. Five years from now, majority of the transactional services will be provided by way of Internet. Net-based banking comes at only 10 percent of the operating costs of conventional banking practices and services. As banks are going to play a key role in IT enabled public services involving electronic money transactions we feel that cooperative banks should consider NET-Banking in a big way.

ROLE OF IT IN THIS PHENOMENAL TECHNOLOGY CHANGE

IT is central to banking. This is one of the major reasons why new private and multi-national banks have been able to survive, thrive, and adapt in an increasingly competitive space. These banks were able to leverage on low-cost channels such as ATMs and Net banking to the optimum levels contributing to reduced operating costs. Banks have realized that shifting customer access to lower cost channels can help bring down operating costs. But this does not mean that branch banking is obsolete. Rather, banks are reinventing their business models to offer new financial services through its branches. Banks are looking at newer ways to make a customer's banking experience more convenient, efficient, and effective. They are using new technology tools and techniques to identify customer needs and are offering tailor-made products to match them. Centralized operations and process automation using core banking applications and IP-based networks improve efficiency and productivity levels tremendously. Core banking applications help a bank to shift from 'branch banking' to 'bank banking.' This basically means that a customer will be treated as a bank's customer than just the customer of a particular branch, which was the case earlier. Also, Internet Protocol based networks let a bank offer multiple services over the same network, resulting in costs savings. CRM solutions, if implemented and integrated correctly, can help significantly in improving customer satisfaction levels. Data warehousing helps in providing better transaction experiences for customers over different transaction channels. This is made possible because data warehousing helps bring all the transactions coming from different channels under a common roof. Data mining helps banks analyze and measure customer transaction patterns and behavior. This can help a lot in improving service levels and finding new business opportunities. Risk Assessment is another area where technology plays a major role. The core issues faced by banks today are on the fronts of customer's service expectations, cutting operational costs, and managing competition. Technology helps banks in meeting these objectives. A data warehouse can help the bank get a single view of its data across disparate systems. This comes in handy since most banks have data spread over several disparate, sometimes legacy systems. If the data is spread across different systems, a transaction done on one system will not be reflected in the other. This is not a very desirable situation when it comes to multi-channel banking. Data warehousing solves these by integrating all the data into a common warehouse (usually an RDBMS). The multiple data coming in from different systems is converted into a common format using the ETL (Extraction, Transformation, and Loading) process. This provides a single repository from which banks can view or use information when required.

THE NEWEST WAY OF BANKING

Internet banking is the most effective way of banking. The bank-to-customer relationship changes significantly, with open standards replacing proprietary front ends, many-to-many networks substituting for single-line links, and traditional locking eroding, so that corporates enjoy lower switching costs. Corporations source globally and seek the best-of- reed. Corporate customers have the freedom to unbundle their corporate banking purchases, selecting the best of breed for each requirement, geographically and functionally, and using integrated front-ends to manage the complexity of multiple providers.

Mobile banking or M-Banking is an extension of Internet Banking. Mobile banking is defined as the "type of execution of financial services which the customer uses mobile communication techniques in conjunction with mobile devices" (Pousttchi and Schurig, 2004). In other words, it means the usage of mobile telecommunication devices for carrying out banking and financial transactions. Since the penetration rate of Mobile phones in India is much higher than the penetration rate of internet, mobile phones is an excellent delivery channel to reach banking customers. In India, only 200 million people have access to a bank account while 811 million have a mobile phone. For a population of 1.2 billion people, this translates into 68 per cent having a mobile phone and only 17 per cent having a bank account. The numbers speak for themselves. When it comes to reaching the 'un-banked' and extending financial inclusion for the larger population, mobile phone is the Key (The Hindu, July 11, 2011). Over a period of nearly 2 years, mobile banking transactions in India have increased by 13 times in volumes and value terms. This shows the growing interest of Indian customers in mobile banking.

CHALLENGES IN E-BANKING

***Implementation of Global Technology*:** There is a need to have an adequate level of infrastructure and human capacity building before the developing countries can adopt global technology for their local requirements. In developing countries, many consumers either do not trust or do not access to the necessary infrastructure to be able to process e-payments.

***Strengthening the Public Support*:** In developing countries, in the past, most e-finance initiatives have been the result of joint efforts between the private and public sectors. If the public sector does not have the necessary resources to implement the projects it is important that joint efforts between public and private sectors along with the multilateral agencies like the World Bank, be developed to enable public support for e-finance related initiatives.

***Confidentiality, Integrity and Authentication*:** These three are the very important features of the banking sector and were very successfully managed all over the world before the coming of internet. Communication across an open and thus insecure channel such as the internet might not be the best base for bank-client relations as trust might partially be lost.

Customer Satisfaction: In today's competitive world, satisfaction of customers is a major challenge for the banking sector because customers have alternative choices in various types of services provided by banks.

Availability of Personnel Services: In present times, banks are to provide several services like social banking with financial possibilities, selective up gradation, computerization and innovative mechanization, better customer services, effective managerial culture, internal supervision and control, adequate profitability, strong organization culture etc. Therefore, banks must be able to provide complete personnel service to the customers who come with expectations.

Non-Performing Assets (NPA): Nonperforming assets are another challenge to the banking sector. Vehicle loans and unsecured loans increases N.P.A. which terms 50% of banks retail portfolio was also hit due to upward movement in interest rates, restrictions on collection practices and soaring real estate prices. So that every bank have to take care about regular repayment of loans.

Competition: The nationalized banks and commercial banks have the competition from foreign and new private sector banks. Competition in banking sector brings various challenges before the banks such as product positioning, innovative ideas and channels, new market trends, cross selling and at managerial and organizational part this system needs to be manage, assets and contain risk. Banks are restricting their administrative folio by converting manpower into machine power i.e. banks are decreasing manual powers and getting maximum work done through machine power. Skilled and specialized man power is to be utilized and result oriented targeted staff will be appointed.

Handling Technology: Developing or acquiring the right technology, deploying it optimally and then leveraging it to the maximum extent is essential to achieve and maintain high service and efficiency standards while remaining cost effective and delivering sustainable return to shareholders. Early adopters of technology acquire significant competitive advances. Managing technology is therefore, a key challenge for the Indian banking sector.

Other Challenges: a) Coping with regulatory reforms b) Development of skill of bank personnel c) Customer awareness and satisfaction d) Corporate governance e) Changing needs of customers f) Keeping space with technology up gradation g) Lack of common technology standards for mobile banking h) Sustaining healthy bottom lines and increasing shareholders value i) Structural changes j) Man power planning.

OPPORTUNITIES

Untapped Rural Markets: Contributing to 70% of the total population in India is a largely untapped market for banking sector. In all urban areas banking services entered but only few big villages have the banks entered. So that the banks must reach in remaining all villages because majority of Indian still living in rural areas.

Multiple Channels: Banks can offer so many channels to access their banking and other services such as ATM, Local branches, Telephone/mobile banking, video banking etc. to increase the banking business.

Worthy Customer Service: Worthy customer services are the best brand ambassador for any bank for growing its business. Every engagement with customer is an opportunity to develop a customer faith in the bank. While increasing competition customer services has become the backbone for judging the performance of banks.

Internet Banking: It is clear that online finance will pickup and there will be increasing convergence in terms of product offerings banking services, share trading, insurance, loans, based on the data warehousing and data mining technologies. Anytime anywhere banking will become common and will have to upscale, such upscaling could include banks launching separate internet banking services apart from traditional banking services.

Retail Lending: Recently banks have adopted customer segmentation which has helped in customizing their product folios well. Thus retail lending has become a focus area particularly in respect of financing of consumer durables, housing, automobiles etc. Retail lending has also helped in risks dispersal and in enhancing the earnings of banks with better recovery rates.

Indian Customers: The growing Indian banking sector with its strong home country linkages, seek a unique combination of Indian ethnicity and global standards that offers a valuable nice opportunities for Indian banks. The biggest opportunity for the Indian banking sector today is the Indian costumers. Demographic shifts in terms of income level and cultural shifts in terms of life style aspirations are changing the profile of the Indian customer. This is and will be a key driver of economic growth going forward. The Indian customers now seek to fulfil his lifestyle aspirations at a younger age with an optimal combination of equity and debt to finance consumption and asset creation. The consumer represents a market for a wide range of products and services he need a mortgage to finance his house, an auto loan for his car, a credit card for on-going purchases, a bank account, a long term investment plan to his children's higher education, pension plans for his retirement, a life insurance policy the possibilities are endless and this consumer does not live just in India's top ten cities. He represents across cities, towns and villages i.e. in rural areas. Consumer goods companies are already tapping this potential it is for the banks to make the most of the opportunity to deliver solutions to this market.

Other Opportunities: a) To enter new business and new markets b) To develop new ways of working c) To improve efficiency d) To deliver high level of customer services.

CONCLUSION

In the past few years, the Indian banking sector has completely transformed. The banks are facing many challenges and many opportunities are available with the banks. Many financial innovations like ATMs, credit cards, RTGS, debit cards, mobile banking etc have changed the face of Indian Banking sector. But still there is a need to have more innovative solutions so that the challenges faced by the e-banking can be solved and opportunities can be availed efficiently by the banks. However e-banking has completely changed the face of the Indian Banking Industry.

REFERENCES

1. Chavan, J. (2013). Internet banking- Benefits and challenges in an emerging economy. International Journal of Research in Business Management, 1(1), 19-26.
2. Geetika, Nandan, T & Upadhyay, AK. 2008 “Internet Banking in India: Issues and Prospects,” The Icfai Journal of Bank Management, Vol. 7, No.2, pp 47-61.
3. Gupta, P., Mishra, C.M. (2012). E-banking- New emerging trends in Indian banking industry. Research Journal of Economics and Business Studies, 1(10), 1-3.
4. Haq, S., Khan, M. (2013). E-banking challenges and opportunities in the Indian banking sector. Innovative Journal of Business and Management, 2(4), 56-59.
5. Jatana, R., Uppal, R.K. (2007). E-banking in India: Challenges and opportunities. New Century Publications.
6. Kamakodi, N. and Ahmed Khan, M. B. (2008), "Customer expectations and Service level in E-banking Era: An empirical study". The ICPAI university journal of Bank Management, Vol. VII, No.4, pp. 50-70.
7. Kaptan, S.S., Choubey, N.S. (2003). Indian banking in electronic era. Sarup and Sons. New Delhi. PP: 16-27.
8. Kumar, R. and Sinha A. B. (2009), "An overview of E-banking in India", Professional Banker, October issue, pp. 35-37.
9. Mavri, M & loannou, G., “Consumer’s perspectives on Online Banking service”, International Journal of Consumer Studies, Vol. 30, No. 6, pp 552-560.
10. Mishra.A. (2011), “Internet banking: knowledge is prevention", http://www. ccaoi. inll11/links/ fwnewsletter 15th%20lan%2()ll%20Sivurity%20Neu'sletter.pdf accessed on 20.08.2013
11. Mohammed, S. and Shariq, S. (2011), "A study of A I'M usage in banks in Lucknow", International Journal of Engineering and Management Studies.Vol.2, No. l, pp.47-53.
12. Mohan, K. (2006), "Information Technology on Indian banking", SCMS Journal of Indian Management, July-Sept issue, pp. 18-24.
13. Sathiye, M. (1999). Adoption of Internet Banking by Australian customers: An empirical investigation. International Journal of Bank Marketing, 17(07), 101–122.
14. Singh, K. (2012). E-banking in India: Progress and Prospects. Lambert Academic Publishing. Srivastava, R. K. (2007). Customer’s perception on usage of internet banking. Innovative Marketing, 3(4), 67-73.
15. Srinivas, S. (2004). Role of trust in e-banking success. Information Management and Computer Security, 12(1), 33–35.
16. Trivedi, M. H., Patel, V. B. (2013). Problems face by customers while using e-banking facilities in India. International Journal of Scientific Research, 2(3), 121-123.
17. www.exim.org
18. www.rbi.org.in
19. www.wikipedia.org

A Study of Channel Innovations and their Impact in Indian Banking

V. Priyadarshini
PhD Scholar
School of Management Studies, University of Hyderabad.

ABSTRACT

Innovations in banking may happen at various levels such as the product level, channel level, process level and business level. Out of these channel innovations are the most influential in changing the banking behavior. Channel innovations refer to new ways of delivering banking services and new distribution infrastructures. However, little focus is given to channel innovations by banking researchers. The present paper tries to address this gap by studying the important channel innovations in the Indian banking sector and their impact on banking customers.

Keywords: *Innovations, channel innovations, banking.*

INTRODUCTION

Growing levels of awareness in the customers has made it imperative for banks to come up with innovations at various levels to attract and retain customers. Innovations in banking may happen at various levels such as the product level, channel level, process level and business level. Out of these channel innovations are the most influential in changing the banking behavior. According to Finale report, 2012 the most number of innovations by banks is happening at channel level.

The advancements in technology have resulted in the creation of multiple banking channels through which customers can get access to banking services and carryout transactions. Some of the recent and prominent channels preferred by banking customers in India are Internet Banking, Mobile Banking, Phone Banking, Video Banking, Direct Sales Agents (DSA), ATMs etc. Innovative channels of banking can help to achieve the Indian government's objective of financial inclusion by making banking services available to the poor and under-served. Therefore banks started using channel innovation and channel integration as a cost-effective strategy to reach a large customer base.

The present paper gives a detailed description of what a channel innovation is, its importance and the various channel innovations in the Indian banking sector along with their impact on banking customer.

OBJECTIVES OF THE STUDY

1. To study the meaning and importance of channel innovations.
2. To list out the various channel innovations in Indian Banking and describe them
3. To study the impact of channel innovations on the banking customer.

WHAT IS CHANNEL INNOVATION?

Channel innovations refer to new ways of delivering banking services and new distribution infrastructures. Channel innovations are means of recognizing new and sustainable channels of distribution that are compatible with the customer's lifestyle. Through channel innovations banks can develop new markets, new offerings and reduce costs.

Kinds of Banking Channels

Banking channels can be categorized into two types. They are direct and indirect.

Direct Channels

Direct channels are owned by the bank and the bank has control over them. Direct channels are again divided into two types: location-based direct channels and remotely-based direct channels. Location-based direct channels generally have a physical presence. Therefore branches, kiosks, roaming vans, and business units fall under this category. Remotely-based direct channels do not have a physical presence and customers cannot have a face to face contact with the bank through these channels. Because of this drawback, it is difficult to gain the trust of rural and poor customers. Internet, call centers, and IVR (Interactive Voice Response) fall under this category.

Indirect Channels

Indirect channels are not fully owned and controlled by the bank. A third party involvement happens to facilitate the functioning of an indirect channel. Examples include issuing a MasterCard prepaid card, working with a mobile operator to facilitate mobile banking, joining a national switch and deploying ATMs, or leveraging a pharmacy chain as part of a banking agent program.

IMPORTANCE OF CHANNEL INNOVATIONS

The significance attached to channel innovations is because of the advantages of massive outreach and dramatic cost reduction. According to a white paper on banking innovations by Infosys, channel innovations stand top in impacting banking customer's behavior. This is because of the fact that any change in delivery processes or distribution infrastructures is directly reflected in the customer experience. Thus channel innovations happen to occupy the highest priority for banking. Research shows that more than half of the banking transactions are conducted through banking channels other than branch banking. And about two thirds of the customers demand a consistent service offering through multiple banking channels. Another finding shows that innovation in the banking channels is a strong customer value proposition across all generations.

CHANNEL INNOVATIONS IN INDIAN BANKING

Rural ATMs

Rural ATMs have the ability to handle used and soiled currency notes. Sensors are used to detect and correct false dispensation. They provide the depositor with secure antiphishing mechanism, secure chest with e-lock activated only by remote-bank server. They have got smart-card based identification, biometric authentication, encrypted secure communication over the internet and real time online communication for 'anywhere banking'.

Biometric ATMs

ATMs with biometric devices are the latest solution in the ongoing effort to offer banking services to the rural masses. To reach the rural masses, and to boost micro financing initiatives, banks are deploying biometric ATMs. Establishing the identity of a rural depositor through biometrics, it makes it convenient for the illiterate to become part of the banking user community. Biometrics establishes identification via face, voice, retina or iris.

Dena Bank has launched the Bio-metric ATMs in Gujarat. Andhra Bank has launched two mobile biometric-access ATMs, one each for the Twin Cities of Hyderabad and Secunderabad. Corporation bank has also introduced 'talking' biometric ATMs. These ATMs 'talk' to the farmers in their local language. Two of India's largest banks, ICICI Bank and State Bank of India, have started setting up 'grammtellers', or low-cost bio ATMs, which use solar light in certain parts of rural Tamil Nadu.

Benefits of Biometric ATMs

- Provides strong authentication.
- Can be used instead of a PIN.
- Hidden costs of ATM card management like card personalization, delivery, management, re-issuance, PIN generation, help-desk, and re-issuance can be avoided.
- Ideal for Indian rural masses.
- It is accurate.
- Flexible account access allows clients to access their accounts at their convenience.
- Low operational cost of the ATMs will ultimately reduce transaction costs.

Green Channel Counter Facility

State Bank of India has launched its 'Green Channel Counter' facility on July 11, 2010, at select branches of the Bank spread across the country as an innovative step towards paperless 'Green Banking' for deposit, withdrawal and remittance transactions in connection with its 204th Birth Day. This facility would give customers ease and comfort in transacting their business at branches. The customers need not fill up any pay-in slips or draw cheques for depositing or withdrawing money from their accounts, saving paper, and thereby contributing to the concept of 'Green Banking'. This facility would be a reducing process time, as duplication in writing/feeding account details and transaction details by the customer as well as the person behind the counter, by simply capturing these details by swiping the SBI Shopping cum ATM Card on a device available at the Single Window (SW) Operator's counter. At the Green Channel counter, there is a Point of Sale Machine (POS), on which the customer swipes his card.

Social Media Banking

Social media is one of the fastest growing channels in banking and banks need to be mindful of several trends in the channel. Social media is dramatically impacting the banking industry, as most banks have established a presence on various social sites. ICICI bank, Barclays Bank, Citigroup, Inc., HSBC and others all engage on social media through Twitter, Facebook, Google+, LinkedIn, etc. Banks can also use social media insights to create pricing models for loans and other banking products, and they can combine traditional scoring elements with data available in the public domain, such as Twitter, Facebook and other social networking sites, to ascertain creditworthiness and price loans. Banks are monitoring customer conversations on online communities and heeding their recommendations and complaints to improve customer service. Some banks have developed a way for customers to securely conduct banking while on Twitter. Customers can also retrieve information on their accounts — such as balances, holds and cleared cheques and even transfer money between accounts.

Immediate Mobile Payment Service (IMPS)

IMPS stands for Immediate Mobile Payment Service or Interbank Mobile Payment Service. Immediate Payment Service (IMPS) is an initiative of National Payments Corporation of India (NPCI). It was launched on 22nd November 2010.

- IMPS is an emphatic tool to transfer money instantly within banks across India through mobile, internet and ATM which is not only safe but also economical both in financial and non financial perspectives.
- Upon registration, both the individuals are issued an MMID (Mobile Money Identifier) Code from their respective banks. This is a 7 digit numeric code. To initiate the transaction, the sender in his mobile banking application need to enter the registered mobile number of the receiver, MMID of the receiver and amount to be transferred. Upon successful transaction, the money gets credited in the account of the receiver instantly.
- Though most banks offer this facility free of cost to encourage paperless payment system, ICICI bank and Axis bank charge for it as per their respective NEFT charges.
- Nowadays, money through this service can be transferred directly also by using the receiver's bank account number and IFS code. In such case, neither the receiver of the money needs to be registered for mobile banking service of his bank, nor does he need MMID code.
- IMPS facility differs from NEFT and RTGS as there is no time limit to carry out the transaction. This facility can be availed 24×7 and on all public and bank holidays including RBI holidays.

USSD (Unstructured Supplementary Service Data) based Mobile Banking

Unstructured Supplementary Service Data (USSD) is a technology unique to GSM (Global System for Mobile Communication). To bring all the Banks under the common platform, NPCI has started common USSD platform called NUUP (National Unified USSD Platform) with a common short code *99# across Telco's and this is a service which has potential to take banking services to every common man in the country.

A great advantage to the customer is that he/she will not be charged for the service which is being used through USSD unlike SMS where he/she will be charged as per the SMS tariff plan of the telecom operator.

The other benefits of USSD are as below:

- GPRS is not required, it works on voice connectivity.
- Works on all GSM mobiles.
- More secure than SMS.
- No application installation is required.
- USSD is application with interactive Menu.

The services currently offered under USSD are as follows

- Balance Inquiry
- Last 3 transactions
- IMPS – Person-To-Person (P2P) funds transfer.
- IMPS – Person-To-Account (P2A) funds transfer.
- Generate MMID
- Generate OTP

Business Correspondents (BCs)

Bank Mitr or Business Correspondents (BCs) are representatives of bank to provide basic banking services i.e., opening of basic Bank accounts, Cash deposits, Cash withdrawals, transfer of funds, balance enquiries, mini statements etc.

- There are more than 1.4 lakh Business Correspondents (BCs) of Public Sector Banks and Regional Rural Banks in the rural areas. In Urban areas too, the Banks would engage Bank Mitr (Business Correspondent) wherever required.
- The Bank Mitr (Business Correspondent) outlets (in both rural and urban areas) would be fully equipped with the required infrastructure including the computers and other peripherals like Micro ATMs, Printer, Web cam and Internet Connectivity.
- Adequate compensation to the Bank Mitr (Business Correspondent) would be ensured for enabling him to provide uninterrupted services particularly in the difficult rural and remote areas.

Banking Kiosks

Kiosks are aesthetically and ergonomically designed cabins containing computers. They are used for advertising, promotion and information purposes. By equipping them with necessary security conditions, Kiosks can be used for viewing or doing banking transactions. Kiosks can perform all non-cash transactions like balance enquiry, internet banking, printing of bank statements, demand drafts, fund transfers, utility bill payments, cheque truncation and information display. Unlike an ATM, which is primarily used for cash transactions like withdrawals, deposits, etc., a kiosk is primarily used for non-cash transactions like cheque book request, printing bank account statements, funds transfer etc. The number of transactions a particular location is expected to be able to support is key here along with the types of transactions required. An ATM and a Kiosk can both easily perform the same non cash and non deposit transactions however the real differentiators come down to how much time/ input the transaction takes (Financial Kiosks have full keyboards and document printers, ATMs generally don`t) and queuing considerations (at an ATM, most people just want to get their cash and go). A unique feature of the banker is its cheque deposit capability. On depositing a cheque at the kiosk, it issues an immediate receipt, with a scanned image of the cheque, with every detail listed. Sources estimate that kiosks can help achieve almost 90% transaction automation in retail banking.

IMPACT OF CHANNEL INNOVATIONS ON BANKING CUSTOMERS

Access to banks and banking services is critical for financial inclusion and a priority for the Government of India. As per a CRISIL report on the state of financial inclusion in India, only one in two Indians has a savings account, and only one in seven Indians has access to bank credit. Channel innovations are the foremost means of achieving financial inclusion.

Many poor customers initially do not trust financial services delivered through technologically-enabled channels. Proper market segmentation, product simplicity, and strategies to increase initial usage can greatly overcome the initial mistrust customers have with innovative channels. There is a need for customer education at the bottom of the pyramid for the effective use of channels. Furthermore, even though there is a significant increase in the use of direct channels like Internet, phone, and mobile, branch banking has not lost its preference. Therefore the significance of branch as a banking channel cannot be undermined. Thus a combination of banking channels has to be used to offer greater transparency and control to the customer.

- Proper design and deployment of IT is an essential element for the success of channels. Indirect channels especially require robust core banking platforms and communication systems. But only few banks have in-house capacity and expertise to successfully implement innovative channels since they require huge capitals. Therefore channel innovations can become economically successful only by generating huge volume of transactions.

Benefits of Channel Innovations to Banks

- Improve customer access.
- Facilitate the offering of more services
- Increase customer loyalty
- Attract new customers
- Increase customer satisfaction.
- Reduction in costs, as the need for physical branches is reduced.
- Reduction in cost, as the need for manpower is reduced.
- Increased transparency and faster response.

CONCLUSION

In conclusion, it is becoming essential for banks to integrate Internet, branch network, and mobile banking channels in order to attract and retain customers. It is apparent that customer loyalty can be significantly influenced by the differentiation that is created through technology-led service innovation across all banking channels. Changing customer behavior and preferences are making multichannel integration as well as customer dialogue and experience management increasingly important. Across all generations, customers are looking for products and services that are consistent, customized, and personalized. Making these available through multiple channels offers banks the opportunity to tailor their customer value proposition. Banking customers are consistently demanding more relevant services and transparent access to information across all channels. Therefore banks should carefully devise channel innovations with a long term view such that optimization of existing infrastructure happens to scale up in a cost effective manner.

Competitive Marketing Strategies in MNC Banks – A Study

JVR Geetanjali[1] and R. Sushma Rani[2]
[1]Research scholar, Osmania University
[2]Student, Bhavan's Vivekananda Degree College

ABSTRACT

Indian banking sector has seen a tremendous growth post independence period. Being the most populous country in the world, India needs to sustain its position to reach the people for the accomplishment of barring BPL. Banking is a boon as well as a better solution to earn the living of a common man. There are currently 27 public sector banks in India, out of which 21 are nationalised banks and 6 are State Bank of India and its associate banks. There are total of 93 commercial banks in India. Importance of these banking sector are very pivotal in a developing country like India and some are like implementation of monetary policy, capital formation and promotion of industry and generating employment opportunities. Globalization on the performance of bank is the emergence and growth of new banking entities, which are clearly a coup in the banking sector. The giant banking entities, by virtue of the enormous economic power relations and the large economic size, and high economic performance, has become a high capability to influence the form and market trends. Among the global giants YES bank has made its entrance in the world of banking sector. The one of the innovative approach by YES Bank is its Yes Bank's wallet, which is designed in a way that the users can send and request money from any of the Facebook friend or phone book contacts. Also, users can split bills among themselves.

Keywords: *Banking, Innovation, knowledge banking and customers.*

INTRODUCTION

The term "Banking Technology" refers to the use of sophisticated information and communication technologies together with computer science to enable banks to offer better services to its customers in a secure, reliable and affordable manner and sustain competitive advantage over other banks. Banking Technology also subsumes the activity of using advanced computer algorithms in unravelling the patterns of customer behaviour by shifting through customer details such as demographic, psychographic and transactional data.

- Evolution of banking took place despite the enormous changes the banking industry has undergone through during the past 20 years – let alone since 1943 – one factor has remained the same: the fundamental nature of the need customers have for banking services. However, the framework and paradigm within which these services are delivered has changed out of recognition. It is clear that people's needs have not changed and neither has the basic nature of banking services people required. But the way banks meet those needs is completely different today. Banking has had to adjust to the changing needs of societies.

- The Indian banking system consists of 26 public sector banks, 20 private sector banks, 43 foreign banks, 56 regional rural banks, 1,589 urban cooperative banks and 93,550 rural cooperative banks, in addition to cooperative credit institutions. Public-sector banks control nearly 80 percent of the market, thereby leaving comparatively much smaller shares for its private peers. Coming to the start up companies in the banking sector, we have seen a tremendous rise in the start ups in banking that is India's banking sector would improve to 12-13 per cent in FY16 from less than 10 per cent in the second half of CY14.

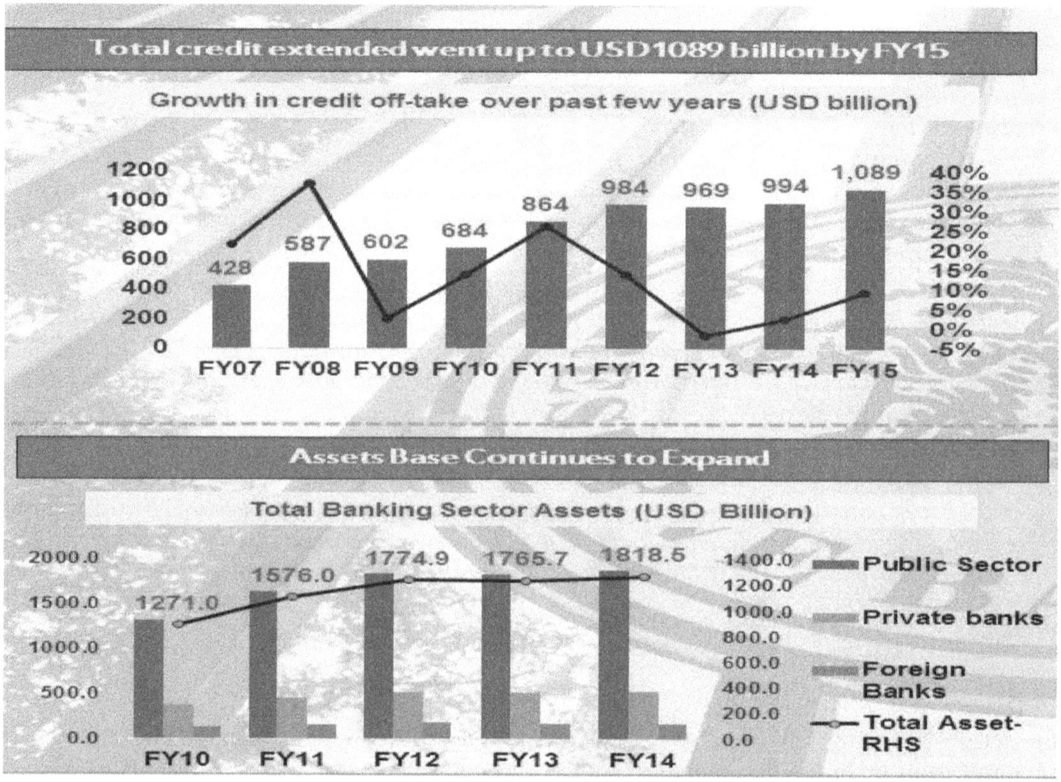

REVIEW OF LITERATURE

The Indian economy's liberalisation in the early 1990s has resulted in the conception of various private sector banks. This has sparked a boom in the country's banking sector in the past two decades. The revenue of Indian banks grew four-fold from US$ 11.8 billion to US$ 46.9 billion, whereas the profit after tax rose nearly nine-fold from US$ 1.4 billion to US$ 12 billion over 2001-10. This growth was driven primarily by two factors. First, the influx of Foreign Direct Investment (FDI) of up to 74% with certain restrictions. Second, the conservative policies of the Reserve Bank of India (RBI), which have shielded Indian banks from recession and global economic turmoil. The solace for Indian banks, however, lies in the fact that India has shown a comparatively robust growth in its GDP over past years, which analysts closely correlate to the performance of the banking industry. The report forecasts that India's GDP growth will take the size of the country's banking sector, to the third largest in the world by 2025.

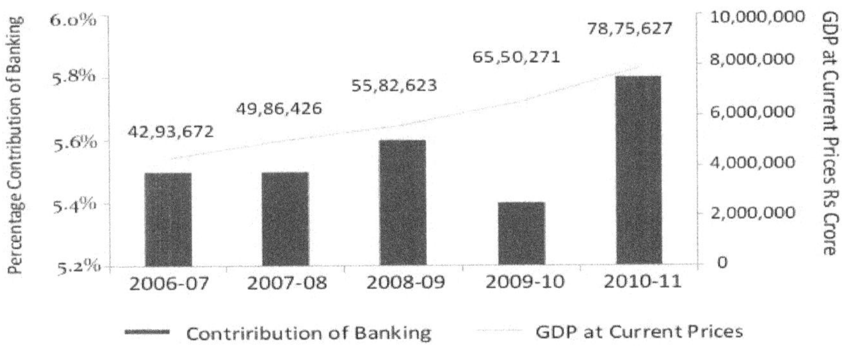

Source: India Budget.nic.in, Reserve bank of India Statistics

Fig. 1 Contribution of banking (including insurance) to the GDP (at current prices)

The explosion of start ups along the intersection of finance, technology and commerce is resulting in rising demand for banking talent, which until now typically moved within the industry or at best into allied areas. There are three new areas attracting talent from banks, namely new payments and small banks, e commerce companies and also this new entrepreneurship revolution, which is attracting people who have ideas and the confidence to execute them. Banks are gearing up for the competition from new kind of lenders like payments banks. We had many new entrants in the Banking sector in the recent years and Yes Bank was one among them and in present YES BANK is India's fifth largest private sector Bank with a pan India presence across all 29 states and 7 Union Territories of India, headquartered in the Lower Parel Innovation District (LPID) of Mumbai, is the outcome of the professional & entrepreneurial commitment of its Founder Rana Kapoor and its top management team, to establish a high quality, customer centric, service driven, private Indian Bank catering to the future businesses of India. YES BANK has adopted international best practices, the highest standards of service quality and operational excellence, and offers comprehensive banking and financial solutions to all its valued customers. Today, YES BANK has a widespread branch network of over 630 branches across 375 cities, with 1150+ ATMs across India.

YES BANK has been recognized amongst the Top and Fastest Growing Banks in various Indian Banking League Tables by prestigious media houses and Global Advisory Firms, and has received several national and international honours for our various Businesses including Corporate Investment Banking, Treasury, Transaction Banking, and Sustainable practices through Responsible Banking. YES BANK is steadily evolving as the Professionals' Bank of India with the long term mission of **"Building the Finest Quality Bank of the World in India"** by 2020.

Need for the Study

The Indian banking industry plays an important role in the economic development of the country and is the most dominant segment of the financial sector. Banks help channel savings to investments and encourage economic growth by allocating savings to investments that have potential to yield higher returns. India's banking system is a robust one and is classified into commercial banks and co-operative credit institutions. In Banking, the services stops not only with the websites but also we have different delivery channels from In-person dealing to Internet banking, Mobile banking, ATM etc. Start-ups have an important role in achieving the vision which is developing in India. The start-up also serves as a national aggregator for the financial institutions. Hence, the present study will focus on the start ups in the Banking sector like YES BANK and also regarding its strategies and modern Banking, which made the Bank India's fifth largest private sector Bank.

Objectives of the Present Study

The present study is compared to analyse about the innovations that have taken place in banking sector and also to analyse the modern ways that are adopted by the start up banks. The present study will also portray the contribution of the banking sector in the present market with a special reference of YES Bank. YES Bank with its innovation have got an edge over other banks and innovation in banking sectors are the most efficient routes in the banking sector and hence, our present study mainly focuses on the start up banks with special reference to YES Bank so as to see the trends in the banking sector.

Scope of the Study

Banking is one of the most exciting industry in current times. The way technology is changing the banking is also changing and for employees, it is giving opportunities to learn a lot of things. Still in India there is a huge untapped potential and RBI along with government t is working on Financial Inclusion. Payment banks and small banks licenses are expected soon which would open up a new era of niche banks. Growth in private sector and MNC bank depends more on performance of individual and that of bank as a whole, growth PSU is largely driven by seniority. From providing plain vanilla banking services, banks have gradually transformed themselves into universal banks. ATMs, Internet banking, mobile banking and social banking have made "anytime anywhere banking". In 2011/12, non-cash payments comprised 91% of total transactions in terms of value and 48% in terms of volume. Within noncash payments, too, the share of payments through cheques has come down from 85% to nine per cent in value, and 83% to 52% in volume between 2005/06 and 2011/12. The growth is not restricted to the metropolitan or urban areas. Financial inclusion has been at the forefront of regulators and policy makers in India, a country where approximately half of the population still does not have access to banking services. There have been occasions when banks have acted beyond their role of finance providers. The entry of new banks could have a significant impact on the Indian banking system. Given the huge unbanked population, there is surely a scope for more banks .With increasing volume and complexity of the banking business, it will be imperative for the regulator to move gradually towards more off site monitoring than onsite. Technology will play a much larger role in the overall supervision of the banking system.

Start ups in the Banking Sector

A lot of start ups in India have entered the Banking industry either unearthing an entirely new market or through gaps in existing markets or product lines. Although there are many successful start ups, here are five, which are growing rapidly and changing how an existing industry works in the process. In recent years, the Indian start up ecosystem has really taken off and come into its own—driven by factors such as massive funding, consolidation activities, evolving technology and an burgeoning domestic market. The numbers are telling—from 3,100 start ups in 2014 to a projection of more than 11,500 by 2020, this is certainly not a passing trend. It's a revolution. And it is going to change the way the markets are working today in India. We have start up banks like GIEOM which helps businesses simplify their view of their operating models. It was established in 2008, GIEOM offers applications to help businesses improve their way of working and decision making. GIEOM claims to help customers increase revenues and profits, create new business areas and reduce operational waste and error. Today over 30,000 users from seven banks operating in 35 countries use the GIEOM software product and also we have banks like **Yes Bank**, which is India's fifth largest private sector Bank, co-founded by Rana Kapoor in 2004. Yes Bank is the only Greenfield Bank licence awarded by the RBI in the last two decades. Yes Bank is a "Full Service Commercial Bank", has steadily built a Corporate, Retail & SME Banking franchise, Financial Markets, Investment Banking, Corporate Finance, Branch Banking, Business and Transaction Banking, and Wealth Management business lines across the country.

A Study on YES Bank Strategies

Yes Bank has pursued a differentiated branding strategy in line with its objective of becoming the Best Quality Bank of the World in India. The foundation of this strategy lies in the name "YES'', which underlines the twin ethos of service and trust and the promise to deliver a truly delightful and unprecedented Banking experiences to all its customers. Though YES bank has entered late to the market, it has entered the market in late 2004 when the banking space in India was already overcrowded with a number of public sector banks, private sector banks, and co-operative banks and also foreign multinational banks, which were growth-constrained, were also waiting eagerly for the sector to open up further in 2009 to make a major foray into this emerging market. However, despite being a late entrant, Yes Bank drew the attention of its competitors and analysts by the speed at which it grew and by increasing its operations throughout the country.

The Growth Story

The bank had grown at a tremendous pace since its inception. In the first two quarters since it began operations in (2004-2005) its balance sheet was standing at Rs.1,300 million, which made it one of the most successful ventures in India. The bank started its operations with just 250 employees and two branches. As of October 2007, it was operating with 60 branches and 3,263 employees. The bank's business size was Rs. 800 million in December 2006.

A Successful Market Entrant

According to the analysts, the bank's competence in terms of using high-end technology, its 'knowledge banking' approach, and emphasis on highly qualified human resources helped it to differentiate itself from other private banks in an increasingly commoditized market.

- In particular, its knowledge banking initiative drew a lot of interest.
- The fact that the bank catered to a niche segment of the market with a differentiated strategy meant that it did not have to compete with other banks on price.

- Banks were gearing up to face the competition. In tune with the developments, Yes Bank wanted to grow into a major bank in India with a presence all over the country. The bank expected to expand mostly in the small and medium towns, where it saw good growth prospects. The opening up of the economy saw many small towns becoming prosperous, but most of these towns had still not been tapped by the private sector banks.

The 12 aspects which we have under KNOWLEDGE BANKING are

- Development banking
- Food and Agri business
- Information technology
- Infrastructure
- Life sciences
- Strategic Government Advisory
- Telecom
- Media
- Reports
- YES SME
- Say YES to education
- Responsible banking

Strategic Government Advisory

It is a dedicated division of YES BANK, designed to deepen the bank's engagement with the Union and State Governments and allied agencies, particularly through advisory services, leadership and developmental support. Knowledge bankers at SGA have cross-functional domain expertise and bring with them significant experience of specific sectors such as Infrastructure, Tourism, Educational and e-Governance amongst others. They have been instrumental in YES BANK's strategic Knowledge Partnerships with Government and Industry organizations, as also in the design of 'Knowledge Publications' focused and strategic research that have been disseminated at leading industry forums in the presence of leaders from Government, industry and other thought leaders. These publications have offered visionary perspectives, documented successful interventions and highlighted investment potential.

Strategic Advisory Services

As a division unique to the banking industry, SGA has extended strategic advisory services and supporting development programs through a wide variety of engagements including Policy Advocacy, Bid Process Advisory, Implementation of specific projects on PPP mode, in addition to the thought leadership, knowledge partnerships and Research & Advisory services to State & Central Government organizations for Specific sectors mentioned earlier. The strength of this approach lies in the bank's capability to effectively integrate all stages of projects – right from conceptualization, structuring of projects, extending to facilitating investments from the private sector.

Facilitating Business with the Government

SGA has been working in partnership with a wide range of stakeholders including Central government ministries, State Governments, Bilateral & Multilateral Agencies, Key Educational Institutions, Think-Tanks, Industry Associations/Chambers, International Trade Bodies, Corporate Partners and Voluntary Groups amongst others.

- Through these efforts YES BANK has been able to build traction with significant Knowledge Partnerships, policy interventions and strategic thought leadership initiatives with Governments and industry organizations. These initiatives have significantly increased mindshare and have been widely appreciated. Knowledge reports that have been distributed amongst key stakeholders and continuously disseminated through YES BANK's extensive branch network have been instrumental in the design of interventions by stakeholders.

CONCLUSION

The Indian banking industry has its foundations in the 18th century, and has had a varied evolutionary experience since then. The initial banks in India were primarily traders' banks engaged only in financing activities. Banking industry in the pre-independence era developed with the Presidency Banks, which were transformed into the Imperial Bank of India and subsequently into the State Bank of India. The initial days of the industry saw a majority private ownership and a highly volatile work environment. Major strides towards public ownership and accountability were made with nationalisation in 1969 and 1980 which transformed the face of banking in India. The industry in recent times has recognised the importance of private and foreign players in a competitive scenario and has moved towards greater liberalisation. Also, the information technology in banking business had a visible impact on the quality of customer service. Banking Sector Reforms have also taken care of the Technology up gradation and its related measures. The RBI had started RTGS, Core Banking solution, INFINET as the communication backbone for the banking sector. The Negotiated Dealing System (NDS) for screen-based trading in government securities and Real Time Gross Settlement (RTGS) System have been the boon for the customers and bankers. All the success stories of banks and innovative services being offered by the banks are the gift of financial reforms.

REFERENCES

1. https://www.yesbank.in/about-us.html
2. http://www.ibef.org/industry/banking-india/infographic
3. http://info.shine.com/industry/banking-financial-services/8.html
4. http://shodhganga.inflibnet.ac.in/bitstream/10603/3712/16/16_chapter%209.pdf
5. http://www.bankingtech.com/181351/innovation-and-opportunity-in-the-banking-sector/
6. http://thenextweb.com/in/2015/07/05/india-the-worlds-fastest-growing-startup-ecosystem/
7. http://www.businesstoday.in/magazine/special/best-banks-2012-indian-banking-challenges/story/189858.html
8. https://www.quora.com/What-is-the-scope-in-the-banking-sector
9. http://www.theinternationaljournal.org/ojs/index.php?journal=tij&page=article&op=view&path%5B%5D=598.

Emerging Trends in Indian Banking – A Review

Durga Prasad Navvulla
Research Scholar, School of Management, National Institute of Technology.

ABSTRACT

Indian banking industry, the largest player of financial sector, has been undergoing a metamorphic change. Today Indian banking industry is strong and capable of withstanding the pressures of global financial turmoil. Indian banking system has seen major financial innovations in the past decades which lead to tremendous improvements in banking services and operations. Various innovations in banking and financial sectors are ECS, RTGS, EFT, NEFT, ATM, Retail Banking, Debit and Credit cards, online banking, internet banking, mobile banking free advisory services and many more value added products and services. Booming of IT industry in India and the implementation of IT solutions to Banking services and Operation has taken the Indian Banking Sector one step closure towards the global technological revolution in banking. This banking technology revolution has a positive impact on the Indian banking sector. This paper gives an insight into the current trends and changes in the technological revolution in Indian Banking Sector.

Keywords: *Indian Banking Industry, Banking Services, Global Technological Revolution, Banking Sector.*

INTRODUCTION

As per the Reserve Bank of India (RBI), India's banking sector is sufficiently capitalized and well-regulated. The financial and economic conditions in the country are far superior to any other country in the world. Credit, market and liquidity risk studies suggest that Indian banks are generally resilient and have withstood the global downturn well. Indian banking industry is expected to witness better growth prospects in 2015 as a sense of optimism stems from the Government's measures towards revitalizing the industrial growth in the country. In addition, RBI's new measures may go a long way in helping the restructuring of the domestic banking industry.

The Indian banking system consists of 26 public sector banks, 20 private sector banks, 43 foreign banks, 56 regional rural banks, 1,589 urban cooperative banks and 93,550 rural cooperative banks, in addition to cooperative credit institutions. Public-sector banks control nearly 80 percent of the market, thereby leaving comparatively much smaller shares for its private peers. As of August 5, 2015, 175 million accounts had been opened under Pradhanmantri Jan Dhan Yojna (PMJDY) and 154 million RuPay debit cards were issued. These new accounts have mustered deposits worth Rs 22,033 crore (US$ 3.31 billion). Standard & Poor's estimates that credit growth in India's banking sector would improve to 12-13 per cent in FY16 from less than 10 per cent in the second half of CY14.

OBJECTIVES OF THE STUDY

1. To study how current banking trends have contributed for the development of Indian banking system.
2. To observe the technological changes in the Indian banks in the changing scenario.

RECENT TRENDS IN BANKING

Real Time Gross Settlement (RTGS) & National Electronic Fund Transfer (NEFT)

Real Time Gross Settlement (RTGS) & National Electronic Fund Transfer (NEFT), National Electronic Fund Transfer (NEFT) and Real Time Gross Settlement (RTGS) allow individuals, companies and firms to transfer funds from one bank to another. Customers can check the RBI website for a list of NEFT and RTGS-enabled branches of his bank. These facilities can only be used for transferring money within the country. To opt for these, they need to fill a form providing your or the beneficiary's details name, bank branch where the account is held, the Indian Financial System Code, a unique code for identifying the branch, and the account number and type. Customers have to submit a cheque while opting for this facility. They can also transfer funds through net banking. These are third-party transfers and the option is available under the same header on your net banking home page.

There is no ceiling on the minimum or maximum amount that can be transferred through NEFT. They can even transfer Rs 1. However, a minimum of Rs 2 lakh must be transferred through the RTGS service. There is no cap on the maximum amount, though. However, banks may restrict the amount you can transfer in one day. For example, HDFC Bank allows a maximum of Rs 10 lakh to be transferred in a day.

Electronic Clearing Service (ECS)

Standard Chartered introduces the Electronic Clearing System (ECS), an innovative facility for busy people. With this facility, customer credit card bill is automatically debited from your savings account, so no need to worry about missing a payment. ECS is an electronic mode of funds transfer from one bank account to another. It can be used by institutions for making payments such as distribution of dividend interest, salary, and pension, among others. It can also be used to pay bills and other charges such as telephone, electricity, water or for making equated monthly installments payments on loans as well as SIP investments. ECS can be used for both credit and debit purposes. This facility is meant for companies and government departments to make/receive large volumes of payments rather than for funds transfers by individuals.

India, the RBI has played a pivotal role in facilitating e-payments by making it compulsory for banks to route high value transactions through Real Time Gross Settlement (RTGS) and also by introducing NEFT (National Electronic Funds Transfer) and NECS (National Electronic Clearing Services) which has encouraged individuals and businesses to switch to electronic methods of payment. With the changing times and technology so have changed the methods of payments in India. E-payments in India have been growing at a fast rate of 60% over the last 3 years.

Electronic Payment Services - E Cheques

An **electronic cheque** is an electronic copy (scanned image) of a real cheque, which is then transferred by email. In addition to the cheque's 'real' signature, the transfer must be digitally signed using the sender's **private key** to authenticate the transfer. It's simply an electronic version of a paper check. When you convert a traditional check into an electronic payment, you can process it through the Automated Clearing House (ACH) Network to save time and money and because electronic checks have more security features than a paper check, they better protect your business and customers. Another way to think of an electronic check is when a customer pays by entering in their bank account information online and electronically sending the money. Electronic checks are becoming increasingly popular because they are so fast, efficient and secure.

Electronic Funds Transfer (EFT)

Electronic Funds Transfer (EFT) is a system of transferring money from one bank account directly to another without any paper money changing hands. One of the most widely-used EFT programs is Direct Deposit, in which payroll is deposited straight into an employee's bank account, although EFT refers to any transfer of funds initiated through an electronic terminal, including credit card, ATM, Fed-wire and point-of-sale (POS) transactions. It is used for both credit transfers, such as payroll payments, and for debit transfers, such as mortgage payments.

Automatic Teller Machine (ATM)

Computerized machine that permits bank customers to gain access to their accounts with a magnetically encoded plastic card and a code number. It enables the customers to perform several banking operations without the help of a teller, such as to withdraw cash, make deposits, pay bills, obtain bank statements, effect cash transfers. There are two primary types of automated teller machines, or ATMs. The basic units allow the customer to only withdraw cash and receive a report of the account's balance. The more complex machines will accept deposits, facilitate credit card payments and report account information. To access the advanced features of the complex units, you will usually need to be a member of the bank that operates the machine. The usage of ATMs increased day by day.

As per Reserve Bank of India (RBI) stats for March 2015, the number of operational ATMs in India is as follows:

Banks	Metro Centres	Urban Centres	Semi urban Centres	Rural Centres	Total
Public Sector Bank	28644	36139	36481	27401	128665
Private Sector Bank	20805	14768	11698	4219	51490
Foreign Banks	835	208	22	32	1097
Total	**50284**	**51115**	**48201**	**31652**	**181252**

Debit Card & Credit Cards

A debit card is also known as a bank card or check card or a plastic payment card that provides the cardholder electronic access to their bank account(s) at a financial institution. Some cards may bear a stored value with which a payment is made, while most relay a message to the cardholder's bank to withdraw funds from a payer's designated bank account. The card, where accepted, can be used instead of cash when making purchases. In some cases, the primary account number is assigned exclusively for use on the Internet and there is no physical card.

A credit card is a payment card issued to users/ cardholders as a method of payment. It allows the cardholder to pay for goods and services based on the holder's promise to pay for them. The issuer of the card usually a bank creates a revolving account and grants a line of credit to the cardholder, from which the cardholder can borrow money for payment to a merchant or as a cash advance.

Point of Sale Terminal

Point of Sale Terminal is a computer terminal that is linked online to the computerized customer information files in a bank and magnetically encoded plastic transaction card that identifies the customer to the computer. During a transaction, the customer's account is debited and the retailer's account is credited by the computer for the amount of purchase.

Tele Banking & Mobile Banking

Telephone banking is a service provided by a bank or other financial institution that enables customers to perform a range of financial transactions over the telephone, without the need to visit a bank branch or automated teller machine. Mobile banking is a term used to refer to systems that allow customers of a financial institution to conduct a number of financial transactions through a mobile device such as mobile or tablet. Mobile banking differs from mobile payments, which involve the use of a mobile device to pay for goods or services either at the point of sale or remotely, analogously to the use of a debit or credit card to effect an EFTPOS payment.

Immediate Payment Service (IMPS)

Immediate Payment Service is an instant interbank electronic fund transfer service through mobile phones. It is also being extended through other channels such as ATM, Internet Banking, etc. Currently majority of interbank mobile fund transfer transactions are channelised through NEFT mechanism. Under NEFT, the transactions are processed and settled in batches, hence are not real time. Also, the transactions can be done only during the working hours of the RTGS system.

With the above context in mind, NPCI conducted a pilot study on the mobile payment system with the banks like SBI, BOI, UBI and ICICI in August 2010. Also the banks like Yes bank, Axis and HDFC bank joined this league in the month of September, October and November 2010 respectively. Immediate Payment Service (IMPS) public launch happened on 22nd November 2010 by Smt. Shyamala Gopinath, DG RBI at Mumbai **and this service is now available to the Indian public.** IMPS offer an instant, 24 × 7, interbank electronic fund transfer service through mobile phones. IMPS is an emphatic tool to transfer money instantly within banks across India through mobile, internet and ATM which is not only safe but also economical both in financial and non financial perspectives.

Cheque Truncation System

Cheque Truncation System (CTS) or Image-based Clearing System (ICS), in India, is a project undertaken by the Reserve Bank of India (RBI) in 2008, for faster clearing of cheques. CTS is based on a cheque truncation or online image-based cheque clearing system where cheque images and magnetic ink character recognition (MICR) data are captured at the collecting bank branch and transmitted electronically. Cheque truncation means stopping the flow of the physical cheques issued by a drawer to the drawee branch. The physical instrument is truncated at some point en route to the drawee branch and an electronic image of the cheque is sent to the drawee branch along with the relevant information like the MICR fields, date of presentation, presenting banks etc. This would eliminate the need to move the physical instruments across branches, except in exceptional circumstances, resulting in an effective reduction in the time required for payment of cheques, the associated cost of transit and delays in processing, etc., thus speeding up the process of collection or realization of cheques.

Electronic Data Interchange (EDI)

EDI (Electronic Data Interchange) is the transfer of data from one computer system to another by standardized message formatting, without the need for human intervention. EDI permits multiple companies -- possibly in different countries - to exchange documents electronically. Data can be exchanged through serial links and peer-to-peer networks, though most exchanges currently rely on the Internet for connectivity. An EDI message contains a string of data elements, each of which represents a singular fact, such as a price, product model number, and so forth, separated by delimiter. The entire string is called a data segment. One or more data segments framed by a header and trailer form a transaction set, which is the EDI unit of transmission (equivalent to a message). A transaction set often consists of what would usually be contained in a typical business document or form.

Progressive Activities

1. In the past few months, there have been many investments and developments in the Indian banking sector
2. The RBI has given in-principle approval to 11 applicants to establish payment banks. These banks can accept deposits and remittances, but are not allowed to extend any loans.
3. The Bank of Tokyo-Mitsubishi (BTMU), a Japanese financial services group, aims to double its branch count in India to 10 over the next three years and also target a 10 per cent credit growth during FY16.
4. State Bank of India has tied up with e-commerce portal Snapdeal and payment gateway Pay-pal to finance MSME businesses.
5. The United Economic Forum (UEF), an organisation that works to improve socio-economic status of the minority community in India, has signed a memorandum of

understanding (MoU) with Indian Overseas Bank (IOB) for financing entrepreneurs from backward communities to set up businesses in Tamil Nadu.

6. The RBI has allowed third-party white label automated teller machines (ATM) to accept international cards, including international prepaid cards, and said white label ATMs can now tie up with any commercial bank for cash supply
7. The RBI has allowed Indian alternative investment funds (AIFs), to invest abroad, in order to increase the investment opportunities for these funds.
8. In order to boost the infrastructure sector and the banks financing long gestation projects, the RBI has extended its flexible refinancing and repayment option for long-term infrastructure projects to existing ones where the total exposure of lenders is more than Rs 500 crore (US$ 75.1 million).
9. RBI governor Mr.Raghuram Rajan and European Central Bank President Mr.Mario Draghi have signed an MoU on cooperation in central banking. "The memorandum of understanding provides a framework for regular exchange of information, policy dialogue and technical cooperation between the two institutions. Technical cooperation may take the form of joint seminars and workshops in areas of mutual interest in the field of central banking," RBI said on its website.
10. RBL Bank informed that it would be the anchor investor in Trifecta Capital's Venture Debt Fund, the first alternative investment fund (AIF) in India with a commitment of Rs 50 crore (US$ 7.51 million). This move provides RBL Bank the opportunity to support the emerging venture debt market in India.
11. Bandhan Financial Services raised Rs 1,600 crore (US$ 240.2 million) from two international institutional investors to help convert its microfinance business into a full service bank. Bandhan, one of the two entities to get a banking licence along with IDFC, launched its banking operations in August 2015.
12. An MoU has been signed between the Yes Bank and the US government's development finance institution Overseas Private Investment Corp (OPIC) to explore US$ 220 million of financing to lend to micro, small and medium enterprises (MSMEs) in India.
13. The RBI has allowed bonds issued by multilateral financial institutions like World Bank Group, the Asian Development Bank and the African Development Bank in India as eligible securities for interbank borrowing. The move is expected to further develop the corporate bonds market, RBI informed in a notification.

Government Initiatives

With the implementation of Core Banking Solutions (CBS), the banking system is now seamlessly integrated. With the basic technology adoption being complete in banks, there is, therefore, a need to move from a transaction processing system to an information processing system. In its IT Vision Document 2011-17, the Reserve Bank of India has highlighted the need for banks to move forward and leverage IT in areas like Management Information Systems (MIS), overall risk management, financial inclusion, customer relationship management (CRM) and enhancing automated data flow within the banks and to the Reserve Bank without manual intervention. Banks need to augment their innovation capabilities in terms of new products, services and strategies which would enable them to maximise their efficiency gains. With the computerisation and adoption of CBS in banks almost reaching the final stage of completion, the focus has now shifted to adoption of more advanced technologies in banking which would enhance their CRM by using appropriate tools, improving internal effectiveness including MIS and managing risks arising out of IT implementation.

There have been a lot of developments in the Indian banking sector. The Government of India announced a capital infusion of Rs 6,990 crore (US$ 1.05 billion) in nine state run banks, including State Bank of India (SBI) and Punjab National Bank (PNB). However, the new efficiency parameters would include return on assets and return on equity. According to the finance ministry, “This year, the Government of India has adopted new criteria in which the banks which are more efficient would only be rewarded with extra capital for their equity so that they can further strengthen their position.”

To facilitate an easy access to finance by Micro and Small Enterprises (MSEs), the Government/RBI has launched Credit Guarantee Fund Scheme to provide guarantee cover for collateral free credit facilities extended to MSEs upto Rs 1 Crore (US$ 0.15 million). Moreover, Micro Units Development & Refinance Agency (MUDRA) Ltd. was also established to refinance all Micro-finance Institutions (MFIs), which are in the business of lending to micro / small business entities engaged in manufacturing, trading and services activities up to Rs 10 lakh (US$ 0.015 million).

The central government has come out with draft proposals to encourage electronic transactions, including income tax benefits for payments made through debit or credit cards. The Union cabinet has approved the establishment of the US$ 100 billion New Development Bank (NDB) envisaged by the five-member BRICS group as well as the BRICS “contingent reserve arrangement” (CRA). The government has plans to set up a fund that will provide surety to banks against loans given to students for higher education.

CONCLUSION

The Indian economy is on the brink of a major transformation, with several policy initiatives set to be implemented shortly. Positive business sentiments, improved consumer confidence and more controlled inflation are likely to prop-up the country’s the economic growth. Enhanced spending on infrastructure, speedy implementation of projects and continuation of reforms are expected to provide further impetus to growth. All these factors suggest that India’s banking sector is also poised for robust growth as the rapidly growing business would turn to banks for their credit needs. Also, the advancements in technology have brought the mobile and internet banking services to the fore. The banking sector is laying greater emphasis on providing improved services to their clients and also upgrading their technology infrastructure, in order to enhance the customer’s overall experience as well as give banks a competitive edge. Many banks, including HDFC, ICICI and AXIS are exploring the option to launch contact-less credit and debit cards in the market shortly. The cards, which use near field communication (NFC) mechanism, will allow customers to transact without having to insert or swipe.

RERFERNCES

1. B.P.Gupta, V.K.Vashistha, H.R.Swami, Banking and Finance, Ramesh Book Depot, Jaipur-New Delhi.
2. http://quickbooks.intuit.com/payments/facts-about-electronicchecks
3. http://www.business-standard.com/article/pf/what-are-neft-and-rtgs-111053100076_1.html
4. http://www.dnaindia.com/money/report-move-over-banks-rbi-pushes-for-smart-wallets-2028550
5. http://www.mudra.org.in/offerings.php
6. Kamlesh Bajaj & Dehjaji; E-Commerce, Tata McGraw hill publications Co. Ltd., New Delhi, 2005
7. S.B. Verma; E- Banking and Development of Banks, Deep & Deep Publications, New Delhi, 2008
8. Various issues of Business week, The Economist, Business Today, The Economic times and Financial Express.
9. www.icicibank.com
10. www.rbi.org.in http://www.ibef.org/industry/banking-india.aspx

Problems and Prospects of Mobile Banking in India

Navyatha Karnati
Lecturer in Commerce, Nizam College.

ABSTRACT

Banks have changed from paper-based banking solutions provider to the latest of the technologies like online-banking, mobile-banking, etc. These advancements in technology are propelling banks to lean more towards web and mobile to offer regular banking services and may be refraining their branches for sales and advisory services. As a result of this advancement, the number of customers who perform banking activities on-the-go has increased considerably and this has made a need to understand how the technology can be used to enhance the services. And this paper helps to understand what is mobile banking, how it emerged and prospered. This paper also studies the density by considering transactions through general mobile banking services in India since the year 2011 to 2015 by application of compounding growth rate and also studies the present challenges and also the future prospects.

Keywords: *Mobile banking, Density of mobile banking, Challenges, Prospects.*

INTRODUCTION

The widespread use of mobile phones and the advent of smart phones have led to a digital revolution worldwide and one of the recent innovation in the field of communication is mobile banking, where a customer interacts with a bank via mobile phone. Today, many financial service organizations including banks as a key component for implementation of their Customer Relationship Management (CRM) have been quick to implement Internet capabilities, and electronic service is becoming feasible. Largely, all banks are pushing ahead the idea of mobile banking to their customers after the introduction of electronic banking and considering modern day requirements mobile banking is expected to give greater scope or contribute to increase the banking adoption especially to rural population. But mobile banking is unknown to most of the population and is in its infancy in India. The banks are using this latest technology to reduce their operational costs and increase customer base. After the launch of mobile banking in India, mobile banking transactions have seen some growth.

The earliest mobile banking services used is SMS services and is known as SMS banking. In 1999 with the introduction of smart phones with WAP support enabling the use of mobile web the first European banks started to offer mobile banking to their customers. Mobile Banking services were first offered by Kenya and Philippines in the world. In Kenya the first mobile banking solution offered was M-PESA in 2007 by telecom operators Safaricom & Vodafone, which captured majority of the market in and has become very popular among customers. Philippines launched SMART money-an electronic wallet and users do most of its banking transactions through mobile only.

In India the RBI in 2006 announced that it would develop a regulatory and oversight framework for mobile banking, and made clear its concern over the safety of transactions through mobile phones. In RBI's Financial Sector Technology Vision: 2008-2010 it included a statement that "adequate steps be taken to ensure safety and security in a mobile based computing /communicating and expected mobile-based services to assume an ever greater portion of banking transactions in general and payment services in particular" and formulated the guidelines that came out in the year 2008 and were modified in 2009 which are (i) Only such banks which are licensed and supervised in India and have a physical presence in India will be permitted to offer mobile payment services to residents of India. (ii) The services should be restricted to only bank accounts/ credit card accounts holders in India which are KYC/AML compliant. (iii) Only Indian Rupee based services should be provided. (iv) Banks may use the services of business correspondents for extending this facility to their customers and guidelines with this regard would be as per the RBI circulars on business correspondents issued from time to time. (v) The 'Risks and Controls in Computers and Telecommunication guidelines will equally apply to mobile payments. (vi) The KYC and AML as prescribed by RBI from time to time would be applicable to customers opting for mobile banking service.

OBJECTIVES

The important objectives of the study are presented as follows:

1. To analyze the Density of the mobile banking transactions in India.
2. To study the problems in adopting mobile banking in India.
3. To study the future prospects of the mobile banking in India.

RESEARCH METHODOLOGY

The research methodology used for this study is presented as follows:

Sources of Data: This study used only the secondary sources of data. The secondary sources of data are drawn from the Reserve Bank of India data base.

Statistical Tools: The selected statistical tools used for study are compounded annual growth Rate.

MOBILE BANKING

According to TRAI, "mobile banking involves the use of mobile phones for banking transactions like fund transfer, balance check, etc. Mobile Banking also refers to provision and availment of banking and financial services with the help of mobile telecommunication devices. Scope of offered services may include facilities to conduct bank and stock market transactions, to administer accounts and to access customized information." According to this, model mobile banking consists three inter-related concepts: (i) Mobile accounting (ii) Mobile brokerage and (iii) Mobile financial information services. Accounting and Brokerage are transaction based and financial information services are non transaction based.

Again Mobile banking transactions can broadly be classified into two: push type and pull type. Push type is a one-way transaction where bank sends information pertaining to account through SMS. Pull type is a two-way transaction, where individual send a request and the bank replies. Push type services involves 1. Inter-bank mobile payment service (IMPS)-fund transfer service through National Payment Council of India (NPCI) to transfer funds from one account to another across banks within the country using mobile phone and IMPS can be used via banks' app, USSD'S dial-in number, encrypted SMS banking or net banking. 2. Bank apps -bank's application or software can be downloaded on mobile phone via internet which works on both GSM and CDMA handsets for Android and iPhone platforms. 3. USSD-based - is a type, in which an individual can dial the bank's service code and ask for information of his bank account. And there is no need of a Smartphone or high end phone to use the USSD platform. 4. SMS-Based - It is the most popular method where one can get account information via SMS. 5. Internet-based mobile banking - This is a way where individual can use mobile screen like a computer monitor. Apart from these there are more options like the mobile wallets, offered by telecom service provider platforms like Vodafone's m-pesa, Bharti Airtel's Airtel Money and Aircel's Mobile Money in which that even an un-banked customer can use this service and for which smart phone and an internet connection are not essential.

DENSITY OF MOBILE BANKING IN INDIA

Due to the highest penetration of mobile phones the mobile banking transactions has increased rapidly. From the table 1, it can be observed that there is a continuous increase in the mobile banking transactions from Aug 2011 to Sep 2015 both in terms of Volume and also Value. And on average for four years we see 9.4 mn transactions through mobile banking which resulted in total worth of 49.82 bn rupees which can be due to adoption of the 2G, 3G and 4G technology and also because of the large shift to using the touch screen mobiles than that of the basic handsets which becomes easy for the people to use the mobile banking application on screen.

And from table-2 it is evident that from Sept 2012 to Aug 2013 we see an average increase of 94.12% Volume of transactions and 65.93% leading to 272.22% worth of transaction, for Sept'13 to Aug'14 there is a 65.98% growth in volume of transactions leading to the overall 246.31% worth in rupee terms with that of the previous year and from Sept'14 to Aug'15 transactions recorded a growth of 99.46% when compared to that of the previous year which is lower than that of the previous year but for the year Sep'2014 to Aug'15 growth rate is 99.46% creating 420.87% growth in worth in terms of rupees.

CHALLENGES WITH ADOPTION OF MOBILE BANKING

Economic Challenges: The rural population in India is spread across 600,000 villages, each with a low transaction value. Hence mobile banking must be inexpensive enough to be attractive for the end-customer over existing methods.

Regulatory Challenges: Although the RBI is supportive of mobile banking in India, there are many regulations that are being put into place such as (i) Restricted to *Financial Institutions and banks*- existing only in India (ii) *Rupee Transactions*-All transactions must be done only in India's national currency, the rupee which act as constraint for interoperability (iii) *Existing Account Holders* - where only customers with valid bank account would be allowed for mobile banking, limits the full potential of mobile banking to extend micro-credit and bring banking to the large number of unbanked customers in India.

Demographic Challenges: India has 18 official languages which are spoken across the country and the state governments also are dictated to correspond in their regional language for official purposes and illiteracy of major population is also creating difficulties in deployment of mobile banking solutions.

***Security Issues with WAP (Wireless Application Protocol)*:** WAP is used for communication between devices like digital mobile phones, internet, PDA etc through which customer can realize more functionality of internet banking and encryption process is currently used for secure data transmission, but it is not good enough for protection of sensitive data between bank and user as data is not encrypted at gateway during the switching of protocol process, which leads to security concern for mobile banking and it is also identified that users are not usually satisfied from mobile commerce over WAP as they encounter the problems like low speed, unreliable connection, and high cost.

***Authentication Risks and Issues*:** One of the authentication method used in mobile banking is the login method where PIN is used and many security issues such as password and id theft were discovered in this method which results in customer's distrust. Bank follows some security mechanisms such as identifying the customer's phone number, SIM card number, pin number etc. But it brings inconvenience to users because of security threat where the hackers may track the customers data where if device gets stolen.

***SMS based Mobile Banking*:** SMS based mobile banking is a convenient and easy way for accessing bank but there are end-to-end security problems such as GPRS protocols and security issues for transaction of money exist in SMS and lacking of privacy, integrity and security. And for *SMS plaintext* end to end encryption is not available and the other threat can be *SMS Spoofing Attack,* the most dangerous where attacker can send messages on network by manipulating sender's number. Due to which, most of the organizations are not adopting mobile banking through SMS.

***Virus Attacks in Mobile Banking*:** There are more than fifty thousand different types of computer viruses, internet malicious program and Trojans. Software like Trojan horses can easily take up password on the web browser or any cached information on operating system. Malicious codes are written for remote communication such as Zeus Trojan targeted mobile bank users. Zitmo has been used by attackers to detect SMS banking. Zeus is commonly used to steal mobile transaction authentication number or password

***Risk with Digital Signature*:** To reduce hardware cost, designer may prefer digital signature which is efficient for authentication, but is computational intensive with unsigned values, for example date, amount, they differ from transaction to transaction. So a signed template can be used with several unsigned values like date, amount etc.

Despite a high base of mobile phone users, the smart phone penetration is limited. This restricts use of full scale mobile banking as users can't download banking app on basic phones and depend on SMS, which is cumbersome. A user can have up to nine mobile phone numbers (allowed by TRAI) but only one mobile bank account (says RBI). And the limit of transactions for mobile payments is Rs 50,000 per month.

Despite being convenient, the cost of Know Your Customer (KYC) for mobile banking or mobile payments is huge - Rs 400 to Rs 500 per person. This is more than the average revenue per subscriber for telcos.

PROSPECTS OF MOBILE BANKING

1. Mobile banking is the future because of its cost effectiveness and ability to reach out to customers in remote areas.
2. *Mobile Network Operators and Large Corporate Houses Co-Venture*: With the popularity of collaborations between mobile network operators (MNO's) and banks live up to the promise of financial inclusion, the RBI and TRAI have announced that they will harmonize and coordinate with each other to avoid any form of regularity conflict. Many large Indian banks have partnered/co-ventured with large mobile network operations (MNO's) and handset.
3. *Under-banked and Un-Banked Population:* Almost half of the country's population is unbanked. Where large section of the Indian population is not just in rural areas but also in many segments of urban markets. This offers a large untapped market with a tremendous business potential.
4. *Demographic Factors:* India has the largest youth population between the age group of 14-29. And also the middle aged group of 30-44 and are among those who are the early adopters of latest technology and new services, which presents a huge opportunity for e/m-banking service providers and financial services is a household need, and not only an individual need, and if the account holder is illiterate, other members of the family are competent enough to execute transactions and use electronic or mobile banking services.
5. The Reserve Bank issued necessary guidelines to banks in December 2014 Where Banks were advised to provide their customers options for easy registration for mobile banking services, through multiple channels, including ATMs, thereby minimising the need for branch visit to avail such services.
6. NPCI (National Payments Corporation of India) is in the process of facilitating mobile banking registration at ATMs. Similarly, NPCI was advised by RBI with regard to setting standards for industry agreements between banks and mobile network operators (MNOs) for handling customer grievances, particularly in the context of the National Unified USSD (Unstructured Supplementary Service Data) Platform (NUUP). Trade Receivables Discounting System (TReDS).

CONCLUSION AND SUGGESTIONS

Though mobile banking is considered at its infancy in India, transactions are growing from time to time since adoption leading to even the Creation of value in rupees to the banks. But it is not so versatile to extend over to the entire population due to the restriction through regulations, Demographic factors, security issues and many other. RBI by taking customer safeguarding approach and friendly guidelines to enhance the usage of mobile services such as providing registration for mobile banking services through ATMs and by collaborating with the mobile network operators for handling customers grievances mobile banking can be made as an effective BC model for even for financial inclusion.

REFERENCES

1. Dr.Vinod Kumar Gupta, Renu Bagoria, *Neha Bagoria, Mobile Banking Services as Adoption and Challenges: A Case of M-Banking in India,* International Journal of Scientific and Research Publications, Volume 3, Issue 1, January 2013
2. Nitin Nayak , Vikas Nath & Nancy Goel, A *Study of Adoption Behavior of Mobile Banking Services by Indian Consumers,* International Journal of Research in Engineering & Technology Vol. 2, Issue 3, Mar 2014, 209-222.
3. Vishal Goyal, Dr.U.S.Pandey, Sanjay Batra, *Mobile Banking in India: Practices, Challenges and Security Issues,* International Journal of Advanced Trends in Computer Science and Engineering, Volume 1, No.2, May – June 2012
4. H R Khan, *Customizing mobile banking in India – issues and challenges,* "BIS central bankers speech on Sustainable excellence through customer engagement, employee engagement and right use of technology", organized by the Federation of Indian Chambers of Commerce and Industry (FICCI) and the Indian Banks Association (IBA), Mumbai, 5 September 2012.
5. Renju Chandran, *Pros and cons of Mobile banking,* International Journal of Scientific and Research Publications, Volume 4, Issue 10, October 2014.
6. Mr. M. Govindarajan, *Financial inclusion in India through mobile banking,* **article in Tax** Management.com, February 21, 2015.
7. Shelley Singh, *why India needs mobile banking & how customers benefit from it,* The Economic Times, Dec 14, 2012.
8. www.rbi.org.i

Linkage between ATMs, Credit and Debit Cards and Employee Productivity: A Study on Indian Public Sector Banks

M. Suvarchala Rani[1], and Dr. U. Devi Prasad[2]
[1]Research Scholar, Gitam University.
[2]Research Guide, Associate Professor, Gitam University.

ABSTRACT

The public sector banks in India account for a major share of business, i.e., deposits and advances of the banking system in the country. The employees play a vital part in carrying out the banking transactions and enabling the banks to function on profitable lines. However, the banks are also seen to open ATMs and issue credit and debit cards for the convenience of customers besides operating through their branch network. This combined operation of banks through branches and ATMs and the use of credit and debit cards by the customers will have implications on the business and profitability of the banks, and the productivity of employees.

It is possible that the more the number of ATMs a bank has and the more the credit and debit cards issued, the larger the scope for the employees to concentrate on the business carried through the branches. Even the number of employees required in branches could be affected in the process. The present study deals with these aspects.

The prime objective is to analyse the relationship and inter-linkages between the ATMs, credit and debit cards, the number and amount of relative transactions, business, number of employees, business per employee, profit and profit per employee, for public sector banks in India. The data are taken for the financial year 2014-15 for each of the public sector banks. The hypotheses have been framed accordingly relating to the ATMs, credit cards, and debit cards and their associations with the business of the banks, the number of employees and the profit of banks. The study uses correlation and regression analysis. The hypotheses have been tested with statistical validity. The results are considered to add to the existing literature on the subject and help in decision making at policy level.

Keywords: *Public sector banks, ATMs, credit cards, debit cards, employee productivity.*

INTRODUCTION

Liberalization, privatization and globalization have led to the flourishing of Indian economy. This includes banking sector as well. Indian public sector banks were presented with a challenge of competing with various private new banks along with foreign banks who integrated new technology into their system. Banks had an uphill task of not only incorporating new technology and introducing creative services but also had a challenge of taking consideration of customers' needs and wants. This led to the adoption of electronic banking which created a wider scope for the customers and the banks as well.

The foreign and new private banks' adoption of new services like plastic cards (credit and debit cards), ATM services, Internet banking, Electronic Funds transfer (EFT), etc. has led to catering to maximum customers inspite of having physical branches. This approach made the public sector banks realize the need to move towards electronic banking to improve their efficiency, customer services, employee productivity and profitability. Thus banks have reengineered their operations to reach maximum customers by their innovative distributive channels.

The business of a bank includes receiving deposits or liabilities. It also creates or invest in assets on the other hand. It is quite important to study the productivity of the banks. To assess bank's productivity, business per employee is considered as a key factor. Some of the performance indicators of this study include business, profit, number of ATMs onsite and offsite, amount of transactions with respect to credit and debit cards, business per employee and profit per employee.

NEED OF THE STUDY

After the advent of electronic banking (ATM centre's, credit and debit cards), the scope for the employees to concentrate on the business carried through the branches has increased. Even the number of employees required in branches could be affected in the process. Hence there is a need to assess the productivity of the employees (Business per employee) with regard to the same.

OBJECTIVES OF THE STUDY

1. To study and compare the employee productivity of public sector banks functioning in India.
2. To analyse the relationship and inter-linkages between business, profit, number of employees, ATMs, credit and debit cards, business per employee and profit per employee, for the public sector banks in India.

RESEARCH METHODOLOGY

The study is based on secondary data collected from the various volumes of banking statistics published by Reserve Bank of India and Indian Banks Association, for the year 2014-15. The variables considered are business, number of employees, ATMs, credit and debit cards, and profit for the public sector banks in India.

REVIEW OF LITERATURE

Bhuvan J. Vyas and Vijay Pithadia (2012) studied on employee productivity in SBI and IDBI bank. The two indicators of productivity used for the study were Income per Employee and Expenditure per Employee for the period of 2006-07 to 2010-11. To measure the productivity ratio analysis and F-test were used. It was concluded that there was a significant difference between SBI and IDBI bank for Income per employee as well as Expenditure per employee.

Geetu Gupta and Amandeep Kaur (2013) have conducted a study on performance and productivity of public sector banks in India on the basis of employee and branch productivity for the period of 1991-2010. To analyse the productivity, statistical measures such as mean, standard deviation and coefficient of variation have been used. It is suggested that banks need to improve their productivity and profitability, maintain efficiency, adopt new technology and look for various cost effective solutions.

Hawa Singh and Kamlesh (2013) did a study on employee's productivity of private sector banks in India during the period 2002-12. The different variables like Deposits per Employee, Advances per Employee, Business per Employee, Total Expenditure per Employee, Total Income per Employee, Spread per Employee, Net profit per Employee, and Burden per Employee were selected to compute the productivity of private sector banks. For the purpose of analysis, statistical measures like standard deviation, coefficient of variation, exponential growth rate, and Trend Analysis have been used. It is observed that the performance of private sector banks has an increased trend during 2004-05 to 2011-12 and also observed that the new private sector banks compete with better performance than the old private sector banks.

Jyotindra M. Jani and Manish B. Raval (2012) presented a paper on employees' productivity in terms of business and profit by using the financial ratios like Business per employee and Profit per employee in four selected Nationalized Banks of India during 2006-07 to 2010-11. F-Test with two-way Anova has been used to analyze the data. The study reveals that there is a significant difference in Business per Employee and Profit per Employee between the banks and there is a significant difference in Business per Employee within the banks over the period of study and there is no significant difference in profit per employee within the banks over the period of study.

Vivek Singala (2013) conducted a study on analysis of productivity in three private sector banks during 2007-08 to 2011-12. Ratio analysis has been used to compare the productivity of Indian banks. The Branch Productivity Ratios and Employee Productivity ratios were selected. It is concluded that ICICI bank is better in employee productivity but less good in branch productivity than other selected private sector banks.

Uppal R.K. (2008) analyzed the quality of e-banking services in the changing environment. The sample size of bank customers is 25. The data is collected through well-structured questionnaire in Ludhiana, Punjab in May 2006.The study concluded that the customers of e-banks are satisfied with the different e-channels and their services in the spread of e-banking services. It also suggests some measures to make e-banking service more effective in the future. The study is mainly concerned with the Indian banking industry in general and particularly those banks that are producing services through e-channels, i.e. e-banking.

Banknet India (2006) conducted an online survey on 316 ATM users during the months of August-September 2006 and the survey is limited to India to get insight into users' perceptions. It is concluded from the survey that the most use (56 per cent) of ATM services is for bill payments and pre-paid mobile recharge where 64 per cent respondents feel comfortable with depositing cash/cheques through ATM but they have to wait in long queues and find no money left in the machine. Most of the respondents (81 per cent) claimed to know about fee charged at other bank ATMs and 20 per cent demand more privacy. Overall, ATMs are preferred over branch banking by majority (95 per cent) of respondents which shows the increasing popularity of e-banking among the public.

Chopra V.K. (2006) highlights the importance of IT and business re-engineering in achieving the objectives of banks. The paper concludes that public sector banks and old private sector banks are slow in imbibing technology in their operations, whereas new private sector banks and foreign banks are early adopters of the technology and they are also increasing the level of competition. The paper emphasizes that IT along with the business process re-engineering can provide ideal technology environment catering to the stated business objectives.

From the broader scanning of the literature on the studies relating to the productivity and the key determining factors, it is found that there is a need for a study of the productivity of the employees in public sector banks in India, and the linkages to profit and other determining factors in this respect. These banks account for a major share of business of the banking system, i.e. deposits and advances, in the country. The employees play a vital part in carrying out the banking transactions and enabling the banks to function on profitable lines. However, the banks are also seen to open ATMs and issue credit and debit cards for the convenience of customers besides operating through their branch network. This combined operation of banks through branches and ATMs and the use of credit and debit cards by the customers will have implications on the business and profitability of the banks, and the productivity of employees. The present study would try to analyse the relationship and inter-linkages between business, number of employees, the ATMs, and credit and debit cards, in respect of all the 26 public sector banks in India.

CONCEPTS

Productivity refers to the amount goods or services produced per unit of labour, capital and other inputs, in a given period of time. In simple words, it is the ratio of output to input. In the case of banking sector, human resources are most vital and valuable assets which show the ability of banks to deliver value to the customers. So, skills of employees or labour or staff play an important role to achieve higher levels of productivity in banks. The Employee Productivity in banks can be judged by using some of the selected financial ratios such as Business per employee and Profit per employee.

In the present study, business refers to the amount of deposits and advances, which represent the major functions of banks of mobilising the resources and lending the same or investing a part of it or using a part of it for meeting the statutory reserves and cash reserves requirements as stipulated by the Reserve Bank of India. Profit is taken to refer to net profit after paying taxes.

HYPOTHESES

H01: There is no significant association across business, number of employees, number of ATM centres and the amount of debit card transactions in the case of public sector banks in India.

H11: There is a significant association across business, number of employees, number of ATM centres and the amount of debit card transactions in the case of public sector banks in India.

H02: There is no significant relationship between profit and business in public sector banks in India.

H12: There is a significant relationship between profit and business in public sector banks in India.

H03: There is no significant relationship between business and credit cards in select public sector banks in India.

H13: There is a significant relationship between business and credit cards in select public sector banks in India.

DATA ANALYSIS AND INTERPRETATION

For the study, data on business, profit, number of employees, number of ATM centers, the amount of debit card transactions, business per employee, and profit per employee, in the case of public sector banks in India, are given in Table 1, for the year 2014-15.

Table 1 Public Sector Banks: Business, Profit and Determinants, 2014-2015

S.No.	Public Sector Banks*	Business (Rs. crore)	Profit (Rs. crore)	Employees	ATMs (No.)	Debit cards (Rs. crore)	Business per employee (Rs. crore)	Profit per employee (Rs. lakh)	Credit cards (Rs. '000 crore)$
1	ALB	343301	615	24007	1168	1244	14	3	NA
2	AB	280967	546	18197	2232	3983	15	3	56
3	BoB	1045625	381	55353	8030	6027	19	7	11
4	BoI	933932	3160	45139	6771	5068	21	7	84
5	BoM	220718	424	14149	1849	1772	16	3	2
6	CanB	803876	2801	56019	8533	5960	14	5	112
7	CBI	444050	597	39029	4835	3172	11	2	40
8	CorpB	344412	585	17999	2933	1966	19	3	6
9	DB	194870	265	13514	1482	806	14	2	NA
10	IB	295089	1012	20450	2336	3222	14	5	13
11	IoB	417805	Loss	31556	3571	2600	13	Loss	6
12	OBC	349271	493	20038	2495	1815	17	2	NA
13	PSB	150585	94	9441	1268	255	16	1	NA
14	PNB	881913	3343	66862	8348	9235	13	5	14
15	SB	458108	1652	29767	3427	2408	15	6	9
16	UCO Bank	361688	1266	26266	2096	1638	14	5	NA
17	UnionB	572524	2016	40319	7020	4527	14	5	5
18	UBI	175581	2433	15228	1912	1554	12	16	NA
19	VB	213039	427	14241	1383	1177	15	3	37

Table 1 ***Contd...***

S.No.	Public Sector Banks*	Business (Rs. crore)	Profit (Rs. crore)	Employees	ATMs (No.)	Debit cards (Rs. crore)	Business per employee (Rs. crore)	Profit per employee (Rs. lakh)	Credit cards (Rs. '000 crore)$
20	SBI	2876820	6017	222033	45502	63659	13	3	344
21	SBBJ	153788	839	13981	1843	2648	11	6	NA
22	SBH	235219	1286	15516	2404	4284	15	8	NA
23	SBM	118090	4034	10085	1334	1620	12	4	NA
24	SBP	171347	2880	14399	1437	1512	12	2	NA
25	SBT	159798	392	13077	1602	3855	12	3	NA
26	IDBI Bank	468213	1250	17864	3000	3512	26	7	NA
	Total	12670629	36013	864529	128811	139518	15	4	

* Full names of the banks are given in Table 2, NA : Not available.

Productivity and Profit per Employee

A measure of productivity per employee is the business per employee. From Table 1, it is found that for all the 26 public sector banks, the average business per employee is Rs.15 crore. The banks have been categorised into three categories as High, Medium and Low, according to the level of business per employee, as shown in Table 2. 'High' includes five banks with business per employee of Rs.16 crore and more. 'Medium' category covers the banks, numbering 13, in the range of Rs.12 crore to Rs.15 crore. The category 'Low' consists of 8 banks in the range less than Rs.12 crore business per employee. Thus, majority of the banks are in the 'Middle' group.

Table 2 Public Sector Banks: Business per Employee for Public Sector Banks in India, 2014-15

Business per Employee (Rs. crore)	Banks	No. of Banks
High (16 & above)	Bank of Baroda (BoB), Bank of India (BoI), Corporation Bank (CorpB), Oriental Bank of Commerce (OBC) and IDBI Bank	5
Medium (12 to 15)	Allahabad Bank (ALB), Andhra Bank (AB), Bank of Maharashtra (BoM), Canara Bank (CanB), Dena Bank (DB), Indian Bank (IB), Punjab and Sindh Bank (PSB), Syndicate Bank (SB), UCO Bank, Union Bank of India (UnionB), Vijaya Bank (VB), State Bank of Hyderabad (SBH), and State Bank of India (SBI)	13
Low (Less than 12)	Central Bank of India (CBI), Indian Overseas Bank (IOB), Punjab National Bank (PNB), United Bank of India (UBI), State Bank of Bikaner & Jaipur (SBBJ), State Bank of Mysore (SBM), State Bank of Patiala (SBP) and State Bank of Travancore (SBT)	8
	Total	26

Business growth is supposed to result in higher profits, which is being examined. From the data on profit per employee (Table 1), the banks have been categorised into High, Medium and Low, according to the level of profit per employee. For the 26 public sector banks, the average profit per employee is Rs.4 crore. 'High' includes five banks with profit per employee of Rs.7 lakh and more. 'Medium' category covers the banks, numbering 15, ranging from Rs.3 lakh to Rs.6 crore. The 'Low' group comprises 6 banks, ranged less than Rs.12 lakh profit per employee. Thus, majority of the banks are in the 'Middle' group.

A comparison of the banks in Tables 2 and 3 reveals that Bank of Baroda, Bank of India and IDBI Bank are in the 'High' category both in respect of business per employee and profit per employee. But, Corporation Bank and Oriental Bank of Commerce have from the 'High' group as per business per employee to 'Middle' and 'Low' groups as per profit per employee respectively. This could be because of a higher level of non-performing assets, or lesser income accruals from investments. Similarly, Dena Bank and Punjab and Sindh Bank slipped from 'Middle' in business to 'Low' in profit per employee.

Table 3 Profit per Employee for Public Sector Banks in India, 2014-15

Profit per Employee (Rs. lakh)	**Banks**	**No. of Banks**
High (7 or more)	BoB, BoI, UBI, SBH and IDBI Bank	5
Medium (3 to 6)	ALB, AB, BoM, CanB, CorpB, IB, PNB, SB, UCO Bank, UnionB, VB, SBI, SBBJ, SBM and SBT	15
Low (2 or less)	CBI, DB, IOB, OBC, PSB, and SBP	6
	Total	**26**

Business and Determinants

For the 26 public sector banks considered for the study, correlation coefficients have been calculated (Table 4) between the business and the determinants viz., employees, number of ATMs and the transactions through debit cards, as well as profit. Credit cards transactions also will have correlation with business but they are analysed separately as data for them are available for only 14 out of the 26 banks considered here. For each of the variables referred above, the inter-correlations are very strong being in the range of 0.74 to 0.99.

Table 4 Correlations between Business and related Variables

	Business	**Profit**	**Employees**	**ATM**	**Debit cards**
Business	1				
Profit	0.88	1			
Employees	0.98	0.84	1		
ATM	0.97	0.80	0.99	1	
Debit cards	0.93	0.74	0.97	0.99	1

For the banks under reference, a regression model has been used regressing business (dependent variable) on the determining variables viz., number of employees, number of ATMs and the transactions from Debit cards. R square is found to be 0.978. The value of Adjusted R^2 0.971 means that 97 per cent of the variation in business is explained by the determining variables which makes the model very explanatory. The Anova output (Table 5), shows that the regression model is a good fit, the significant F value1.12E-17 being less than the level of significance of 0.05.

Table 5 Anova Results for Business and Determining Factors

	df	**SS**	**MS**	**F**	**Significance F**
Regression	3	7.41E+12	2.47E+12	280.5605	1.12E-17
Residual	22	1.94E+11	8.81E+09		
Total	25	7.61E+12			

The regression statistics (Table 6) reveal that the p-values for the coefficients are less than 0.05 level of significance for employees and debit cards, and at par for ATMs at 0.10 level of significance. These values are interpretable. The p-value for the intercept is more than even the 0.10 level of significance. But this is the case, when the value of the intercept is given the value of zero as well. Hence the value of the intercept is included in the regression model assuming that the value accrues on account of credit cards and any other relevant independent variables left out of the regression model. The, the regression model is formulated as equation (1).

$$Y = 35520 + 10.86X_1 + 47.34X_2 - 2.68X_3 \qquad \text{... (1)}$$

We find from equation (1) that an addition of an employee will result in an increase in business by Rs.10.86 crore, and an ATM added will contribute Rs.47.34 crore to business. This implies that adding ATMs is more beneficial (as they are operative with no time limits) than recruiting additional persons (as they work for fixed hours), though manpower is crucial for banks as they supervise the working of ATMs, besides doing other functions which cannot be done by ATMs. In the case of debit cards, the relationship is inverse with business growth, as debit card transactions involve outflow of money from the banks resulting in a corresponding decline in deposits (with an impact of Rs. 2.68 crore), though a part of the withdrawals may come back to the banking system through subsequent non-card transactions.

Table 6 Regression Statistics: Coefficients and Test Results for Business and Determinants

	Coefficients	**Standard Error**	**t Stat**	**P-value**	**Lower 95%**	**Upper 95%**
Intercept	35520.39	36815.82	0.96	0.345	-40831	111871.7
Employees	10.86	3.56	3.05	0.006	3.47	18.26
ATMs	47.34	27.62	1.71	0.101	-9.95	104.63
Debit cards	-2.68	1.08	-2.47	0.022	-4.93	-0.43

Profitability

Now, turning to the relationship between business and profit, for the 26 banks considered, the correlation coefficient is found to be 0.88. When business (dependent variable) is regressed on profit, R square is found to be 0.77. The value of Adjusted R^2 0.76 implies that 76 per cent of the variation in profit is explained by business which makes the model well explanatory. The Anova output (Table 7), shows that the regression model is a good fit, the significant F value 3.31E-09 being less than the level of significance of 0.05.

Table 7 Anova results for Business and Profit

	df	SS	MS	F	Significance F
Regression	1	3.99E+11	3.99E+11	81.94	3.31E-09
Residual	24	1.17E+11	4.87E+09		
Total	25	5.16E+11			

The regression statistics (Table 8) reveal that the p-value for the coefficient for business is less than 0.05 level of significance and thus coefficient value is interpretable. The p-value for the intercept exceeds the 0.05 level of significance, and this is also the case when the value of the intercept is taken as zero. Hence the value of the intercept is included in the regression model assuming that the value arises from sources of profit other than business such as sale of assets. The regression model is formulated as equation (2) below.

$$Pr = 26946 + 0.23B \qquad \text{... (2)}$$

Equation (2) indicates that business of Rs.1 crore increases profit by Rs.23 lakh.

Table 8 Regression Statistics: Coefficients and Test Results for Business and Profit

	Coefficients	Standard Error	t Stat	P-value	Lower 95%	Upper 95%
Intercept	26946.03	18413.42	1.46	0.16	-11057.4	64949.5
Business	0.23	0.025	9.05	3.31E-09	0.18	0.28

Credit Cards

Credit cards transactions will influence the level of business. These should have been included in regression equation (1) itself, but are analysed separately here, as data for them are available for only 14 out of the 26 banks considered earlier (Table 1).

The regression of business (dependent variable) on the amount of credit card transactions (independent variable), has given the value of R square as 0.81. The value of Adjusted R^2 0.79 means that 79 per cent of the variation in business is explained by the amount of credit card transactions which makes the model well explanatory. The Anova output (Table 9), shows that the regression model is a good fit, the significant F value 1.26E-05 being less than the level of significance of 0.05.

Table 9 Anova results for Business and Credit Cards

	df	SS	MS	F	Significance F
Regression	1	4.93E+12	4.93E+12	50.30754	1.26E-05
Residual	12	1.18E+12	9.81E+10		
Total	13	6.11E+12			

The regression statistics (Table 10) reveal that the p-values for the coefficients are less than 0.05 level of significance for the intercept as well as the credit cards. Thus, these values are interpretable. The regression model is formulated as equation (3).

$$B = 339447 + 6824Cr \quad \text{... (3)}$$

Equation (3) shows that a unit (Rs. 1000 crore) increase in credit cards' transactions will increase business by Rs. 6824 crore. This indicates a six multiple in business per Rs 1 crore credit card transaction incorporating the ripple effects in the nature of such business. This perhaps explains why the banks follow up much the credit cards activity.

Table 10 Regression Statistics: Coefficients and Test Results for Business and Credit Cards

	Coefficients	Standard Error	t Stat	P-value	Lower 95%	Upper 95%
Intercept	339446.7	97858.91	3.47	0.005	126230.5	552663
Credit Cards	6824.19	962.13	7.09	1.26E-05	4727.9	8920.5

CONCLUSION

The study deals with an analysis of the productivity of employees, and the association between business and key determinants such as the number of employees, ATM centers, debit cards and credit cards, in the case of public sector banks in India. The relationship between business and profit has also been examined. A majority of the public sector banks are found to be in the 'Middle' level category in the case of business per employee, as well as profit per employee. Some banks have slipped from a higher category of business per employee to a lower category of profit per employee. Analysis has shown that there is a significant association between business, number of employees, number of ATM centers, the amount of debit card transactions and credit cards.

REFERENCES

1. Bhuvan Vyas and Vijay Pithadia. (2012). "Productivity in Service Sector: SBI and IDBI Bank", Indian Journal of Applied Research, 2(2): 107-108.
2. Geetu Gupta and Amandeep Kaur. (2013). "A Study on Productivity and Performance of Public Sector Banks in India" Universal Journal of International and business Management 1(4): 117-136 |
3. Hawa Singh and Kamlesh. (2013). "Employee Productivity of Private Sector Banks in India", International Journal of Management and Social Science Research, 2(10): 64-79.

4. Jyotindra M. Jani and Manish B.Raval. (2012). "An Analytical Study of Employees Productivity in Some Selected Nationalized Banks in India", Indian Journal of Applied Research, 1(9): 19-20
5. Vivek Singala. (2013). "Analysis of Productivity of Indian Banks: A Comparative Study of Selected Private Banks", International Journal of Computing and Business Research, 4(2).
6. Uppal R.K. (2006). Indian Banking Industry and Information Technology. New Delhi: New Century Publications.
7. Banknet India. (2006). 'ATM User Survey report 2006'. Survey conducted by Banknet India. Mumbai.
8. Chopra V.K. (2006). 'IT and Business Process Re-Engineering'. Indian Bankers – Special Issue on e-payments and Commerce. 1(3). March 2006.

WEBSITES

www.rbi.org.in

www.iba.org

An Analytical Study on Technological Advancements in Banking Sector

A.V.B.N.H. Saroja[1] and Dr. Raavi Radhika[2]
[1]Research Scholar, GITAM University.
[2]Research Guide, Assistant Professor, Hyderabad Business School.

ABSTRACT

In today's world technology support is very important for the successful functioning of the banking sector. Technological innovation in India will lead the way for innovation in banking sector. Information technology is one of the most important facilitator for the transformation of the Indian banking industry in terms of transactions processing as well as various other internal systems and processes. The research focus on usage of technology in banking sector for effective functioning of banks. Banks will use technology to facilitate and serve customers across the world. The technological development of modern banking can be traced from 1960, when Charles Sanford joined Bankers Trust. During his tenure he introduced check encoders, check scanners, currency counters, currency discriminators, check strippers. Post 80's banking sector witnessed technological developments such as use of Computers, ATMs, Mobile Banking and Cloud Computing. The technological development in the banking sector with usage of Advanced Ledger Posting Machines (ALPM) in the 1980s and later used Core banking solutions (CBS) for providing better services to their customers. The various innovations in banking sector are ECS, RTGS, NEFT, ATM, Retail Banking, Debit & Credit Cards, funds transfers, internet banking, implementation of standing instructions of customers, payments of utility bills, issue of free cheque books, free advisory services, traveller's cheques and many more value added services. Now the branches are working on the concept of 24 × 7 *working without having to hire higher manpower.* 24 × 7 *working made possible to Tele banking, ATMs, Internet Banking, Mobile and E- Banking. This research paper focuses on the way how technology is effective in the banking sector by the usage of IT products which changed the face of banking in India. New Technology facilitates the banks to introduce new products and services in banking sector which helps bankers in complete digitalization.*

Keywords: *Information Technology, Banking Sector, Internet Banking, Mobile Banking, ATMs.*

INTRODUCTION

The study presents broader overview of towards the incorporation of advanced technology in the current banking industry in India. The innovations in financial sector and banking sector are ECS, RTGS, EFT, NEFT, ATM, Debit & Credit cards, retail banking, internet banking, tele banking, mobile banking, selling insurance products, issue of travel cheques and free cheque books, implementation of standing instructions of customers, fund transfers, and many other value added services. Financial innovation associated with technological change totally changed the philosophy of banking industry. The major benefits out of centralization of transaction process, centralization customer information, centralization accounting process, real-time information availability, basic MIS reporting. Today, most of the banking transactions can be done from the home and customers need not visit the bank branch for anything. The information technology implanting today is being leveraged to customer acquisitions, delivering ease and efficiency to customers, driving automation and process efficiency. For banks, information technology plays an important role in decision-making by creating a means to collect and codify experiences and solutions in such areas as customer services, relationship development and financial management. The implementing technologies include distributed computing, networking, and data warehousing and client/server. Many of the IT initiatives of banks started in the late 1990s or early 2000 with emphasis on the adoption of core banking solutions (CBS). The banks have to use the right technology to provide timely information, will give productivity increase and thereby gain a competitive edge. Information technology offers a chance for banks to build new systems that address a wide range of customer needs including many that many be imaginable today.

The Following are the innovative services offered by banking sector:

(a) Real Time Gross Settlement (RTGS): RTGS, introduced in India since March 2004, funds can be transferred from their account to the account of another bank through electronics instructions. RTGS is maintained and operated by the RBI and provides a means of efficient and faster funds transfer amount banks facilitating their financial operations. In RTGS as the name suggests, funds transfer between banks takes place on 'Real Time' basis. Therefore money can reach the beneficiary account within two hours.

Table 1 Growth of RTGS in India

Item	Volume (000's)			Value (Rupees in Crores)		
	2007-08	2008-09	2009-10	2007-08	2008-09	2009-10
RTGS	5840	13366	3321	2,73,18,330	3,22,79,881	3,94,53,359

As on 30th October, 2015 there are more than 1, 23, 423 RTGS enabled bank branches.

(b) Automatic Teller Machine (ATM): ATM is the most popular devise in India; it enables the customers to withdraw their money 24 hours a day, 7 days a week. In addition to cash withdrawal, ATMs can be used for payment of funds transfer between accounts, utility bills, deposit of cheques and cash into accounts, balance enquiry etc. ATM card performs routine banking transactions without interacting with a human teller.

Table 2 No. of ATMs in India as on 31st March, 2013

Bank Group	Rural	Semi-Urban	Urban	Metropolitan	Total
Public sector Banks	8552	18445	22518	20137	**69652**
Old Private sector Banks	768	2760	2354	1684	**7566**
New Private sector Banks	2214	6484	10995	15842	**35535**
Foreign Banks	30	21	244	966	**1261**
Total	**11564**	**27710**	**36111**	**38629**	**114014**

(c) Tele Banking: It facilitates the customer to do non-cash related banking on telephone. Under this devise Automatic Voice Recorder is used for simple queries and transactions.

(d) **Electronic Funds Transfer (EFT):** It is a system whereby anyone who wants to make payment to another person/company etc., can approach his bank and make cash payments or give instructions / authorization to transfer funds directly from his own account to the bank account of the beneficiary. This service is provided by RBI (Reserve Bank of India).

(e) **Electronic Clearing Services (ECS):** Electronic Clearing service is retail payment system that can be used to make bulk payments / receipts of a similar nature, where each individual payment is of a repetitive nature and of relatively smaller amount

The Evolution of Technology adoption in Indian Banking Sector

1. It started off with computerization of a few key functions and departments in main branches through adoption of advanced ledger posting machines. These systems were designed to take care of the accounts related functions of the banks for accuracy and control.
2. Implementation of branch automation enabled setting up of "Single Window Service "facility to the customers.
3. Another important stage in the evolution of the user friendly technology were development of ATMs and adoption of Core Banking solutions transformed by way of banking was done by both bankers and customers.
4. Introduced network based operations to provide interbank connectivity.
5. Most important technology were created INFINIT in 1999, implementation of PKI based electronic data transfer and Structured Financial Messaging System (SFMS) which facilitated the development of secured payment practice in India.
6. Innovations like internet banking, mobile banking, pre-paid cards issued by non-banking entities emerged.

Challenges ahead for Banking Sector

Technological changes in the Indian Banking sector give unique opportunities and challenges for the banking industry. Deploying , developing or acquiring suitable or right technology and maintain high servers and maintaining efficiency standards were a key challenges before the Banking industry. The primary challenge is to give prompt and consistent service to customers. Retention of customers is going to be a major challenge. Banks need to emphasis on retaining customers and increasing market share. Even now with ATM machines and Internet Banking, many consumers still prefer to have personal touch of their neighborhood branch bank. Technology makes it possible to provide services throughout the branch bank network, providing instant updates to check accounts. However, this dependency on network brought Information Technology department's additional responsibilities and challenges in managing, maintaining and optimizing the performance of retail banking networks. The increasing use of technology in banks has also brought up 'security' concerns. To avoid frauds and mishaps on the account, banks have to maintain a well-documented security policy including network security and internal security. There are network management challenges, whereby keeping these complex, distributed networks and applications operating properly in support of business objectives becomes essential. After passing of the Information Technology Act-2000, it has come as a boon to the banking sector, and banks should now ensure to abide strictly by its covenants.

Some of the challenges that the banks are facing today are:

- Changing needs of the customer.
- Keeping pace with technology up-gradations.
- Closing down and/or merging of unviable branches particularly in urban and metropolitan branches;
- Restructuring and reorganizing banks' setup towards thinner and leaner administrative offices
- Coping with regulatory reforms.

ADVANTAGES & DISADVANTAGES OF TECHNOLOGY

Advantages

- **Online Banking**: Many banks integrated information technology systems to improve on their customer service. Today, it is very easy to withdraw money using an ATM card or smart money card, because of this customer can save time lining up in banks.
- RFED payment.
- **Fast Credit**: Technology used in banks help in collecting of financial details and credit scores about customer, the information collected can be used when a customer applies for credit the bank.

Disadvantages

- **Money laundering:** Cases of online money laundering are on the rise and this has exposed many online users to the predators.

Technology and its implementation Anti-money laundering

Technology is one of crucial component in an efficient anti-money laundering (AML) compliance frame work. The banking organizations can leverage the current technology tools and boost their ability to mitigate financial crime risk.

OBJECTIVES OF THE STUDY

1. To analyze the usage of technology in the banking sector.
2. To study the awareness of the technology in banking sector.
3. To determine the influencing factors of a customer towards technology usage in banking services.
4. To suggest how to improve effective utilization of technology in banking services.

RESEARCH METHODOLOGY

The research is about the usage of technology in banking sector and to find the factors that attracts the people to use technology effectively in banking services. Descriptive research design has been used for the study. Chi Square Test used. The sample constituted about 47% of male and 52% are female. 48% of the respondents are within the age group of 21-30. About 31% of the respondents are post graduates.

Table 3 In 2009, the number of total branches in the country stood at 80,200. The following table shows the growth of the branches in the country in last five years.

As on	Rural	Semi-Urban	Urban	Metropolitan	Total
March 31,2009	31476	19126	15273	14325	**80200**
March 31,2010	32493	20855	16686	15446	**85480**
March 31,2011	33905	23114	17599	16419	**91037**
March 31,2012	36356	25797	18781	17396	**98330**
March 31,2013	37953	27219	19327	17844	**102343**

- There are 6 lakhs villages in India as per 2001 census. The Average Population per Bank Branch (APBB) as on 31.3.2013 stands at 12,100.
- As per census 2011, 58.7% households (67.8% urban & 54.4% rural) are availing banking services in the country. A significant proportion of the households, especially in rural areas, are still outside the formal fold of the banking system.
- Though there has been tremendous development in information technology adopted by banking sector, the level of penetration is low in rural areas. Trust and human touch are the key aspects in banking sector. Due to lack of human touch in new technologies there is a high possibility to lose a customer.

CONCLUSION

The study emphasizes on the percentage of awareness on maximum utilization of technology. The banking sector in India has undergone significant transformation in the past few years. As per census records, only 30.1 % of the rural households are availing banking services may be due to non-availability of bank branches in neighborhood. Banks have to go for mobile banking services for a cluster of villages. Alternatively, technological institutions have to come out with low-cost, self-service solutions/ ATMs. Banks should take effective measures in creating awareness towards the effective usage of technology. The government and the RBI should actively support such research efforts. Implementation of New Trends in Information Technology promise to change the pace of banking to the next few years.

REFERENCES

1. http://www.asmgroup.edu.in/incon/2015/FIN/INCN15_FIN_016.pdf
2. http://www.gktoday.in/blog/number-of-branches-and-atms/

3. http://www.ijmbs.com/24/sreelatha
4. *http://www.myresearchpie.com/*
5. https://www.rbi.org.in/scripts/PublicationsView.aspx?id=15449
6. Role of Technology in Development of Banking by Dr C. Rangarajan Chairman Economic Advisory Council to the Prime Minister
7. Technological Innovation In Indian Banking Sector – Use of it Products *Dr. Kanhaiya Singh, Professor, Fore School of Management, New Delhi, India ;Dr. U. S. Pandey, Associate Professor University of Delhi, New Delhi, India Priya Gupta, Asst. Professor, SSCBS, University of Delhi, Research Scholar, BIT(Mesra) Ranchi*
8. http://rbidocs.rbi.org.in/rdocs/RTGS/DOCs/RTGEB0815.XLSX
9. http://www.useoftechnology.com/advantages-disadvantages-information-technology/

E - Banking: A Tool for Technological Development in Modern Era

Smriti Nagaria
Assistant Professor, St. Joseph's Degree & PG College.

ABSTRACT

The advent of IT has brought about a dynamic change in today's business operations. With the rapid spread of technology where internet is used as the best channel for introduction of new business paradigm, development and rendering services in various sectors specially the banking sector. Bank plays an important role in Indian financial markets as the biggest purveyors of credit, attracts savings from people and acts as a backbone for economic development. Banks operate in a globalized, liberalized and privatized environment where IT is used as a tool to sustain in the competitive world. E-banking has emerged from such an innovative development which refers to the use of electronic channels for delivery of banking products and services.

E-banking has revolutionalised the way the bank operates, deliver and compete in order to have a competitive advantage. It has replaced traditional banking practices where there is no limit to its area of operation and this facility can be used from office or home for 24 x7x365 days. The objectives of this paper is to study the functioning of e-banking, various products and services available, models or systems, benefits available for e-banking and challenges faced and is concluded by giving suggestive measures for the growth of e-banking which should not become unacceptable but a preferred mode of banking.

Keywords: *Dynamic, business operations, economic development, competitive environment and growth.*

IT plays a predominant role in today's modern business functioning acting as an important tool for any organization. Dynamic development of information, telecommunication and their application has made functioning of organizations fast, easy and far reaching. Tremendous advances and aggressive infusion of IT has bought a shift in banking operations.

Banking sector acts as a backbone of modern business and development of any country which depends upon its banking system. To cope up with the pressure of growing competition banks have adopted e-banking as an initiative for maintaining share of market and retaining its customers. E-banking refers to the use of modern information and telecommunication technologies in carrying out business transactions from home, office or business trip for 24 hours a day and 365 days in a year.. It also refers to the electronic connection between bank and customer to manage and control financial services. Computerization of operations has made an impact on internet, customers and banking system. Three basic facilities that e-banking provides is convenience, no waiting in queue and 24 x7 service.

What is electronic banking?

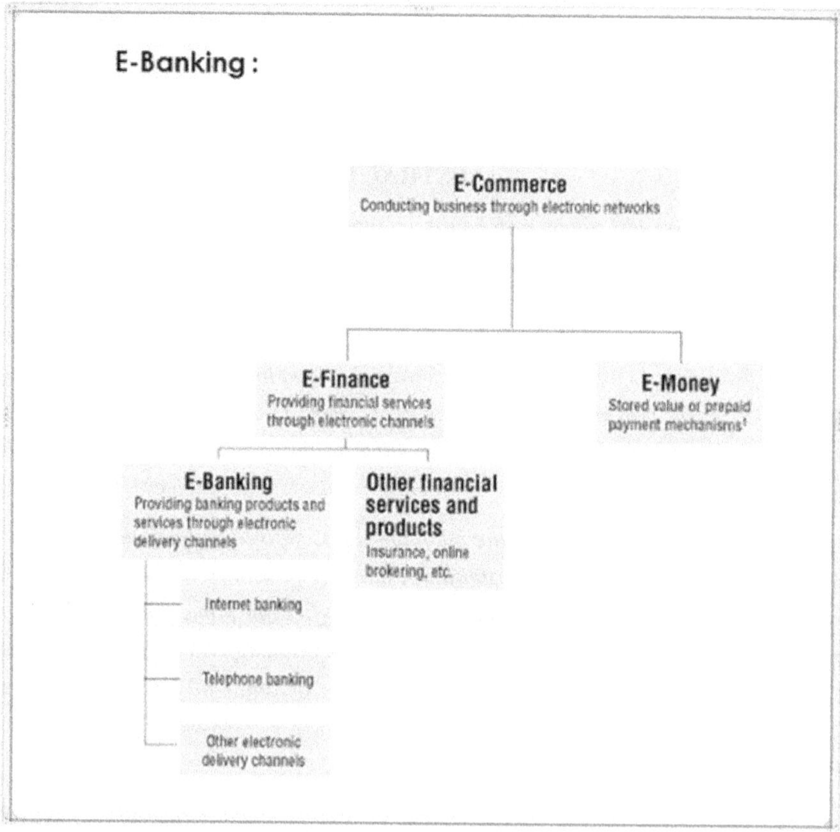

DEVELOPMENT OF E- BANKING

It involves various stages:

1. **Initiative Phase:** Usage of information and telecommunication technologies for competitive advantage
2. **Interactive Phase:** Transition from the provision of banking services from offline to online
3. **Personalization Phase:** Online banking services take the lead role in providing services to clients
4. **Virtualization Phase:** Emerges as a new trend

FACTORS AFFECTING E - BANKING

1. **Transactional Factors:** It deals with providing financial transactions such as fund transfers, payment of bill and it facilitates loan applications.
2. **Non – Transactional Factors:** It deals with viewing account balances, downloading periodic account statement and ordering cheque books.

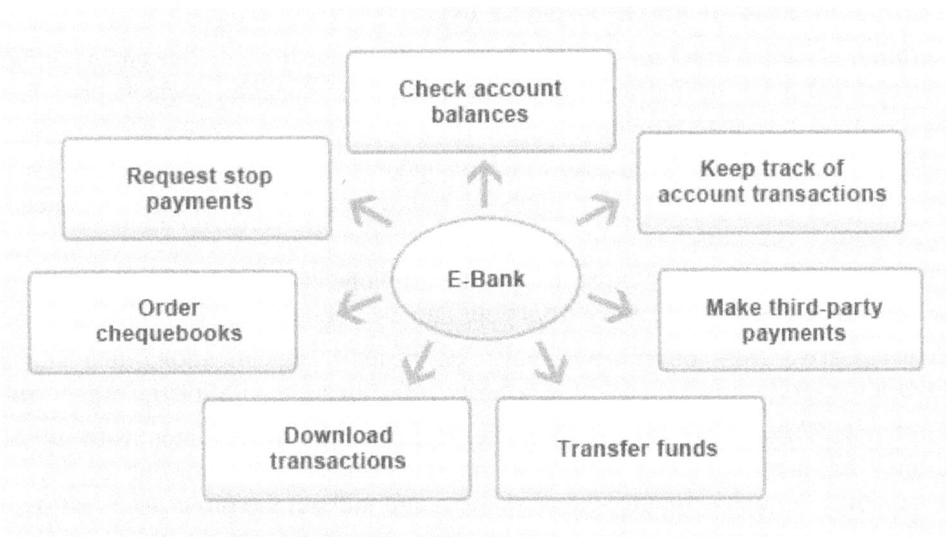

FUNCTIONING OF E – BANKING

This includes the following:

1. **Inquiry about Information of the Account:** Clients needs information about his account details which includes balance and historical records.
2. **Card Account Transfer:** This enables transfer of funds to other person's credit card in the same city.
3. **Bank Securities Account Transfer:** It facilitates transfer between capital account in Securities Company and bank saving account.
4. **Transaction of Foreign Exchange:** It relates to enquiry about exchange rate, trade in foreign exchange and cancellation of orders.
5. **Client Service:** This facilitates modification of password and credit card information.
6. **Reporting Loss in Account:** The client can report in case credit card or pass book is stolen or lost.

TYPES OR FORMS OF E –BANKING

1. Usage of ATM for deposits, withdrawals, inter-account transfer and payment of linked accounts.
2. Buying and paying for goods and services using debit cards or smart cards without carrying cash or a cheque book.
3. Using a telephone to perform direct banking to make balance enquiry, inter-account transfers and pay linked accounts.
4. Using a computer to perform direct banking

PRODUCTS AND SERVICES OF E- BANKING

- **Automated Teller Machine (ATM):** It is a cash dispensing machine and a computerized telecommunication device seen at banks and other location which give facility to customers to draw cash anytime.
- **Internet Banking:** It is an electronic payment system that enables customers of a financial institution to conduct financial transactions on a website operated by the institution.
- **Mobile Banking:** It refers to the use of a Smartphone or other cellular device to perform online banking tasks while away from your home computer.
- **Smart Card:** They provide personal identification, authentication, data storage and application processing with a strong security authentication within large organizations.
- **Electronic Fund Transfer:** It refers to electronic transfer of money from one bank account to another, either within a single financial institution or across multiple institutions, through computer-based systems and without the direct intervention of bank staff.

(A) **ONLINE SERVICES:** This service is provided using internet which includes the following:

- ➢ Account Summary
- ➢ Overdraft Details
- ➢ Transactions Details
- ➢ Online Requests
- ➢ Funds Transfer between own Accounts
- ➢ Adding of Account in Beneficiary List
- ➢ Viewing of Beneficiary Accounts
- ➢ Fund transfer to other Beneficiary Account
- ➢ Standing Order
- ➢ E-Payment Facilities

Online Enquiry includes

- **Cheque Enquiry:** User may enquire status of a Cheque or range of Cheques issued in an account.
- **Cheque Books:** User may enquire for Cheque books issued in an account.
- **Outward Cheques Enquiry:** User may enquire status of specific Cheque or all Cheques deposited in an account.
- **TDS Detail:** User may view the Tax Deducted at Source details.

OTHER OPTIONS

- **Contact Details:** User may view address details

- **Change Login Password:** User may change login password as per guidelines available on website.
- **Change Transaction Password:** User may change transaction password as per guidelines available on website
- **Change User Preference:** User can change their User-id, however the same can be changed only once
- **Login History:** User may view login history

(B) OFFLINE SERVICES

- Deposit Account Opening
- Deposit Amend/Renewal
- Closure of Deposit Account
- Issuance of demand drafts and delivery options
- Account Statement
- Cheque Book Issue
- Funds Transfer Facility
- Account Transfer
- Phone Banking
- SMS Banking
- Loan Account Opening
- Request Status Enquiry

MODEL OF E –BANKING

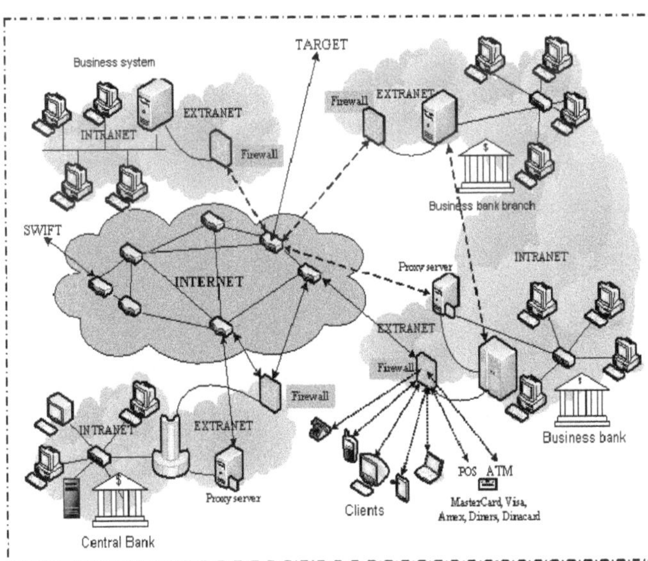

Model of Information and Telecommunication System of Banking

Today, in modern banking systems there exist the following models and systems of electronic banking:

- Home Banking
- Office Banking
- Online Banking
- Internet Banking
- Mobile Banking
- Telephone Banking
- SMS Banking

BENEFITS

1. **Convenience** –Easy to operate 24 x7 with internet connectivity
2. **Transaction Speed** – Executes and confirms transaction at quicker speed than ATM processing
3. **Efficiency** – To access and manages all bank accounts
4. **Cheap Alternative** – The cost is low hence considered cheap than physical banking
5. **Customer Service and Satisfaction** – Provides flexibility where the customer need not go to the branch to avail banking services
6. **Increases Comfort and Time Saving** – Provides facilities for 24 hours without physical interaction with the bank
7. **Better Cash Management** – E- banking facilities speed up cash cycle and increases efficiency of business
8. **Convenience** – All the banking transactions can be performed from the comfort of the home or office or from the place a customer wants to.
9. **Speed** – The response of the medium is very fast; therefore customers can actually wait till the last minute before concluding a fund transfer.
10. **Funds Management** – Customers can download their history of different accounts and do a "what-if" analysis on their own PC before affecting any transaction on the web. This will lead to better funds management.

CHALLENGES

1. Lack of proper installation of e- delivery channels
2. Not safe and lacks confidentiality, integrity and authentication
3. Lack of preparedness on part of bank and customer in adoption of technological change
4. The ability to adopt global technology to local requirements
5. The ability to strengthen public support for e-finance

REGULATORY TOOLS TO OVERCOME CHALLENGES

1. **Adaption** – Staff should be trained to access changes in risk in electronic transactions
2. **Legalization** – Development of new instruments, services and methods for conducting transactions
3. **Harmonization** – Cross border cooperation between coordinating laws and regulatory practices
4. **Integration** – Coordinating between IT issues and operations risk in bank supervision and safety.

CONCERNS OF E-BANKING

- **Customer Support** – This is achieved by creating a customer support desk to help solve queries
- **Security** – Customer worries about protection and security so assure the customers about safety measures
- **Software Issues** – Updation of software which enables smooth flow of work
- **Lack of Knowledge from Customer End**

RECOMMENDATIONS

1. Make people literate about the use of e - bank products and services
2. Ensure full security of customer funds
3. Amount to be spent by the Government for building necessary infrastructure for carrying out e banking activities
4. Seminars and workshops to be organized

CONCLUSION

Technology is allowing banks to offer new products, operate more efficiently, raise productivity, expand geographically and compete globally which has changed the business of banking.

E-banking has revolutionalized the banking operations by making it fast, easy and far reaching and today it is known as a survival weapon for changing businesses. E- banking has become a convenient mode for young generations for which banks are also making sincere effort to popularize their products and services in order that e –banking should not become unacceptable but a preferred mode of banking. In order for E-banking to continue to grow, the security and the privacy aspects need to be improved and resolved in order to be successful and to become leading player in the business world.

References

1. Research Articles on E- Banking
2. International Journal of Research in Business
3. Online Material

Websites – www.wikipedia.com

www.investopedia.com

www.scribd.com

Privatization of Banking Sectors in India with Special Reference to Goa: A Critical Review

Badruddin
Associate Professor, PES's Shri Ravi Sitaram Naik College of Arts & Science.

ABSTRACT

Transformation of e- governance needs the establishment of true entrepreneurship at local levels where banking sectors remain the priority area of interest. Naturally reserved and resource rich state like Goa, often called as paradise of 'Sea Beach Tourism' attracts over millions of tourists from India and the world. It helped to expand banking sectors in three phases: Liberation of Goa 1961; creation of statehood 1987 and the emergence of globalization 1991, both private as well as public undertakings.

Goa offers an ideal example of corporate world of fiscal management and remains a model example for companies, business tourism and best banking services in India. According to periodical surveys by various corporate agencies and Government of Goa economic reports, Goa remains the top most destination for private banking sectors. Various economic indicators like per capita income, higher literacy rate, standard of living and ancestral properties do indicate the highest status of Goa in India. Goa has witnessed boom in profiting the private banking sectors that stands 237 by 31st March 2015 an average highest in India. Besides there are also privately controlled commercial banks, multinational banks, cooperative banks and scheduled banks apart some independent banks associated with corporate business.

This paper will examine various infrastructural facilities and local conditions as how Goa has become a hub in prompting private banking sectors with inbuilt facilities and business minded people' motivation. A comparative study of banking sectors with other rich sectors of banks in Chandigarh, Delhi, Mumbai, etc will make information more interesting. Besides, the paper will also analyze the aggregate deposits, transactions and business rotations in private banks of Goa. Several factors like annual growth, domestic, NRE deposits, periodical dividends, shares and various attractive schemes are also important. Data will be collected from various primary and secondary sources apart from online agencies which are readily available. At this stage, there is an urgent need to have a critical view as how private banks are more competent and comfortable than nationalized banks.

Keywords: *Goa Tourism, Corporate, Private Banking, Infrastructure.*

BACKGROUND

Privatisation refers to the transfer of government services or assets to the private sectors either for larger benefits or speedy action. In most cases, the State-owned resources may be sold to private owners or statutory restrictions on competition between privately and publicly owned enterprises may be lifted. Services formerly provided by public sectors may be contracted out or supervised. The objective is often to increase government efficiency; implementation may affect government revenue either positively or negatively. Privatization is the opposite of nationalization, a policy resorted to by governments that want to keep the revenues from major industries, especially those that might otherwise be controlled by foreign interests.

India is the largest democracy in world with massive human resources, labour management and capital flow. The impact of globalisation in private sectors in form of free flow of capital, ICT revolution, patent law and corporate governance, all have changed the economic profile of banking sectors in India. Four major parameters: ownership, operational and organisational measure have helped the large number of private banks including agricultural, rural, foreign and insurance banks and companies. All these helped to increase efficiency, competitive power of the enterprises, reduction of deficit financing and strengthening of banking knowledge management. These also helped to promote better customer services with expanded market by reducing burden sharing.

Banking system refers to transfer of fiscal resources required by the individuals, business communities and the public organizations which are essential conditions to meet the daily expanses for buying and purchasing capital. Most banks work on the management of appreciative capital formation, mobilization of savings and investment policies. Banks also play a very important role in the economic life of the nation. The health of the economy is closely related to the soundness of its banking system. Although banks create no new wealth but their borrowing, lending and related activities facilitate the process of production, distribution, exchange and as such become very effective partners in the process of economic development. In a nutshell, economy remains the channel of communication in various streams of life.

India is the 5th largest economy in the world followed by USA, China, Japan and Germany and the second largest man force followed by China that played greeter role in deciding the financial management. In terms of banking management and financial resources, India is still too backward compared to several European, Gulf and Asia countries like China, Japan, Hong Kong, South Korea and Malaysia. However, the impact of neo-liberalization, emergence of highly complex web of interconnectivity and interdependence world order changed the financial atlas of India in late nineties. Thereafter, globalised agencies contributed powerful impetus to economic liberalization and corporate the international economic system where the poor countries including India continue to face odd challenges. Gradually, however, globalization and World Trade Organization (WTO), as an enlightened economic freelancing also embarked serious scholarly debates in various forums where banking sectors became the most important to contemporary scholarly debate in corporate world. Obviously, money, capital, finance or dollar culture continue to play the significant role and determine the fate of countless people in the world.

Banking System in India: From Ancient to Modern

Historians believe that the oldest banking systems existed in China, England and India but these were entirely different as what we have now. Banking system in India since the ancient days have played greater role though there have major changes in transaction policy time and again. It gradually moved from ancient, medieval, colonial to modern era covering over four thousand years of history (2000 BC to 2000 AD). During Medieval Mughal India, the finance system rather remain loosely organized and directly controlled by the ruler or king. The Mughal Empire was one of the biggest centres of attraction for trade and commerce all over the World. There were great flourishing trade canters in Lahore, Agra, Ahmadabad, Sironj, Berhampore, Jaipur, Dhaka, Patna, Benares, Golconda, Deccan, Bijapur, and Daulatabad. Banking and trade routes crisscrossed the country, the vibrant trade route of Surat-Agra passed through Sironj and Burhanpur. In fact Burhanpur had trade connections with Iran, Turkey, Russia, Poland, Arabia and Egypt. These urban centers of trade contributed about 19% to Mughal tax revenue. [1]

British India Model of Banking System in India: Modern Way of Banking

There was no clear-cut demarcation of public and private banking system during British Raj as all banks in English India worked on common parameters. However, it is duly noted that large number of banking during colonial phased were converted into public banks during post independence India and finally most of them became public undertakings during the phase of nationalization in 1969.

British India implemented several financial policies when the establishment of General Bank of India with Joint Stock Bank was started in 1786 which followed the establishment of Bank of Hindustan (1809), Bank of Bombay (1840), Imperial Bank (1921), Reserve Bank of India Act (1934) and Central Bank (1935). During freedom struggle of India against British colonialism, large number of banks were established. [2] The prominent ones included: Punjab National Bank Ltd., Bank of India Ltd., Canara Bank Ltd., Indian Bank Ltd., Bank of Baroda Ltd., and Central Bank of India Ltd. But most of these banks were not properly organized. During the post independent India, the banks have moved from Post colonial banks (1950s), nationalized banks (1960s) to the present stage of and globalization (1990s till date). Physical as well as virtual expansion of banking through mobile banking, internet banking, tele-banking, bio-metric and mobile ATMs have been phenomenally expanded and are taking place in various corporate and social sectors.[3]

During Indira Gandhi Ministry, most of these banks were nationalized and finally implemented on 19 July 1969. Altogether 26 semi- public sectors banks limited started with full operation. It included: Allahabad Bank, Andhra Bank, Bank of Baroda, Bank of India, Bank of Maharashtra, Central Bank, Central Bank of India, Corporation Bank, Dena Bank, IDBI Bank, Indian Bank, Indian Overseas bank, Oriental Bank of Commerce, Punjab & Sindh Bank, Punjab National Bank, Union Bank of India, United Bank of India, Vijaya Bank, State Bank of Bikaner & Jaipur, State Bank of Hyderabad, State Bank of India, State Bank of Mysore, State Bank of Patiyala and State Bank of Travancore. [4]

Private Banks in India

Unlike USA, UK, Germany and Japan, Private Banking system in India is too young which papered in 1980s. By 1990 and 2000 during the intermediate phase of globalization, large number of private banks became home to India. Several multinational companies found India as resource rich, cheap labour source and highly competent qualified Indians. It attracted large number of foreign banks to invest in India. It appeared in the forms of purely private, semi private (cooperative and rural banks) and international banks which can broadly be classified under group B: Private Banks . There briefly include: Catholic Syrian Bank, City Union Bank, Dhanlakshmi Bank, Federal Bank, ING Vyas Bank, J&K Bank, Karnataka Bank, Karur Vyas Bank, Lakshmi Vilas Bank, Nainital Bank, Ratnakar Bank, South Indian Bank and Tamil Nadu Mercantile Bank are also operating in India. Some well established multinational banks like Axis Bank, ICICI Bank, HDFC Bank, Indus land Bank, Yes Bank and Kotak

Mahindra are also doing successful business in India. It is rather difficult to discuss in details about the banking system in India. Let us have a brief overviews of broadly private banks in India in the Table 1.

Table 1 Private Banks in India- A Broad Classification

Private Sector Banks	**Cooperative Sector Banks**	**Foreign Private Banks In India (Selected ones only)**
Old Generation Private Banks	State Cooperative Banks	ABN AMRO,
New Generation Private Banks	Central Cooperative Banks	Abu Dhabi Commercial Bank,
Foreign Banks in India	Primary Agriculture Credit Societies	Antwerp Diamond Bank
Scheduled Cooperative Banks	Land Development Banks	Australia and New Zealand Banking Group,
Non-Scheduled Banks	Urban Cooperative banks	Bank International Indonesia, Bank of America,
	Primary Agriculture Development Banks	Bank of Bahrain and Kuwait
	Primary Land Development Banks	Bank of Ceylon
	State Land Development Banks	The Bank of Tokyo-Mitsubishi UFJ
		Barclays
		Deutsche Bank
		Citibank India
		Credit Suisse
		The Royal Bank of Scotland
		Standard Chartered
		Scotia bank
		HDFC
		ICICI

Source: *Manorama Yearbook 2013*, Kottayam, pp.691-92,

Above table is only an indicative one. Within the private sector banks like Old Generation Private Banks, New Generation Private Banks, Foreign Banks in India, Scheduled Cooperative Banks and Non-Scheduled Banks are major themes only. For example, Old Generation Private Banks has more than 100 branches followed by equal number of new generation, foreign and scheduled banks. However for reference some banks are listed below:

These briefly include: Andhra Pragathi Grameena Bank, Kerala Gramin Bank, Bangiya Gramin Vikash Bank, Gramin Bank of Aryavart, North Malabar Gramin Bank, Pallavan Grama Bank, Pandyan Grama Bank, Paschim Banga Gramin Bank, Sarva UP Gramin Bank, South Malabar Gramin Bank, Uttar Bihar Gramin Bank and Vananchal Gramin Bank. The list of defunct banks is also exhaustive in India. Some of these are: Alliance Bank of Simla, Arbuthnot & Co, Bank of Bombay, Bank of Calcutta, Bank of Chettinad, Bank of Madras, Bank of Madura, Bank of Rajasthan, Bengal Central Bank, Bharat Overseas Bank, Centurion

Bank of Punjab, Chartered Bank of India, Australia and China Commercial Bank of India, Dass Bank, Exchange Bank of India & Africa, Global Trust Bank, Grindlays Bank, Imperial Bank of India, Lord Krishna Bank, Madhavpura Mercantile Cooperative Bank, Mercantile Bank of India, London and China, Nath Bank, Nedungadi Bank, New Bank of India Oriental Bank Corporation, Oudh Commercial Bank, Palai Central Bank, Pandyan Bank, State Bank of Indore, State Bank of Saurashtra and United Industrial Bank.[5]

There are many odds and corners like business man, *Aam Admi*, farmers, professionals, service class and even layman who require fund transfer to meet various contingencies. The need therefore is to meet the expanses on goods and services. Currently, banking management in India is working fairly on good terms and is doing successful business in various streams while maintaining parity with western Banking system. While considering the quality of works and assets, most banks in India are based on clean management despite several corrupt practices reported by media time to time. Economic indicators like currency management, labour policy, banking infrastructure, insurance, customer catchments, share bazaars, dividends and fiscal programme: all are working within the banking parity to target human resource management. While RBI acts as a coordinator and successfully handling the borrowing policies and the union and state governments. RBI also formulates and administers monetary management to promote policy stability while giving due incentives to higher production in various sector besides maintaining the currency system and several ventures while global management including International Monetary Fund. [6]

Though there are still challenges as large number of banks of are based on urban sectors only. The needful therefore is to established decentralized accountability of banking system in India covering every state, districts and villages. Public and Private Finance especially the banking management play crucial role in deciding the destiny of any nation. During the age of globalization and competitive liberalism as highly complex web of interconnectivity and interdependence world order. India, the largest democracy in the world with unlimited human and material resources accepted the process of globalization in *toto*. [7]

Banking System in Goa

Banking in Goa took steps in 1980 during the crucial phase of economic reformation in India when it was a part of Union Territory. Between 1982 to 1986, Goa struggled to establish some corporate business when large number of nationalized banks like SBI, BOI, UBI, Dena Bank and Bank of Baroda started foot printings. Soon Goa became the major tourist attraction where banking managements played crucial role. Since then Goa is going through major transformation in the field of banking sectors. The creation of statehood in 1987 was a major step forward.

Since new millennium 2000, the State Government adopted sustainable commercial polices where future visions are being revised by every Goan. The pride of economic prosperity through banking networks are helping to show the right path of love, tolerance and harmony. To achieve the economic prosperity, Goa's attractive business ventures and corporate banks are playing dynamic role and trying to redefine the development paradigm. By developing commercial banking infrastructure and polices have helped significantly.

Since its liberation in 1961, Goa has made tremendous progress in both economic and social fields. Growth of banking offices in Goa steadily increased many fold from a mere 5 in 1962 which jumped to 81 in 1973, 300 in 1987 that touched to 694 as on 31st March 2014. The Table 2 shows the trends of banking offices in Goa from 1980 till 2014 that include banks of all categories. The rapid expansion of banks offices from 258 (1980) to 681 (2014) show significant growth. The Table 2 shows the upward trends of nationwide nationalized banks in Goa from 1980 till March 2014.

Table 2 Year-wise number of Banking Offices (Semi Government and Private)

Year	Number of Banking Offices
1980-1981	258
1990-1991	306
2000-2001	444
2009-2010	547
2010-2011	598
2011-2012	643
2012-2013	674
2013-2014	694
2014-2015	701*

Source: *Economic Survey: Government of Goa*, 2014-2015, Panaji, p.39.

*Projected Data as exact number is not documented.

The data includes nationalized, private, cooperative and international banks. Data wise, SBI remains on top most having 78 branches all over Goa. Every Taluka of Goa with average population of one Lakh represents six SBI branches higher than any other part of India. Considering the demographic profile, there is only one SBI branch covering just 2250 people at national level, while there are total 14816 branches covering average one bank against 87850 people.[8] Similar is the case of other nationalised banks in Goa. In fact number of private and scheduled banks in Goa is comparatively doing better business than nationalised ones. It clearly shows that the Goans are economically well off and have much better banking transactions showing vey high Per Capita Income (PCI) and high standard of living. In fact, human resource management has been important mechanism that has harnessed the creativity of Goans. Expansion of banking sectors since 1980 till 2014 has encourage large number of other sectors like tourism, mines, fisheries and wine business. Obviously, it has added dimensions to other thrust areas like employment generation, social security, health, education, environment and e-banking in Goa and have taken aggressive steps to computerize the administrative set ups in commercial banks. It also provided information and access services to citizen portals. Large number of banks in Goa of diverse categories have successfully established hi-tech habitats, Software Technology Park and cyber connectivity to develop customer friendly atmosphere. SBI, HDFC, ICICI and Axis banks are the leading examples in such references. As a result, high rate turn over and 'Mini Silicon City' software are being modelled. Nationalised banks like Bank of India, Corporation Bank, Dena Bank, Bank of Baroda, Maharashtra Bank, Union Bank of India and Central Bank are also doing excellent business in Goa.

Rise of Private Banks in Goa

So is the case of private and international banks like ICICI, HDFC, Axis Bank, Kotak Mahndra etc. Scheduled and cooperative banks like Goa Urban Co-operative Bank Ltd., Mapusa Urban Co-operative Bank Ltd, Bicholim Urban Co-operative Bank Ltd and Goa State Cooperative Bank Ltd are doing fairly good business. Cities of Goa like Panaji, Margao, Vasco-da-Gama, Mapusa, Ponda, Bicholim, etc. have good number of commercial banks. Large number of cooperative banks are well established in Goa. For example, Goa State Co-operative Bank Ltd (GSCBL), most leading private bank, established in 1963, an apex financing agency people oriented banks, has network of 67 branches all over Goa and fully connected with online sources. GSCBL actively promotes conferences, workshops, contact programmers besides NRI services, trade and finance while personnel fiancé depart deals agriculture loans, Non-agriculture loans, Housing, Car, Urban loans and subsidies. GSCBL as being the top most also supported through bank of directors, budget report, and finance position all over Goa. GSCBL- KYC norms are sustained through Registration, Commencement of Business, Apex Financing Agency, Multi-State Status, Apex Bank Status and Branch Locators. As on 31 March 2014, the total asset liability of GSCBL stands 1,17,3 million. [9]

On the parallel line, the Mapusa Urban Co-operative Bank of Goa Ltd., is the first Urban Co-operative Bank of North Goa, established on 9th December, 1965 and has 65 branches. The Reserve Bank of India granted the Scheduled Bank status on 30th January, 1998, and a deemed Multi-State Co-operative Bank on 6th January, 1998. The Bank has a network of 24 branches and one Extension Counter covering the entire State of Goa and works on the parallel line of GSCBL. Lately, it has adopted the Core Banking Technology wherein our customer can avail the facility of "Any Branch Banking". [10] Large number of cooperative banks have MoU with several nationalized banks and have their close networking in rural areas too. There are also large number of non- institutional local types of banks of miscellaneous business that can be seen even in villages and mini-towns operating off the circle of mainstream. Even if a laymen moves around Panaji , Margao, Mapusa and Vasco- Da- Gama city, every tenth building has some bank or corporate office. Several private banks have started attractive schemes which include: Housing Loan, Education Loan, Pradhan Mantri Jan Dhan Yojana, Kisan Credit Cards (KCC), and Credit Flow To Minority Communities.

Goa is often called as state of bankers and businessmen apart from being a major tourist destination in India. Strong support system with good connectivity are the added advantage. Goa also means – business and banks – a centre of flourishing trading culture and so small is beautiful. If we have on overviews of local population about their financial status that come from ancestral properties, local business (cashews, fenny, mines, tourism and fisheries, etc), Goa is the second richest state in India in terms of per capita income which stands 1,60,000/- compared to national PCI that stands 75,000/-monthly while national capital Delhi has 1.91 Lakh PCI as highest in India as there are several other economic indicators too. [11] Or otherwise, as per latest information, Goa earns the credit of being the richest in terms of Tax Deduction at Source (TDS) while considering the population, where chunk of amount holders come from private banking sectors only. Just during the financial year 2015-2016 the TDS collection was 263.4 millions. [12]

Status of Banks in Goa: District and Taluka –wise Distribution

Geo-politically, Goa is divided between two districts: North Goa and South Goa followed their Head Quarters at Panaji and Margao respectively. Panaji is also the capital city and has major tourist attraction. Most corporate offices of Goa are located in Panaji. According to periodical survey, Panaji has distinction of having the highest number of commercial banks: including all categories stand 227 while considering its population just (115,000) and area (36 Sq Kilometres) which remain surprising. Panaji has all best infrastructure: banking, business, adventures, frolic and fun: is a rare example in India.

A look at the District-wise and Taluka-wise, number of bank branches functioning in the State as on 31st March 2013 given in Table 3. It is seen that 58.46% of the total number of bank branches in the State are in North Goa District and that South Goa District accounts for only 41.54 percent. Among the Talukas of the State, Bardez and Salcete regions account for around 21 percent each out of the total banking office in the State (Bardez 21.52% and Salcete 21.36%). Tiswadi Taluka accounts for only 18.10% of the total bank branches, followed by Mormugao and Ponda Talukas which account for 11% and 10% respectively. The remaining seven Talukas of the State account for only a small share in the total banking network in the State, which ranges from 1 to 4 percent due to poor infrastructure. The Table 3 gives an overview of various banks by 31st March 2013.

Table 3 District-wise and Taluka-wise Number of Banking Offices as on 31st March 2014 (Public+ Private)

State/District/Taluka	No. of Branches	Total %age
North Goa District	**394**	**58.46**
Tiswadi	122	18.10
Bardez	145	21.52
Pernem	19	2.82
Bicholim	29	4.30
Sattari	13	1.93
Ponda	66	9.79
South Goa District	**280**	**41.45**
Sanguem	10	1.48
Canacona	19	2.82
Quepem	28	4.16
Salcete	144	21.36
Mormugao	73	10.83
Dharbandora	06	0.89
Grand Total	674	100

Source: *Economic Survey: Government of Goa*, 2014-2015, Panaji, p.40

Several studies show that the dramatic expansion of banking branches in Goa have significantly boosted employment opportunism - the most sustainable means. Tiswadi and Bardez Taulkas for example have earned rich dividends in employing 2250 youths under various schemes like Jana Dhana Scheme, Students Scholarship Schemes, Swarna Jayanthi Shari Rozgar Yojana, Swarnajayanthi Gram Swarozgar Yojana, Swarna Jayanthi Shahari Rozgar Yojana, etc. So is the case of other branches in Ponda, Salcette and Mormugao. Bank managements have taken several steps by providing variety of incentives. Several banks are also linked with various productive services like Kamdhenu, Krishinagar, Retrenchment Benefits and Training-cum-Production initiatives. [13]

N.R.E. Deposits in Goa

In India banking terminology, the term Non-Resident External or NRE Account refers to funds deposited with a financial institution that allows for the efficient conversion and transfer of Indian and foreign currency both within and outside of India. Goa being a major tourist destination, has earned credible support from NRE sources as large number of Goan Diaspora are working in Gulf, UK, USA, Australia and Portugal. By a conservative estimate there are over five lakh Non-Resident Indians (NRIs) from Goan origin. NRI Commission, Government of Goa is globally well connected through Non-Resident Goans Emergency Repatriation Fund for the benefit of NRE-Goan origin. Various provisions for NRE funds in Goa are being carried on through various official orders and circulars. [14]

Goa has shown upward and down words trends in NRE Despite schemes. For example, during the year 2012 (by 31st March), the NRE despots stood 4912.30 which was slightly higher in 2010-2011 (5,046.90 crore). The gross NRE deposits, which stood at 583.47 crore in 1992-93, have been boosted considerably. The N.R.E. deposits during the period 1992-93 to 2011-12 have increased from 583.47 crore to 4912.30 crore. The percentage contribution of N.R.E. deposit to the total deposit stood at 12% during 2011-12 which was less by 2% as compared to the year 2010-11. SBI, Syndicate and Canara Banks remain the key partners with NRE deposits representing over 50% total share. [15] NRE accounts remain protected in number of ways. NRE deposits in Goa remain exchequer for domestic and local economy by enhancing the economic productivity of banks and promote better customer relationship. Goa being an international tourist destination, offers various opening for NRE deposits. Goa State Infrastructure Development Corporation Limited with coordination of NRI Goa Commission have been helpful in identifying various priority area including NRE deposits.

FINDINGS

Goa has earned credible support from customer services and infrastructure of banking management. The expansion of phenomenal growth of branches have taken up door to door people in both rural and urban conglomeration. Large number of locals of higher, middle and lower class people do prefer to have banking transactions unlike large number of other states of India. It attracts the peer teams too to have investment and savings opportunities. As an average Goa adds 25 branches of commercial banks every year which is normally much higher than any other part of India while considering the size of geography and demography. The recent move to have more private and cooperative banks while considering stability and higher returns, Chunk of Goan population prefers to have business with private banks where a sizeable sections have been encouraged to invest with private banks including bank lockers, bullion, ornaments, cash deposits and property documents. All these have helped to expand banking business in Goa as the favourable economic conditions and unpredictable growth of banking sectors. Despite tough competetion with nationalized and international banks in Goa, local attitude about professional interest on banking sectors cannot be easily changed. But the expansion of globalizations and liberal capitalism have stiff competetion between public and private partnership where global banking business are more attractive due to IT revolution, quality works, competitive market and talent management which are lacking in Goa. The scope of mutual funds, loan guarantee and safety, role of leasing and investment companies, and several risk factors are now changing the attitude of young minds who prefer safe and social banking and thereby attract nationalized banks in Goa.

Besides, several attractive schemes of nationalized banks - social banking like interest free loan for students, incentives for senior citizens, schemes for women, higher subsidies for farmers and rural sectors, are now imperatives and thereby change the attitude of Goans about the role of commercial banks. Under the directives of RBI and the Banking Regulation Act, the policy of diversification like role of merchant banks, mutual fund transfer, retail banking, ATMs, concept of anywhere banking, factoring and venture capital funds, be it Goa or India, the commercial banking system have come SMART business. Reforms in Banking sectors like statutory liquidity & cash reserve ratio, prudential & capital adequacy norms, access of capital market, freedom of operation and local banks are actively involved in operating the financial management in Goa. The question of awareness about banking services and usage, Goa is the best state in India whether it is online banking services, tele-banking and SMS banking. Important parameters like cheque books & DD services, utility of bill payment through e-banking, transfer of funds, request for opening new accounts, inter-bank transactions through SWIFT, ECS, NEFT, ETGS, RTGS, IFSC and MICR are measured much higher in Goa, India's tiniest state. Besides, Goa is also rated among the best in India in terms of FDs, ATM card holder services, cash withdrawal, Kiosks series, business facilitator agents and even financial literacy programme.

While considering the pluses and minuses, banking system in Goa offers an 'Ideal Corporate Model' due to access of asset reconstruction, higher statutory liquidity ratio, certified deposits and flexible business hours in banks as all are important. Even a young mind in Goa is well conversant about banking management due to money minded attitude. Being highly professional, most locals want to earn speedy and early money without putting hard works or talents. As a result, large number of locals lack highly skilled jobs in various banking sectors as key profile jobs in Banks (mostly nationalized) are owned and designated by outsiders who come through All India Test. In a way, Goans at any cost do not want to sacrifice money transactions and gold business where the commercial banks of varied categories have wider options and prospective market avenues. Despite odds and challenges, large number of Goans are well adjusted in various banking and financial sectors due to strong supports from their elders, peer atmosphere and ancestral properties.

Goa really presents a unique case of private banking system in India which significantly differs in several ways. Goans no matter from any caste or community, think to start some private business and proudly cooper or coordinate with some private banks. Such private banks offer big lump sum even without any surety or bonds and easily lend money to the borrower at maximum risk factors. Large number of fraudulent cases are reported time and again. Banks also lends money on silver, gold and diamond bonds. In several cases, private banks simply mortgage the original documents while other simply ask for surety. Secrecy behind the success of private banks depends on social security, transparency of serve sectors and accountability in work performance where Goa can be cited as the best example in India. In term of transfer of assets, management, functions and responsibilities in private banking sectors, Goa is a classical example.

REFERENCES

1. http://livelystories.com/2014/05/21/banking-mughal-india/\
2. Srivastava, Samir K, "Expansion of banking in India", *The Economic Times,* 7 June 2008, pp. 8
3. http://en.wikipedia.org/wiki/Commercial_Bank_of_India
4. Ibid.
5. Ibid.
6. *Manorama Yearbook*: Kottayam 2013, pp 692.
7. Gaurav Datt & Ashwani Mahajan (2013), *Indian Economy*, New Delhi: S. Chand & Company Ltd, p.878.
8. www. *en.wikipedia.org/wiki/State Bank of India*
9. http://www.gscbgoa.com/index.html
10. http://www.mucbankofgoa.com/
11. *For their details, see,articles.economictimes.indiatimes.com/2014.../47126380_1_2004-05-price..*
12. Goa Rates Highest in TDS Collection" *The Times of India*, 28 November 2015, p.3.
13. Sanjay Hegde (2012), *Destination Next Goa*, Panaji, Shri Multimedia Vision, pp. 78-80.
14. http://www.nri.goa.gov.in/orders&circular1.html
15. *Economic Survey: Government of Goa, 2013-2014*, Panaji, p. 42.

Impact of E-Banking on Online Markets

B. Lakshmi[1] and Rafath Begum[2]
[1]Lecturer, Department of Pharmaceutical Management, NIPER.
[2]2nd year MBA Student, Department of Pharmaceutical Management, NIPER.

ABSTRACT

Today most of the shopping happens while you are in office or at home or on the way. Banking is at your fingertips. Banking cards like debit cards and credit cards are more preferred to be carried than currency notes in customer's wallets. Banking services are available 24 × 7, 365 days. Electronic devices have become more reliable for banking irrespective of the customer's location. Banks today operate in a highly competitive environment. In order to survive in this environment banks have adopted various strategies to succeed. Electronic banking has emerged from such innovations of services. The objective of the present paper is to study and analyze the trends of E-banking and impact of E-banking on online markets. The study is based on primary and secondary data. E-banking contributes for the growth of GDP which has impact through online marketing. Online markets are customer centric by providing E-banking services. Challenges and benefits of E-banking are discussed in this paper. The paper concludes that in years to come E-banking will be the only mode of dependent banking.

Keywords: *E-banking, online markets, Impact, Security, Customer Adoption.*

INTRODUCTION

E-banking means any user with a computer (personal / official) and a browser can get connected to his/her bank's website in which they have an account to perform any of the banking functions. In today's organizations Information Technology has become a critical tool. In internet banking system the bank has a centralized database which is web-enabled. Menu of all the services are displayed on the internet for which banking is permitted. Once when the branch offices of bank are interconnected through land line cables or satellite links, there would be no physical identity for any branch. It would act as a borderless entity which permits for anytime, anywhere and anyhow banking. Intranet is the network that connects the various locations and gives connectivity to the central office within the organization. These networks are limited to organizations for which they are set up. In today's generation banks are operating in a highly privatized, liberalized, globalized and a competitive environment. In order to overcome this competition and sustain in this environment banks have to use IT. New business platform was been introduced by IT. IT is increasingly playing a critical role in improving the access to the services in the banking industry. Tremendous developments due to sweeping changes that are taking place in. The information technology has an impact on banking industry. Electronic banking has emerged in recent times. E-banking provides enormous benefits to consumers in terms of ease of access, security, customer benefits, service, cost of transactions through internet. In the financial industry E-finance has become one of the most essential changes in technology. E-finance is a means of financial services and markets which does communication and computation through electronic mode. In general, E-finance includes e-payment, e-trading etc. Internet has changed the era, which includes the behavior pattern of shopping, and lives of the people. Internet usage has grown rapidly and has become a common means for marketing, trading information, services and goods. In recent years, shopping online has become frequent and all over the world consumers prefer to shop online as it has many benefits to customers. Internet-based electronic business/online business environment enables customers to search for information and purchase goods and services through direct interaction with online stores which is enabled through different online markets. Although, purchasing online is still growing, most business analysts expect that it will increase drastically with the introduction and implementation of E-banking services. Web-retailers can only offer certain ranges of products and services to web-shoppers, including technology gadgets, cosmetics, clothing, and the booking of airline tickets etc., which are favored through E-banking services. This study aims to examine the effect of E-banking services on marketing environment, online markets, customer online shopping behavior, customer satisfaction, customer perception, contribution to GDP, pros and cons of E-banking services.

OBJECTIVE

- To examine customers of which age group are actively involved in online shopping.
- To understand the adoption percentage of E-banking services.
- To evaluate the awareness of people about the necessity of E-banking in online markets.
- To understand the impact of E-banking on online business which contribute to GDP
- To understand pros and cons of E-banking.

METHODLOGY

A secondary research was performed initially in which the data available on various parameters of E-banking and online markets used in marketing environment was collected. This illustrated the knowledge of Consumer Online Shopping Behavior, technology adoption by customers, impact of E-banking on traditional banking, various modes of online purchasing and the Effect of Internet on Marketing Environment.

Primary research was conducted with the help of a Survey of different people. The survey was conducted online which included 101 respondents. A structured Questionnaire was used to collect the primary data. Structured, undisguised, open and close ended questions were included. Data collected was compiled for analysis and the observations are discussed.

Table 1 Data Collection - Parameters

S.No.	Parameter	Description
1	Research type	Quantitative and qualitative
2	Tool of data collection	Structured questionnaire containing both open and close ended questions
3	Mode of data collection	Online Survey
4	Sample selection	Random Sampling
5	Target respondents	All age group people
6	Sample size	101

Limitations of the Research

- The **respondent bias** can be a major limitation in the research. There could have been difference between the information generated and the information wanted due to the way in which the respondent must have interpreted the question.
- Limited number of questions to understand overall perception of the respondent.
- The research was carried out only through few respondents of different age groups which did not involve all the people. The primary data collected may not be a representative of the entire population.
- Sample size of 101 respondents may not reflect the same results in **actual size.**

To decrease non-responsive rate following corrective steps were taken:

- All questions were made compulsory
- Constant follow up was done to get maximum responses

LITERATURE REVIEW

ICICI Bank is the credit taker for the launch of internet banking in India. In 1999 Citibank and HDFC Bank followed with internet banking services. Government of India as well as the Reserve Bank of India had come up with several initiatives to facilitate the development of E-banking in India. The Government of India enacted the IT Act, 2000 with effect from October 17, 2000 which provided legal recognition to electronic transactions and other means of electronic commerce. A high level Committee under chairmanship of Dr. K.C. Chakrabarty and members from IIT, IIM, IDRBT, Banks and the Reserve Bank prepared the IT Vision Document- 2011-17, for the Reserve Bank.

To overcome the pressure of competition, Indian commercial banks have adopted several initiatives and E-banking is one of them. E-banking transactions are much cheaper than branch or even telephone transactions. This could change yesterday's competitive advantage - a large network of branches - into a comparative disadvantage, allowing E-banks to undercut traditional in-house banks. E-banks are easy to set up, so threats of new entrants will arrive. E-banking gives customers much more choice. Loyalty of the consumers is less inclined towards non-adoption. E-banking providers are likely to attract the most significant share of banking profits. They would simply bring two parties together e.g., buyer and seller, payer and payee. The goods and services will be provided by experts in their fields.

Online shopping has eliminated on the consumer's side of traditional shopping inconveniences such as moving in crowds, standing in long queue lines, and searching and paying for parking spaces at busy shopping places. The customers are able to evaluate the available goods and services and their prices from diverse options and diverse outlets through the Internet. These comparison shopping sites may save customers time and money because they can see which retailer has the best price without visiting many websites. Thus, it allows customers to browse online shopping websites in the privacy of their home, and prefer online mode of banking for online purchasing. Online shopaholics will soon have one more reason to avoid the crowd. Non-bank finance companies are working on interest-free installment plans for online purchasers. This option is now available only for buying from large online stores.

A study revealed that online shopping prevents work-related stress and several types of health issues caused by it like hypertension and depression. The study, conducted over a period of six months, has also showed that over 40 percent of professionals worldwide consider online shopping as solution for their stress and depression caused due to their work and this survey was conducted across major cities including Mumbai, Chennai, Delhi and Pune and 45 percent of the people in India voted online shopping to be the best way to ensure temporary distraction from anxieties caused by the work. According to the health ministry, 40 percent of the people in cities and 20 percent in rural India suffer from hypertension and the number was fast increasing due a sedentary lifestyle and hectic working official working hours. Medical experts rate hypertension and depression as the leading factor for a slew of diseases including heart attacks, paralysis, renal failure and thickening of the arteries. "While shopping, their level of oxytocin, the hormone of love and happiness, increases due to excitement. This helps in decreasing stress levels and relieving shoppers who get a feeling of achievement," Kulpreet Kaur, co-founder of Shoppirate.in, said in a statement – "Most companies are finding it tough to maintain their discounted factory outlets as consumers are increasingly turning to shopping online due to the lure of bigger discounts". Megamart from Arvind Brands, for instance, recently rebranded its large format stores that have been struggling to shed their 'discount format' image. Bengaluru-based discount-led garment chain "Coupon" was sold to Future group's discount format Brand Factory, while some discount chains such as The Loot and The Grab Store have completely shut operations in the past two years. "This model has become stagnant. Going forward, there will be closures and we will soon see the end of factory outlets," said J Suresh, chief executive of Arvind Brands. Discounted factory outlets started coming up about a decade ago and offered extraordinary savings on merchandise that was two to three seasons old. These outlets were mainly used by companies to attract new customers who could not otherwise afford the brand. According to industry experts 5-10% of the store merchandise is routed through factory outlets.

Offline retailers blame online players for getting "more enquiries and less sales" at their stores. "The growth of discounted format has fallen from high double digits to 7% since the advent of online platform. There are too many offline and online sales that have impacted the factory outlet model," said a senior executive of a Bengaluru-headquartered retail company. "Not many brands are looking to expand in this segment any more. The roll-out of factory outlets will be gradual now."

S Raghunandan, an independent retail consultant and former chief executive officer of Xander Retail, said e-commerce offers current season stocks at discount, "which is suicide", to build customer engagement. "With this model, these outlets become meaningless," he said.

"It becomes inconvenient for customers to go to each and every store individually. In case your sales of a particular year go well, there will be no stock at the stores making these stand-alone stores unprofitable," said Suresh Sadhwani, head of business at Brand Factory.

According to a Crisil report, as online shopping increases in the country, the brick-and-mortar retailers are expected to see their growth rate moderate to 13-15% over the next two-three years from an annual average growth rate of 24% seen over the past five years. After the launch of mobile app, State Bank Buddy, SBI Card has launched Simply CLICK, a credit card targeted at the online shopper. In collaboration with seven leading e-retailers -- Amazon India, Clear trip, Fab Furnish, Food Panda, Book My Show, Lens kart and Ola Cabs -- it has brought out a card to leverage the popularity of e-commerce in India and expand its existing base of 3.2 million credit card holders.

It is a culmination of our efforts to address the evolving needs of the consumers and has been inspired by the aspirations of a generation that is always online," said Vijay Jasuja, CEO, SBI. The card comes for a fee of Rs 499, but new customers will get an Amazon e-voucher worth Rs 500. The renewal fee will be reversed if the customer crosses an annual spend of Rs 1 lakh. Loaded with other benefits, it offers rewards to the tune of 5X on all online spend and 10X on purchases made on partner sites. The customer can also get Rs 4,000 worth of vouchers on spends of Rs 2 lakh annually. This way online marketing and E-banking services are being promoted in the market.

ADVANTAGES OF E-BANKING

- **Information of Account:** Real time balance information and summary of day's transaction can be easily obtained
- **Transfer of Fund:** Managing of purchasing and distribution of the goods and services effectively by using online transfer mechanism. Effect of fund transfer on a real time basis across the bank locations is enabled.
- **Request:** Make a banking request online while doing online shopping
- Customers can Integrate the System with his own ERP
- Bill Payment through Electronic Banking
- The Electronic Shopping Mall
- Effecting Personal Investments through Electronic mode.

LIMITATIONs OF E-BANKING

- Danger of giving your card number when buying online.
- Refund of amount is possible but requires time to recover the money.
- Sometimes goods and services ordered and delivered are not matched which again consumes time for returning back.

DATA REPRESENTATION & ANALYSIS

Sample distribution based on age group:

Table 2 Sample distribution based on age group

Age Group	Number of Respondents
<20	11
21-40	81
41-60	6
>60	3

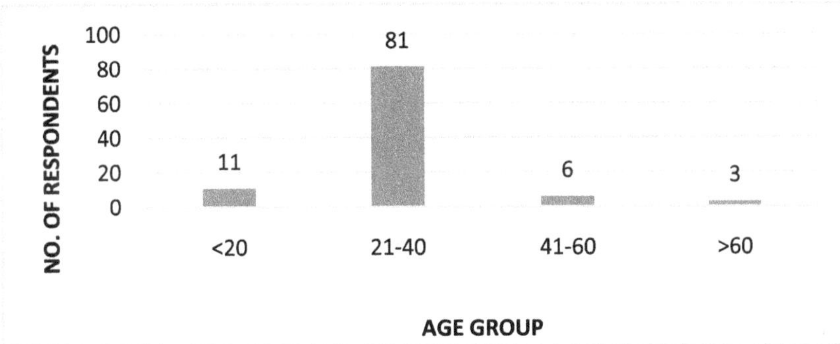

Fig. 1 Respondents distribution-Age Group

INFERENCE

Out of 101 respondents

- 81% respondents are from age group 21-40 yrs, it infers that most of the respondents that use E-banking services for online shopping are from this age group.
- 11% respondents are from age group < 20 yrs
- 6% respondents are from age group 41-60 yrs
- Only 3% respondents are from age group > 60 yrs

Sample distribution based on age group and gender

Table 3 Sample distribution based on age group and gender

Age Group	Male	Female
<20	4	7
21-40	42	39
41-60	4	2
>60	3	-

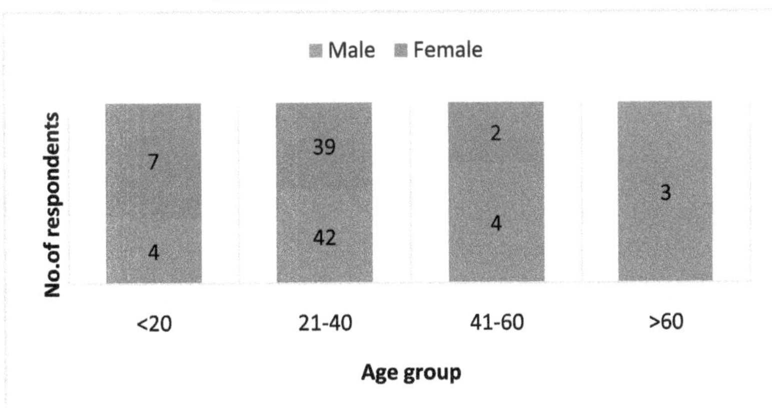

Fig. 2 Respondent distribution- Age Group and Gender

INFERENCE

Out of 101 respondents,

- 53% respondents are males and remaining are females.
- In the age group of < 20 yrs females are more compared to males, which indicate that teen age girls are more prone to online shopping.
- In the age group of 21-40 yrs, 42 respondents are males and 39 respondents are females
- In the age group of 41-60 yrs, 4 respondents are males and 2 respondents are females
- 3 respondents of age group > 60 yrs are only males
- From this study it can be inferred that male respondents are high in number.

Table 4 Frequency of online shopping

Approximately how frequently you do online shopping?

Frequency	Number of Respondents
Daily	4
Weekly Twice	5
Weekly Once	11
Monthly	47
Rarely	34
No online shopping	-

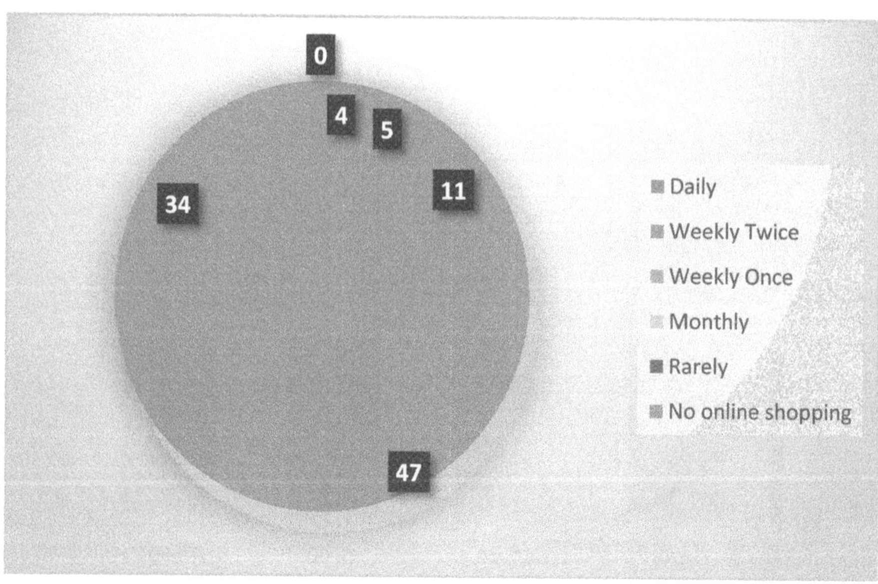

Fig. 3 Respondent Distribution- Frequency of online shopping

INFERENCE

Out of 101 respondents,

- 47% respondents do online shopping monthly
- 34% respondents do online shopping rarely
- 11% respondents do online shopping weekly once
- 5% respondents do online shopping weekly twice
- Only 4% respondents do online shopping daily
- It infers that most people opt doing online shopping but very less on daily basis

Which mode of payment you use for online shopping?

Table 5 Mode of payment used

Mode of payment used	Number of Respondents
E-banking services	14
Cash on delivery	19
Both	68

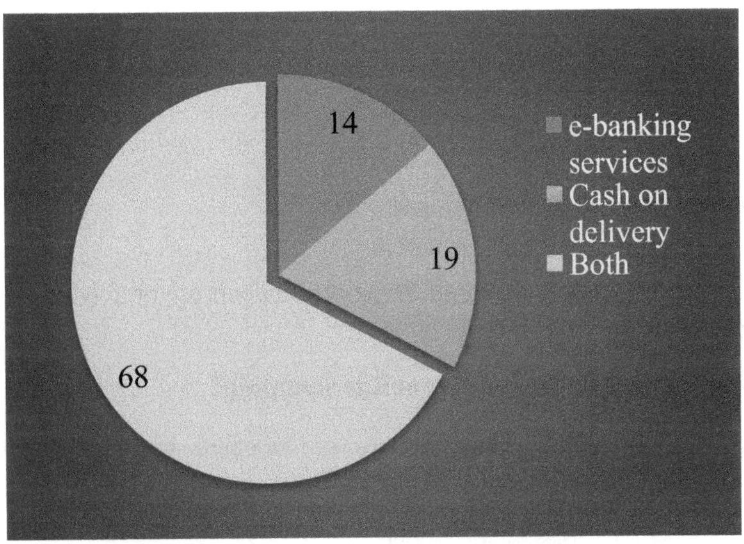

Fig. 4 Mode of Payment used by the Respondents

INFERENCE

Out of 101 respondents,

- 68% of the respondents opt for both the modes of payments i.e.,. E-banking services and cash on delivery
- 19% of the respondents are opting cash on delivery for online shopping

- 14% of the respondents are opting E-banking services
- It can be inferred that both the payment modes are widely used.

If both the mode of payments are used for online shopping then which is mostly used comparatively?

Table 6 Type of service used

Type of service	Number of Respondents
E-banking services	64
Cash on delivery	37

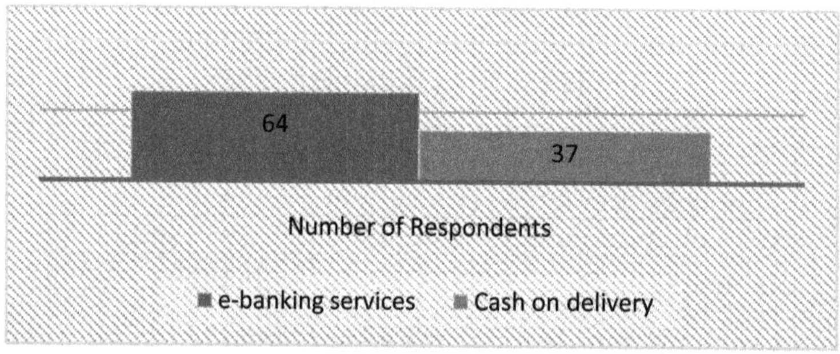

Fig. 5 Type of Service used by the Respondents

INFERENCE

Out of 101 respondents,

- 64% respondents are using E-banking services
- 37% respondents are using cash on delivery
- It can be inferred that more than half of the respondents are preferring E-banking services over cash on delivery for online shopping.

Which E-banking services do you use for online shopping?

Table 7: E-banking services used for online shopping

Type of Service	Number of Respondents
1. Debit card	37
2. Credit card	6
3. Net banking	11
Only 1 & 2	15
Only 1 & 3	12
Only 2 & 3	1
All	19

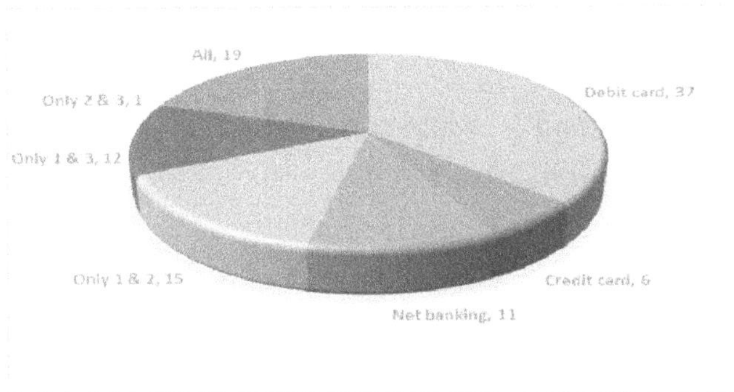

Fig. 6 Respondent Distribution-E-banking services used for Online Shopping

INFERENCE

Out of 101 respondents,

- 37% respondents use debit card
- 11% respondents use net banking
- 15% respondents use both debit card and credit card
- 12% respondents use both debit card and net banking services
- 19% respondents are using all the 3 facilities i.e., debit card, credit card and net banking
- It infers that most of the people use debit card.

How frequently do you use these E-banking services per month?

Table 8 Frequency of usage of E-banking services

	I never use this service	1-3 times	3-8 times	8-12 times	>12 times
Debit card	10	58	22	8	3
Credit card	56	35	5	2	3
Net banking	39	45	10	4	3

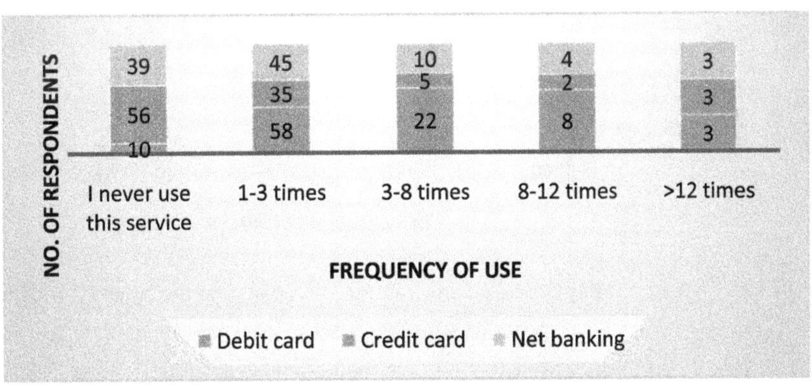

Fig. 7 Frequency of usage of E-banking services

INFERENCE

Out of 101 respondents,

- 58 respondents use debit card 1-3 times per month
- 56 respondents do not use credit card facility
- 22 respondents use debit card 3-8 times per month
- 8 respondents use debit card 8-12 times per month
- >12 times, equal number of respondents i.e., 3 use debit card, credit card and net banking

From above graph it infers that frequency of usage of debit card is more than all the 3 available E-banking services.

What amount (In Rupees) of transactions you do per month through E-banking?

Table 9 Purpose of using E-banking Transactions

	<1000	1001-5000	5001-10000	>10000	N/A
Online shopping	31	45	16	8	1
Pay bills	42	31	8	3	17
Bank transfer	12	23	12	13	41
Loans and mortgages	17	7	8	8	61
Others	27	9	4	2	59

Fig. 8 Purpose of using E-banking Transactions

INFERENCE

Out of 101 respondents,

- 45 respondents have reported spending in online shopping in the range of Rs.1001-5000 per month
- 31 respondents are spending in online shopping an amount of < Rs.1000 per month
- 16 respondents have reported spending in online shopping in the range of Rs.5001-10000

How do you rank E-banking?

Table 10 Ranking of E-banking services

	Worst	Bad	Good	Very Good	Excellent	N/A
Service		1	31	35	34	-
Security	1	1	31	38	30	-
Ease of access	-	1	21	41	38	-
Benefits to Customer	1	1	36	31	30	2

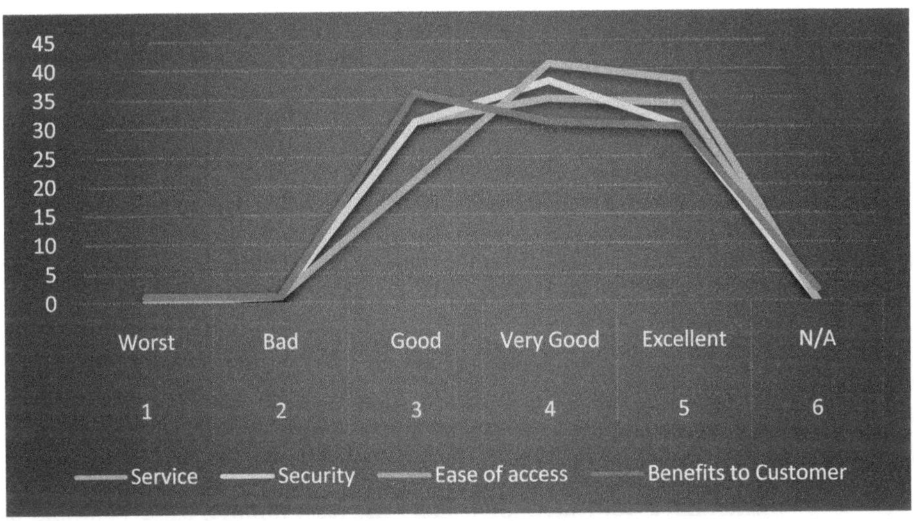

Fig. 9 Respondent Distribution-Ranking of E-banking services

INFERENCE

- 100% of the respondents have ranked E-banking service and ease of access in the range of good, very good and excellent
- 99% of the respondents have ranked E-banking security in the range of good, very good and excellent
- 97% of the respondents have ranked E-banking benefits to customer in the range of good, very good and excellent

In your opinion what would be the impact of E-banking on online marketing? (Growth in online purchasing)

Table 11 Impact of E-banking on online market

Growth in online marketing	Number of Respondents
Very little impact	6
Less impact	11
No impact	4
High impact	53
Very high impact	27

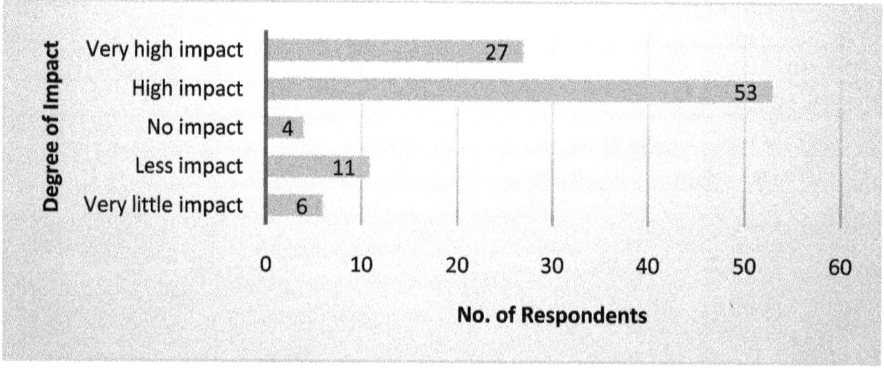

Fig. 10 Respondent Distribution-Degree of Impact of E-banking on online market

INFERENCE

Out of 101 respondents,

- 53% respondents have indicated that there is high impact of E-banking on online marketing
- 27% respondents have indicated that there is very high impact of E-banking on online marketing
- 11% respondents have indicated that there is less impact of E-banking on online marketing
- 6% respondents have indicated that there is very little impact of E-banking on online marketing
- Only 4 respondents have said that there is no impact of E-banking on online marketing
- Majority of the respondents have indicated that there is high impact of E-banking on online marketing

KEY FINDINGS

- According to this survey, customers are likely to adapt to changing technology of shopping in coming years

- Majority of youth are engaging in online shopping
- 80% of the respondents of age group 21-40 yrs are indulging in online shopping
- More than 50% of respondents are preferring for E-banking services rather than cash on delivery
- It was found that most of respondents are doing online shopping monthly which is having great indication of economic growth
- Respondents are using all the E-banking facilities like debit card, credit card and net banking but most of the respondents consider security, usability, rewards/offers/discounts, and no transaction cost and customer benefits while implementing the usage
- 37% of the respondents are using debit card
- 19% of the respondents are using all the facilities of E-banking services i.e,. debit card, credit card and net banking
- Majority of respondents are aware of online marketing
- 58% of the respondents are using debit card for 1-3 times per month
- 45% of the respondents are using net banking service for 1-3 times per month
- 45% of the respondents do online shopping with transaction amount of Rs.1001-5000 per month
- Debit card usage for 8-12 times is 8%.
- 31% of the respondents do online shopping with the transaction amount of < Rs.1000
- 8% of the respondents do online shopping with the transaction amount of > Rs.10000
- 53% of the respondents are having the opinion that there is high impact of E-banking on online markets
- Highest ranks for various parameters like security, service, customer benefits and ease of access are given in the scale of good, very good and excellent

RECOMMENDATIONS

- E-wallet: A digital wallet refers to an electronic device that allows an individual to make electronic commerce transactions. This can include purchasing items on-line with a computer or using a smart phone to purchase something at a store. According to the current study the e-wallet can be offered by the banks, rather than 3rd party vendors. Also, most offers come with terms & conditions, instead of that even simple offer with lower discounts or cash back options will get better response in online marketing.
- E-commerce and E-banking are very good initiatives that have come in the recent years but proper implementation in rural areas is required with the support of good internet facilities.

- There is a drastic change the online marketing trend due to E-Banking but proper awareness and effectiveness need to be built within the customers through various campaigns, promotions, offers etc.
- E banking and online marketing are mutually beneficial to the online shopping customers.
- It contributes to customer satisfaction through better service which saves time.
- Online marketing through the support of E-banking services should be done in an uninterrupted manner to reduce dissatisfied customers who may impact the total business.
- People of all age groups and income groups are using online sources but the frequency of use is very low so proper modes of access should be provided.
- Youth is more engaged in online shopping hence this segment should be targeted for best utilization of e -resources for augmenting profits.

CONCLUSION

In a country like India, there is a need for providing better and cost efficient banking services to public. With the stated objectives of the survey, responses have been collected from people of different age groups. Secondary data indicates how E-banking services have helped the growth of online markets. This shows that the introduction of E-banking has made a significant impact on online markets. The growth percentage would further increase if the marketing environment provides effective services, benefits to customers and efficient shipments to reduce delivery time. Major parameters of online markets and customer perceptions have been considered to understand the E-banking effectiveness. Despite of challenges in terms of providing all the details of bank account or debit card during online shopping, the security is ranked well by the respondents. To conclude the concept of E-banking has made a significant effect on online marketing and online shopping. With things available at the touch of button, online shopping and E-banking would become more prevalent in the market.

REFERENCES

1. "Overview of E-Banking", E-Banking: A Global Perspective Bankers, Gupta V, (2002).
2. Acceptance of E-Banking among Customers, K.T. Geetha & V.Malarvizhi, Journal Of Management And Science Vol .2, No.1
3. An Implementation Of Core Banking Solution With Special Reference To SBI, Shivamoga, Manjushree S, Sai Om Journal Of Commerce & Management, Published By: Sai Om Publications, Volume 1, Issue 2(2014)
4. BANKERS' PERSPECTIVES ON E-BANKING, Dr. Himani Sharma, NJRIM VOL.1, NO.1, JUNE 2011
5. Consumer Online Shopping Behavior: The Effect Of Internet Marketing Environment, Product Characteristics, Familiarity And Confidence And Promotional Offer, Norazah Mohd Suki,

Norbayah Mohd Suki, International Journal Of Social, Behavioral, Educational, Economic And Management Engineering Vol:7, No:3, 2013

6. E-Banking: The Indian Scenario, Dr. Roshan Lal;Dr. Rajni Saluja, Asia Pacific Journal Of Marketing & Management Review, Vol.1 (4), December (2012)
7. http://articles.economictimes.indiatimes.com/2015-09-25/news/66884593_1_factory-outlets-brand-factory-arvind-brands
8. http://articles.economictimes.indiatimes.com/2015-11-07/news/68089904_1_online-shopping-hypertension-40-percent
9. http://articles.economictimes.indiatimes.com/keyword/online-shopping
10. Impact of E-Banking on Traditional Banking Services, Shilpan Vyas, School Of Computer Science And Information Technology.

Journey of E-Banking in the Demanding Environment

T. Vijaya
Research Scholar, Centre for Economics and Social Studies (CESS).

ABSTRACT

The sphere of banking and financial services has been changing in the demanding environment of globalization, where conventional models like " brick and mortar" systems are paving way for modern techniques of customization, with 24/7/365 uptime service provision for the customers. All these would be possible with perfect combination of all the stakeholders like bankers, IT regulatory mechanisms, financial houses, business houses and RBI. Different e-banking solutions in the form of ATM'S, NEFT, RTGS, ECS, and MOBILE BANKING are present forming the e-banking system. In this demanding environment there are innovative opportunities and path breaking challenges to be faced. This paper reveals all the ins and outs of e- banking from the time period 2011-2015.

Keywords: *E-banking, globalization, e-banking solutions, stakeholders.*

INTRODUCTION

The fast advancing global information infrastructure (including information technology and computer networks such as the Internet and telecommunications systems) enable the development of electronic commerce at a global level. The nearly universal connectivity which the Internet offers has made it an invaluable business tool. These developments have created a new type of economy, which many call the 'digital economy'. This fast emerging economy is bringing with it rapidly changing technologies, increasing knowledge intensity in all areas of business, and creating virtual supply chains and new forms of businesses and service delivery channels such as e-banking. As a direct consequence of the emergence of the 'digital economy', the balance of power seems to be shifting to the customers. Customers are increasingly demanding more value, with goods customized to their exact needs, at less cost, and as quickly as possible. To meet these demands, businesses need to develop innovative ways of creating value which often require different enterprise architectures, different IT infrastructures and different way of thinking about doing business. This transformation of business from an old company to a new agile electronic corporation is not easy and requires a lot of innovative thinking, planning and investment. This paper will cover many of these issues in e-banking context.

Evolution of E-banking

There have been significant developments in the e-financial services sector in the past 30 years. According to Devlin (1995), until the early 1970s functional demarcation was predominant with many regulatory restrictions imposed. One main consequence of this was limited competition both domestically and internationally. As a result there was heavy reliance on traditional branch based delivery of financial services and little pressure for change. This changed gradually with deregulation of the in- E-Banking Management, IGI Global, distributing in print or electronic forms without written permission of IGI Global is prohibited. Industry during 1980s and 1990s, whilst during this time, the increasingly important role of information and communication technologies brought stiffer competition and pressure for a faster pace of change. The Internet is a relatively new channel for delivering banking services. Its early form 'online banking services', requiring a PC, modem and software provided by the financial services vendors, were first introduced in the early 1980s. However, it failed to get widespread acceptance and most initiatives of this kind were discontinued. With the rapid growth of other types of electronic services since mid 1990s, banks renewed their interest in electronic modes of delivery using the Internet. The bursting of the Internet bubble in early 2001 caused speculation that the opportunities for Internet services firms had vanished.

REVIEW OF LITERATURE

Raj preet kaur (2013) this paper aims to explains about the reason behind the security breaches and the participation of both customers and the banks to enable the hackers or crackers to access others network. The present study aims to find various types of flaws in the security of online banking that result in loss of money of account holders and financial institutions. Security breaches are not only because of banks faults and banks inadequate polices but customers are equally responsible for it, because customer's awareness regarding security is equally important.

Majid Karimzadeh (2012): This paper provides a possible six factor model centered upon the following: infrastructure, knowledge, legal-security, socio-cultural, economic and management and banking issues. The results of the study indicate that legal and security, socio-cultural, and management and banking issues are accepted as challenges for the development of e-banking but there is less awareness regarding new technologies and unsuitable software which are ranked respectively as the highest and lowest obstacles in India.

OBJECTIVES

1. To study the challenges and benefits of e-banking.
2. To analyze and compare the current status of different payment systems in e-banking sector.

METHODOLOGY

The present study is descriptive in nature. The data used for the study is secondary.

Sources: Data collected from RBI Bulletin, journals, books, news papers.

Tools: Averages, Growth rates, CAGR used to calculate and analyze the data.

1. **To study the benefits and challenges of e-banking.**

   E-Banking Importance: Understanding e-banking is important for several stakeholders, not least of which is management of banking related organizations, since it helps them to derive benefits from it. The Internet as a channel for services delivery is fundamentally different from other channels such as branch networks, telephone banking or Automated Teller Machines (ATMs).

   Choice and Convenience for Customers: In the fierce battle over customers, providing a unique experience is the compelling element that will retain customers. Most of these aspects of customer service cannot be automated. The adequacy of staff members serving customers can be expected to directly influence the customers' satisfaction. However, e-banking backed up by data mining technologies can help in better understanding customers' needs and customizing products/services according to those needs.

Attracting High Value Customers: E-banking often attracts high profit customers with higher than average income and education levels, which helps to increase the size of revenue streams.

Challenges in E-Banking: Based on 'best practices' in developed countries, United Nations Conference on Trade and Development (UNCTAD) report has identified four challenges that developing countries, in general, are expected to overcome to achieve the advantages that E-banking initiatives can bring about.

The ability to adopt Global Technology to Local Requirements: An adequate level of infrastructure and human capacity building are required before developing countries can adopt the global technology for their local requirements.

The ability to Strengthen Public Support for E-finance: Historically, most e-finance initiatives in developing countries have been the result of cooperative efforts between the private and public sectors. For example, Singapore's successful Trade Net system was a government-sponsored project.

The ability to Create a Necessary Level of Regulatory and Institutional Frameworks: The lack of regulatory frameworks, trust, security and privacy standards, high trade barriers, customer and investor protections impede progress in implementing e-banking initiatives on a larger scale in many developing countries.

2. **To analyze and compare the current status of different payment systems in e-banking sector**

Bank Wise Volumes in ECS/NEFT/RTGS/Mobile Banking Transactions (2011)

Table 1 Data (in Billions)

2011	ECS(CREDIT)	ECS(DEBIT)	NEFT	RTGS	MOBILE BANKING
JAN	91.46	61.05	938.88	38239	0.6277
FEB	191.67	49.72	905.8	38081	0.6161
MAR	95.10	58.63	1503.81	59916	0.846
APR	158.26	62.9	1302.94	38185	0.76
MAY	136.54	65.14	1145.32	41901	0.91
JUNE	166.20	66.8	1319.95	47690	0.98
JULY	160.7	65.3	1283.54	40564	1.2
AUGUST	221.53	67.66	1225.679	38446	1.364
SEP	130.1	66.15	1365.51	46839	1.464
OCT	171.21	70.4	1420.33	38885	1.606
NOV	102.43	70.5	1362.15	38710	1.739
DEC	154.01	73.423	1603.45	51920	1.97

Bank Wise Volumes in ECS/NEFT/RTGS/Mobile Banking Transactions (2012)

Table 2 Data (in Billions)

2012	ECS (CREDIT)	ECS (DEBIT)	NEFT	RTGS	MOBILE BANKING
JAN	187.153	72.486	1705.7	45883	1.9
FEB	114.83	75.41	1765.03	43110	1.96
MAR	134.92	77.47	2403.89	67174	2.32
APR	151.13	79.13	1954.96	49945	2.34
MAY	114.5	80.12	1994.27	50408	2.86
JUNE	156.89	81.42	2070.26	64584	3.06
JULY	207.28	83.5	2109	54735	3.37
AUGUST	179.67	83.29	2107.76	52367	3.54
SEP	136.37	85.48	2272.914	57997	4.1
OCT	163.17	88.51	2534.21	54459	4.97
NOV	146.61	88.03	2301.55	46775	5.38
DEC	124.8	90.11	2667.68	57278	5.9

Bank Wise Volumes in ECS/NEFT/RTGS/Mobile Banking Transactions (2013)

Table 3 Data (in Billions)

2013	ECS (CREDIT)	ECS (DEBIT)	NEFT	RTGS	MOBILE BANKING
JAN	133.69	90.79	2814	58002	6.2
FEB	131.06	92.73	2560	52883	8.07
MAR	170.55	95.22	3602	77410	9.91
APR	191.59	94.84	3247	61061	9.86
MAY	153.57	95.47	3289	58723	11.94
JUNE	207.63	102.72	3253	62383	11.47
JULY	274.8	101.89	3444	62423	12.8
AUGUST	238.79	99.21	3150	55083	14.12
SEP	210.16	107.13	3434	62835	15.65
OCT	241.04	100.57	3860	58824	19.54
NOV	170.62	105.05	3332	52505	19.63
DEC	242.95	108.56	3929	63850	22.61

Bank Wise Volumes in ECS/NEFT/RTGS/Mobile Banking Transactions (2014)

Table 4 Data (in Billions)

2014	ECS (CREDIT)	ECS (DEBIT)	NEFT	RTGS	MOBILE BANKING
JAN	170.3	113.41	3871.54	61921.84	26.25
FEB	176.51	119.95	3656.05	52867.91	26.36
MAR	217.79	126.34	5312.25	81773.84	34.07
APR	186.26	123.01	4219.56	58109.41	32.96
MAY	170.33	130.77	4307.38	58381.63	38.82
JUNE	155.77	130.89	4509.52	66242.97	39.85
JULY	147.79	134.88	4577.84	57378.87	44.21
AUGUST	181.66	196.61	4520.4	55570.27	46.81
SEP	211.58	140.09	5393.36	71529.23	77.3
OCT	151.6	141.54	4781.5	56828.29	84.05
NOV	154.53	140.99	4616.75	54644.76	102.32
DEC	183.51	147.44	5573.36	68744.01	113.23

Bank Wise Volumes in ECS/NEFT/RTGS/Mobile Banking Transactions (2015)

Table 5 Data (in Billions)

2015	ECS (CREDIT)	ECS (DEBIT)	NEFT	RTGS	MOBILE BANKING
JAN	165.5	148.83	5084.73	61648.02	129.17
FEB	159.01	149.79	5046.41	57414.11	140.66
MAR	151.26	155.17	7173.09	87421.48	169.14
APR	127.1	145.63	6043.75	65199.89	188.69
MAY	98.51	150.55	5536.03	60051.45	199.18
JUNE	85.92	149.63	6324.58	74181.48	202.91
JULY	0	0	6289.37	68891.04	214.56

Growth Rates of Different Payment Systems in E-Banking System

Table 6 (Percentages)

Year	ECS (CREDIT)	ECS (DEBIT)	NEFT	RTGS	MOBILE BANKING
2011	4.43	1.54	4.56	2.58	10.00
2012	-3.32	1.83	3.79	1.86	9.90
2013	5.10	1.50	2.82	0.80	11.38
2014	0.62	2.21	3.08	0.87	12.95
2015 JULY	-10.35	0.04	3.08	3.08	7.5

Compiled Data from the Figures of RBI

Interpretation of Data

1. From the above data we can interpret that among the different payment mechanisms, one can observe that **mobile banking** is growing Y-O-Y basis at a faster pace from 2011 (10%) to 2014 (12.95%).
2. On observation **ECS (credit and debit)** payment mechanism is declining Y-O-Y basis from 2011 (4.43%), (1.54%) to 2014 (0.62) (2.21%) in a negative format, at a faster pace.
3. On observation **NEFT and RTGS** mechanisms are also declining Y-O-Y on a slow basis compared to **ECS from.**
4. On observation **MOBILE BANKING** has grown on a robust basis from the year 2011 to 2014 altogether at a 470.779 %, (from the above tables given).

Future of E-Banking

- **Web Calculator:** You can use the Web Calculator for stock exchange transactions to figure out quickly and easily the brokerage fees for transactions you are planning or you have already executed
- **PayPen:** Reads Swiss payment slips easily and quickly. With a quick brush of the hand payment slip may be imported into the e-banking system of the bank or payment software in seconds.
- **GIROMAT 130:** With GIROMAT 130 you can process all Swiss payment slips. It can read orange payment slips with the new or old dimensions.

CONCLUSION

The future phase of e-banking will change, but the change should be concrete and categorical in nature. Metamorphosis of change should catch the modern customization, meeting all the levels of consumers, clearing all the challenges, like bettering the technologies and to be in stride with newer technology.

REFERENCES

1. Raj preet kaur (2013). "Online Banking Security Flaws: A Study", Volume 3, Issue 8, August 2013.
2. International Journal of Advanced Research in Computer Science and Software Engineering. www.ijarcsse.com
3. Majid Karimzadeh (2012). "Electronic Banking Challenges in India: An Empirical Investigation", June 2012 VOL 4, NO 2. Www. ijcrb.webs.com.
4. Deloitte (2010). Mobile banking A catalyst for improving bank performance. www2.deloitte.com.
5. https://rbi.org.in/scripts/AnnualReportPublications. Das(2011). "Electronic Remittance System in India– Rationalization". ww.math.iitb.ac.in/.../TechReport_National_Electronic_Funds_Transfer.

Trends in Modern Banking

Balaji Vidadala[1] and Dr. Raavi Radhika[2]

[1]Research Scholar, GITAM University.
[2]Research guide, Hyderabad Business School.

ABSTRACT

The banking industry has experienced a series of significant transformations in the last few decades. Among the most important of them is the change in the type of organizations that dominate the landscape. Since the eighties, banks have increased the scope and scale of their activities and several banks have become very large institutions with a presence in multiple regions of the country.

In order to provide a thorough understanding of the subject, this study begins by looking at the traditional theory of banking. A bank is a financial firm which offers loan and deposit products on the market. The intermediary role played by banks, another area of our interest, is the reason why banks exist in modern economies.

Where banking is going in the future? What do they expect customers to want from the new and exciting delivery channels that are coming into being? What major trends are going to matter during the next five and ten years? How do institutions see their own financial future? These are main probing questions that we have been asking ourselves during the course of the research. The presentation of this work is organized to give flexible means of understanding the major trends of the Global banking development. The material is largely non-technical--it is the ideas and concepts that are challenging, not the statistics.

This paper / article explore the new trends in banking sector both in India and abroad.

Keywords: *Latest trends in Banking sector, Evolution of Modern Banking, Changing channels in Banking sector, Virtual Banking, Digital Banking.*

INTRODUCTION

At the beginning of the 21st century, the biggest banks in the industrial world have become complex financial organizations that offer a wide variety of services to international markets and control billions of dollars in cash and assets. Supported by the latest technology, banks are working to identify new business niches, to develop customized services, to implement innovative strategies and to capture new market opportunities. With further globalization, consolidation, deregulation and diversification of the financial industry, the banking sector will become even more complex.

Although, the banking industry does not operate in the same manner all over the world, most bankers think about corporate clients in terms of the following:

- Commercial banking: Banking that covers services such as cash management (money transfers, payroll services, bank reconcilement), credit services (asset-based financing, lines of credits, commercial loans or commercial real estate loans), deposit services (checking or savings account services) and foreign exchange;

- Investment banking: Banking that covers an array of services from asset securitization, coverage of mergers, acquisitions and corporate restructuring to securities underwriting, equity private placements and placements of debt securities with institutional investors.

Over the past decade there has been an increasing convergence between the activities of investment and commercial banks, because of the deregulation of the financial sector. Today, some investment and commercial banking institutions compete directly in money market operations, private placements, project finance, bonds underwriting and financial advisory work.

Furthermore, the modern banking industry has brought greater business diversification. Some banks in the industrialized world are entering into investments, underwriting of securities, portfolio management and the insurance businesses. Taken together, these changes have made banks an even more important entity in the global business community.

THE EVOLUTION OF MODERN BANKING

Times are changing, and today's digital world is having widespread effects on an array of consumer behaviors, including how we handle our finances. Electronics and mobility are key trends for financial institutions to keep track of, but consumers aren't ready to sever all ties with their local bank branches just yet.

According to Nielsen data from a custom study conducted in November 2013, the vast majority of U.S. consumers (82%) have entered the digital arena, stating that they banked online at least once in the last 30 days. The high percentage speaks to the prevalence of the digital world in consumers' lives, especially when compared against the 68 percent of people who said they had visited a physical branch in the same period.

E-Banking is an Electronic Payment System

E-Banking is an **electronic payment system** that enables customers of a financial institution to conduct financial transactions on a website operated by the institution, such as a retail bank, virtual bank, credit union or building society. Online banking is also referred as **internet banking**, **e-banking**, **virtual banking** and by other terms.

To access a financial institution's online banking facility, a customer with Internet access would need to register with the institution for the service, and set up a password and other credentials for customer verification. The credentials for online banking is normally not the same as for telephone banking. Financial institutions now routinely allocate customers numbers, whether or not customers have indicated an intention to access their online banking facility. Customers' numbers are normally not the same as account numbers, because a number of customer accounts can be linked to the one customer number. The customer number can be linked to any account that the customer controls, such as cheque, savings, loan, credit card and other accounts.

To access online banking, a customer visits the financial institution's secure website, and enters the online banking facility using the customer number and credentials previously setup. Online banking services usually include viewing and downloading balances and statements, and may include the ability to initiate payments, transfers and other transactions, as well as interacting with the bank in other ways.

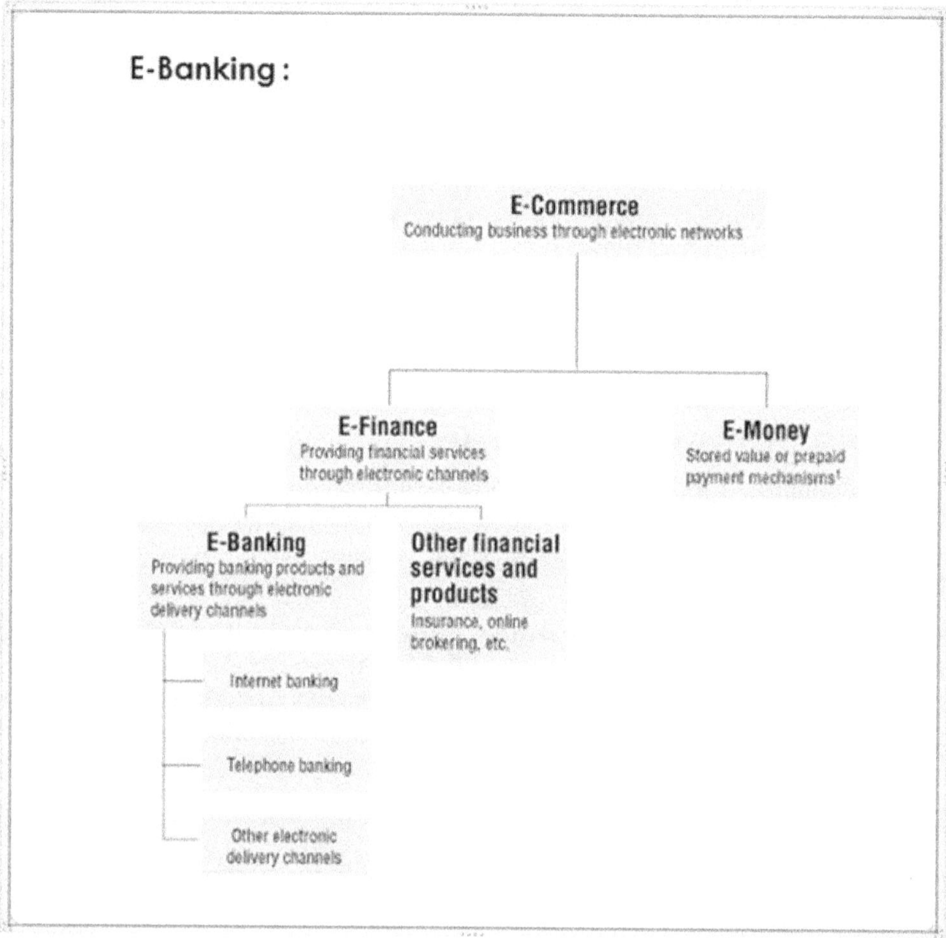

Mobile Banking

Mobile banking – either via tablet or Smartphone it is a distant preference compared with the other more traditional channels, but it is gaining momentum. The use of call centers, however, is trending the opposite direction, making it the least-utilized channel among consumers. So the bottom line for financial institutions is that staying abreast of consumer banking preference will help maintain loyalty, engage new customers and serve consumers wherever they want to bank.

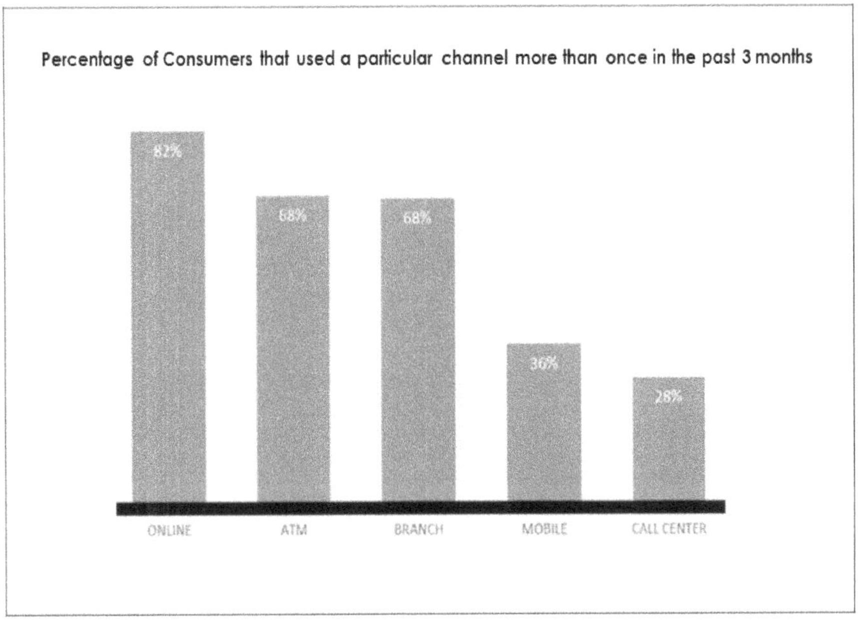

CHANGING CHANNELS

Identifying banking preferences in aggregate only tells part of the story. In order to truly understand preference, financial institutions need insight into which channels consumers use for their specific banking activities. For example, banks won't have much luck touting their automated drive-up teller technologies to customers that prefer banking via smartphone app.

In today's world, companies and brands need to be online. And that includes banks and financial firms. In fact, 77 percent of consumers say they prefer to pay their bills online. Mobile consumers prefer checking their account balances using their smartphones or tablets, and most consumers prefer to make deposits and seek investment advice in the branch.

And when it comes to cold hard cash, there's currently no substitute for the physicality of an ATM that dispenses paper currency—the preferred method for withdrawing money. Got a problem? That's what the call centers are for, which is how most consumers say they seek to resolve any questions or issues they have with their accounts.

After all, there's less benefit in trying to engage a Web-savvy consumer with a highway billboard. And the same is true when it comes to banking. If it's not convenient or feasible for a customer, he or she is bound to find the convenience they're looking for somewhere else. And with myriad choices available, consumers won't have to look far to find what they're looking for.

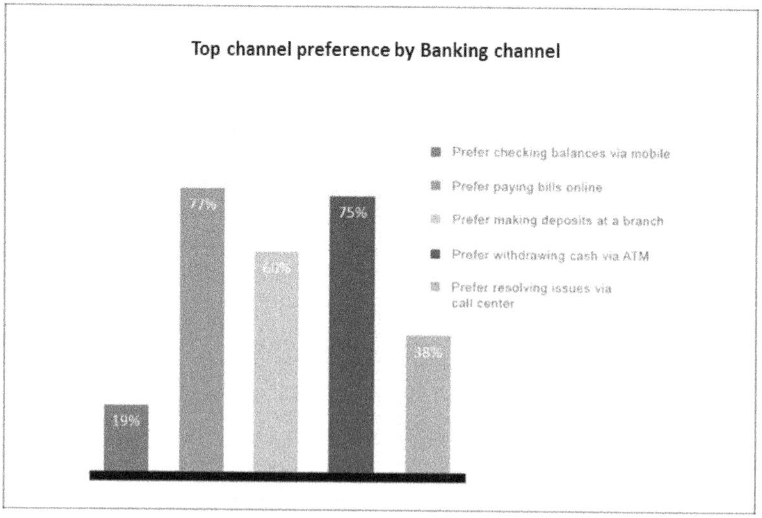

LATEST TRENDS IN BANKING

Today's bank doesn't look a whole lot like yesterday's bank. From smart technology to online and mobile banking, how consumers interact with their financial institutions is more revolving door than teller wall.

This constant motion in the industry has led to some exciting, interesting innovations. For bank brands, the goal is now how to capitalize on these trends and ensure consumers keep coming back for more.

But which changes are getting the most traction? To find out, take a look at this list of the six latest trends in modern banking.

Innovation labs -- *"Innovation labs let banks experiment with new ideas."*

All those creative branch redesigns, smart technologies and seamless mobile tools have to come from somewhere. That "somewhere" is usually an innovation lab, a technique employed by a number of major banking institutions across the country. These labs are where designers can test out their new ideas on employees and consumers alike. Labs are often futuristic, over-the-top centers full of toys and gadgets, all in the hopes that something sticks and can make it into bank branches all over.

Faster Queues

Standing in line is one of the worst parts of the bank experience. That is no more, however, thanks to a cool trend known as the digital queue management system. One popular option, QMatic, lets bank customers join a digital queue before they arrive at the branch, or even book appointments ahead of time. This technology can remove long lines at the branch and increase customer satisfaction. Not to mention, it is simply cool to queue up in line before you ever set foot in the branch itself.

Interactive Tools

Gone are the days of standing around waiting to be helped. Banks are now providing a number of interactive tools for consumers, and this is one cool trend in the industry. Some options include free use of tablets, computers and the Internet. One step farther is the interactive wall, a massive touch screen where consumers can click around industry news and events while they wait to be served.

From tablets to touch walls, banks are offering a wide range of interactive tools.

The Teller Kiosk

One of the least cool parts of any bank is the teller wall. This is why so many branches are doing away with the idea, in favor of a much cooler teller kiosk. Kiosks are self-contained pods where tellers can perform a wide range of functions for the consumer. Where the cool factor really kicks in is with the options kiosks afford in the way of a branch redesign. Without being bogged down by the wall, banks can get creative with their design and really change the look and feel of their branches.

Multiple Services

Another cool way banks are looking toward the future is with multiple services. Once, banks were only there for banking. Today, banks are also offering up coffee shops and restaurants as a new approach, so consumers can grab a cup of joe while they make a deposit. The branch design here is focused on the coffee shop, not the bank, so it doesn't look like your average branch. This ups the cool factor, and creates a novel, exciting experience for consumers.

Smart Technology

Technology can do a lot to improve the consumer experience. One of the coolest trends around today is interactive gesture technology. This smart bit of design senses when a person walks through the door, sounding a greeting and bringing up an interactive screen where the consumer can check out the branch's products and services. Thanks to this technology, a bank's customers will have a user experience that is hard to find elsewhere.

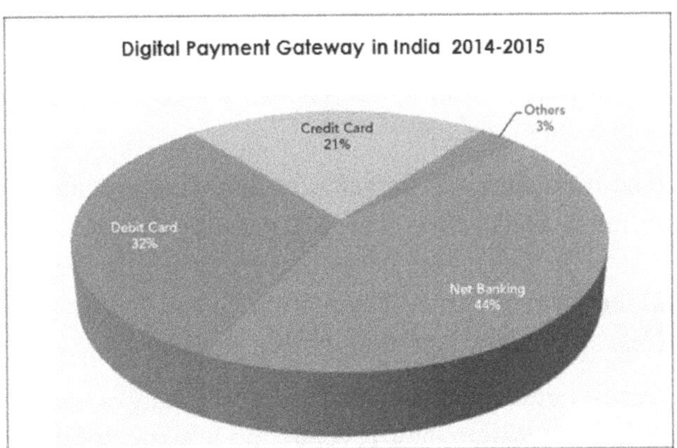

MODERN GLOBAL BANKING TRENDS

The Rich get Richer and the Poor get Poorer

Rates on low interest cards have been falling for a while, and we're seeing an uptick in balance transfer and other promotional offers. Banks are offering juicy rewards for those with good credit, in an effort to get the penalty-dodging-APR crowd spending money. For those who front the cash for annual fees, rewards credit cards are improving too – see, for example, the new deal out of **Capital One for 100,000 bonus miles.** This kind of deal hasn't been seen in years.

Vitally, credit card merchant exchange fees are not regulated by the Durbin Amendment, and often bring in higher fees than debit cards. Rewards credit cards command the highest swipe fees of all, so look for banks to push customers to get rewards cards and then to use them often.

On the other hand, interest rates have spiked for those with bad credit. The Credit CARD Act of 2009 prohibited "risk-based pricing," in which card issuers changed the interest rate of a card if the customer's risk profile changed. They can also no longer charge overdraft fees unless customers opt-in, and even then can do so in a limited fashion.

Unable to hike interest rates and denied lucrative overdraft penalties, banks now charge a higher rate upfront. Some banks even charge a flat fee for poor credit histories, irrespective of consumer behavior and in addition to the annual fees that come standard with poor credit. No one expects interest rates to be as low as they were in the pre-recession days, but those with bad credit will be hit harder and longer.

More Fees, Less Free

This is where financial reform comes in. The Dodd-Frank bill banned overdraft fees unless customers opt in, curtailed rate hikes in credit cards, and per the Durbin Amendment, authorized the Fed to limit debit interchange fees. In years past, "free" checking was paid for by "swipe fees" and by overdraft charges on small segments of the population.

Now, banks cannot earn as much money from the overdrawing crowd. The cost of free checking, which was never truly free to begin with, will be spread over a broader customer base. Rob Windsor, president of First Financial Services Credit Union, says, "Consumers are used to getting all these services for free, including free checking, debit, credit. But none of these things are free. We need revenue to pay for them."

The revenue will come from charging for services that were previously free. Free checking is already on its way out: many banks now charge a monthly fee, or for services such as paper statements and teller assistance. Others are becoming creative with their fees: **Bank of America demands a $59 annual fee** for credit card customers with bad credit, while Citibank levies a fee for customers who put less than $2,400 on their cards a year.

Debit interchange fees, interest rate hikes and overdraft charges were extremely lucrative for banks. Now, they are forced to change their revenue models and spread fees over more of their customers.

Pruned Debit Rewards Programs

Banks make money off different customers in different ways. Those with poor credit pay in the form of high annual fees and high interest, penalty and cash advance rates; debit cards previously yielded overdraft and swipe fees; and rewards credit cards offered juicy premiums on merchant fees and the occasional annual fee.

As we mentioned before, only the last revenue stream is still in place. Therefore, while banks spice up their rewards credit cards to get the cardholders spending and swiping rewards debit cards are nowhere near as lucrative.

A number of banks now charge annual or monthly fees for debit rewards programs, or have removed them altogether. PNC did away with free rewards checking, and Chase and Wells Fargo have axed their entire debit rewards program for new customers. Other banks are expected to follow. Rewards checking still exists; free checking still exists. Both in the same account, however, is a feature likely to become history.

New Toys Online and New Fees Offline

The financial industry is not immune to technological innovation, which offers greater and easier access to consumers. A number of banks now have mobile apps that allow users to check their balance, make transfers and even scan checks.

In the wake of the financial crisis, some are offering online financial tools to help customers make and stick to budgets, and to help students use their **first credit card.** Citibank will soon introduce its 2G cards, which feature a smart chip instead of a magnetic strip for security. Users can, with the touch of a button, pay for their purchases with rewards or with their credit account. Starbucks is testing a prepaid card smartphone app, and Visa and Master card are developing systems that require only a smartphone to pay. **PayPal** and startup **Bling Nation** are testing a pilot program in Silicon Valley that does just that.

Online banking has benefits for banks as well: online statements and support documentation are far cheaper than mailed statements and salaried tellers. As a result, some checking accounts charge for paper statements and for receiving teller assistance. Still, the move to online banking is a net positive for consumers, who can access their account easily, transfer funds, and save paper. The new technology in the works is likely to be rolled out in the next couple of years; look for more developments and introductions as banking finds its way onto smartphones.

The Rise of Retail Finance

Banks make their profits off financial services and pass them on to their shareholders. Credit unions make their profits off financial services and pass them back to their customers. Retailers, on the other hand, make profits when people buy their merchandise, and so make an effort to drive traffic to their stores.

In particular, retailers love in-store shopping; people are more likely to browse the shelves and make a few more impulse buys. If a retailer can use a credit card to increase sales, and spend some of its profit to lower interest rates or offer better rewards, then both the retailer and the cardholders win.

Target offers a rewards debit card, it's one of the few remaining free rewards debit cards, that gives a 5 percent in-store discount with no annual fee. It also offers a credit card with the same rewards rate, no annual fee, and an APR that's slightly above industry average. According to a Target spokesman, the store will keep its rewards program regardless of the Durbin Amendment outcome, since they don't rely on a third-party payment processor for transactions.

Wal-Mart, too, began its foray into the murky waters of finance. It offers **prepaid debit cards** at $3 a pop, with 1 percent back on gas purchases, and $3 for check cashing services. Its prepaid debit card fees are significantly lower than those of other providers, but serve Wal-Mart's goal of being a one-stop shop for its consumers. The company also partnered with Jackson Hewitt to provide tax services to shoppers, and acquired an equity interest in prepaid card supplier Green Dot. Sam's Club, a Wal-Mart subsidiary, now makes small-business loans.

Other retailers have financial products that more directly benefit their sales or bring in fees. Best Buy, along with Tio Network, now has bill-paying services that cater to Hispanic customers who typically avoid traditional financial services. Kmart began a similar pilot program aimed at un- or under-banked shoppers who lack or do not use checking and savings accounts. Last year, Kmart and Sears dusted off their Layaway Programs, in which the store holds an item while customers pay the cost over 8 weeks for a small fee. Many other retailers offer "Christmas savings accounts," which yield savings of 0 percent to 3 percent and can only be spent in-store after a certain date.

The companies mentioned above are already expanding their services or piloting new ones, while others experiment with bill paying and rewards programs. In 2011, more retailers who serve low-income households with a limited credit history, and retailers who make their profits on the volume of their transactions, are sure to join these frontrunners.

FINDINGS

Cost-saving, time-saving and convenient way of banking. Accessible all the time and operative from anywhere. Risks associated with stolen cheques and forged signatures are avoided.

Makes possible to do online shopping. There is less chance of confidentiality of your account status and transactions being compromised as there is minimum human interference with the transactions conducted online. Transfer funds between your accounts of different classification so that you gain maximum returns on your deposit.

Though online banking portal is secure and user friendly, there are people who are beginners in using internet and therefore are exposed to the dangers of stolen passwords and website phishing when using public computers.

NEED AND OBJECTIVES OF THE STUDY

- To Study the impact of Trends in Modern Banking
- To Study the adoption and utilization of Digital Banking
- To Study the Innovative ideas in banking sector
- To Study the encouraging factors of customers for utilizing E-Banking

CONCLUSION

The study of this paper explores the modern/latest trends in banking sector. It explores the possibilities of different trends that are available in banking sector to satisfy the customers and their needs in a secured manner. The study brings the awareness and reveals the changes from traditional banking to Digital banking.

REFERENCES

1. http://www2.deloitte.com/us/en/pages/financial-services/articles/2015-banking-outlook.html
2. https://www.iisd.org/business/banking/sus_trends.aspx
3. https://www.bai.org/bankingstrategies/article.aspx?Id=1e4c97e3-cf98-48cf-9442-45d55f8ba7b6
4. http://www.pwc.com/gx/en/industries/financial-services/banking-capital-markets/banking-2020/emerging-trends.
5. http://www.strategyand.pwc.com/perspectives/2015-retailbanking-trends
6. http://www.ey.com/GL/en/Industries/Financial-Services/Banking---Capital-Markets/8-trends-shaping-the-bank-of-2030
7. http://www.ibef.org/industry/banking-india.aspx
8. http://www.ey.com/Publication/vwLUAssets/EY-global-banking-outlook-2015-transforming-banking-for-the-next-generation/$FILE/EY-global-banking-outlook-2015-transforming-banking-for-the-next-generation.pdf
9. https://www.in.capgemini.com/resource-file-access/resource/pdf/Trends_in_the_Global_Banking_Industry.pdf
10. http://www2.deloitte.com/global/en/pages/financial-services/articles/2015-banking-outlook.html

Study on Consumer Satisfaction in Indian Retail Banking

Preeti Jaiswal
Associate Professor, Aurora's PG College, Ramanthapur, Hyderabad.

ABSTRACT

The advent of Liberalization, Privatization and Globalization in the Indian economy served as the gateway for the global and private players to introduce their products and services in the Indian market. The organized retailing industry was a relatively late entrant which started occupying most of the market share in the Indian context. Introduction of retail banking, a process of customizing the services of the banks to individual customers by offering the extra frills of services like online banking, credit, debit/ATM, phone, mobile and other facilities stands as a landmark feature in the Banking industry of India. The banking system is one of the oldest and the most conservative systems followed by the people globally. Asians, as pointed out by most of the researchers, are a set of people who strongly believe in saving their hard earned money for any future exigency. They do the same by investing their money in any of the trusted financial institutions. Indians were of the view that the financial institutions are the best places to safeguard their money and other transferable assets and showed keen interest in depositing them in post offices and some banks which had options of personal transactions. This facility was accessible only to the rich and affluent and required a security deposit. This clearly was a hindrance for many interested in banking to shy away from the same.

Retail banking ever since its inception has been striving to attain customer satisfaction and carve a niche for its services in the minds of the consumers. The introduction of various schemes and services like the floating interest rates on loans and higher fixed interests rates on the various kinds of accounts, are few of the valid examples of their efforts to gain a clear competitive advantage. Customer Relationship Management and the retention of loyal customers has been posing a great challenge to the retail banks globally, owing to the ever growing stiff competition from local, national and global players. The study tries to acknowledge these attempts of the Retail banks and gain an insight into the factors which are necessary from the viewpoint of consumers, to enrich the services of the Bank and achieve ultimate customer satisfaction.

INTRODUCTION

The growth of the disposable income among the upper and middle classes in India have opened a galore of opportunities to the retailing industry, which is fast growing with the economy of the nation. Retailing is considered as one of the strongest pillars of the Indian economy within the services economy. The cut throat competition and the ever changing needs of the consumers is posing a great challenge to all the sectors in the retailing industry. Retail banking is one of the fastest and the most reliable sectors in the Retailing industry. Growing awareness in the consumers regarding the banking services and its advantages has clearly proved that the conservative approach in banking is being sued by all the concerned parties. The primitive notion that the banking transactions are primarily for the affluent and the employed is being overpowered by almost all the individuals having a bank account in any of the various types of banks to their credit.

Retail banking is the form of banking which intends to serve the consumers by directly transacting with them and offering them a range of value added services like personal loans, ATM/debit cards, phone banking, online banking, to name a few, apart from the traditional savings, fixed deposits, lockers facilities and the like. The main objective of retail banking worldwide has been to reduce the transactional time and increase customer satisfaction by improving the efficiency and effectiveness of the services offered to the end users. A research into the history of banking and its development in India over the twentieth century gives us a clear idea that consumers are the top priority for the existence of the banks. Though banking has its roots in serving institutional needs catering mainly to organizations and public sector enterprises, changes in the post independence phase of the nation and particularly in the early 1990's has been a far cry from its basic motives to only cater to corporation or industrial needs. The emphasis on customized banking started taking shape in the post LPG (Liberalisation, Privatisation and Globalisation) phase.

History and Evolution of Banking in India

The origins of banking in India dates back to the last lap of the eighteenth century with two major players serving the banking needs of the nation, namely The General bank of India and The Bank of Hindustan, which are not functional anymore. The British East India Company was instrumental in setting up of the a bank named the Bank of Calcutta in the early decades of the nineteenth century i.e., June of 1806, which was renamed as the Bank of Bengal thereafter. The Company was also influential in setting up of the Bank of Bombay and Bank of Madras, which along with the Bank of Bengal were considered as the three Presidency banks of the British ruled India. The three presidency banks merged in the year of 1921 to form the Imperial bank of India, which is better known as the State Bank of India, post independence. The other quasi-central banks established under the British rule in the mid eighteenth century and functional till date include the big brands like the Allahabad Bank (Joint stock bank), Punjab National Bank (established in Lahore). A few multinational brands like Hong Kong Shangai Banking Corporation (HSBC) and The Comptoire d'Escompte de Paris also started setting up their branches in India during this period. The twentieth century, particularly the post independence era saw the emergence of National and local banks like the Bank of India, Corporation Bank, the Indian Bank, Bank of Baroda, Canara Bank and Central Bank of India. Many other efforts to establish new banks later on, either were futile or resulted in a merger with the other brands which were prevalent in that epoch. The formation of the Reserve bank and further nationalization of the banks which are 27 in number including the State Bank group, have been the milestones in the history of banking in India. Retail banking started unfolding in the early 1990's with the government headed by Sri. P. V. Narasimha Rao, opening the gates of Indian economy to Global markets. The liberalization and privatization played a major role in impacting the economy of the country and the banks being a great contributing factor in the same were also affected. The entry of Private and global brands started giving a tough time to the nationalized banks and this competitive environment in the sector made many a banks to start revising their policies and procedures to gain a competitive advantage over the others.

The introduction of personal accounts and further introduction of customized services marked the inception of retail banking in the nation. The boom of information technology and internet services clearly left a positive impact on the retail banking sector. Banks irrespective of their kind started concentrating their efforts on creating and retaining a large customer base in the form of individual consumers. The ever growing competition globally, has thus left the retail bankers with the only option to offer the best of the kind services to its patrons. The article makes an earnest effort to surface few of the factors which are essential for an efficient customer service management by the retail bankers. An extensive study on a sample of members in the population has been done to get a clear concept on the retail banking services and customers expectations of the same.

OBJECTIVES OF THE STUDY

1. To understand the evolution and growth of Retail banking services in India.
2. To recognize the actual practices adopted by the sector to achieve customer satisfaction.
3. To analyze the expectations of the customers regarding service provided by the retail bankers.
4. To draw conclusions and bridge the gap (if any) between the expectations and actual, on the basis of the sample study.

RESEARCH METHODOLOGY

The analysis of the study was planned on a primary data clubbed with inputs from secondary data, mainly from the internet and newspaper studies. The primary data has been collected from a study executed on a sample of 100 members in the population. A questionnaire containing around eleven questions of open ended and closed ended types was formatted and administered to all the respondents. The mixed questionnaire was designed to help elicit the best and unbiased responses from the sample, which would benefit the study. The sample units included people of age groups ranging from 18 years to 75 years and have been selected on a random basis.

LIMITATIONS OF THE STUDY

Though thorough care was taken in executing the study in the best possible manner, some limitations have crept in inevitably, owing to the inadequacy of resources and geographical constraints. The following have been identified as the limiting factors to our research:

1. The sample of the population is very low. The sample consisted of 100 respondents, who were randomly chosen.
2. The respondents were chosen from within the confines of the city Hyderabad.
3. The responses were grouped into various broad categories for easier interpretation and analysis of the data.

Data Interpretation and Analysis

The data collected from the exercise has been analyzed and has been depicted in the following manner:

The first two questions in the instrument intend to know the number of respondents across all age groups with respect to them holding an account in the bank and the kind of bank they have an account with. It is noticed that the demographic factors like gender, profession, organization, and the like had minimal bearing on the choice of banker. The age of the respondents was instrumental in deciding the kind of account to be owned in any of the banks.

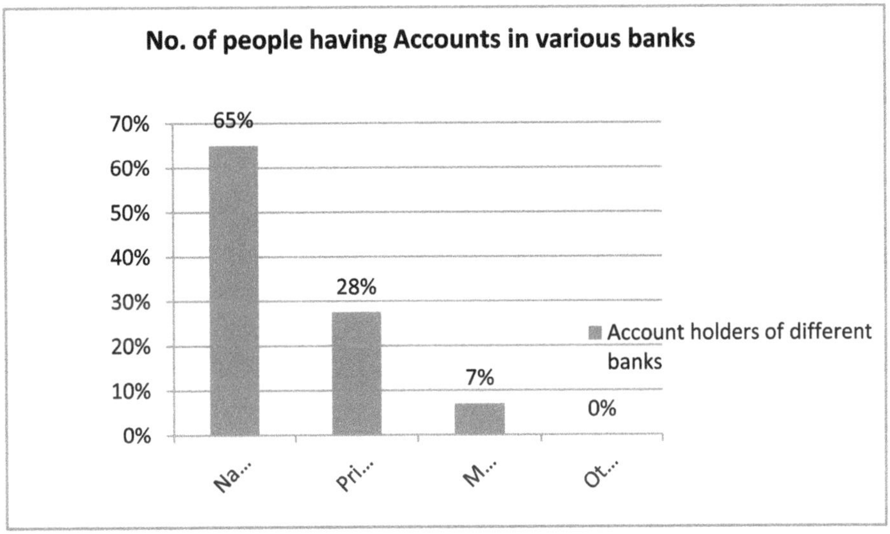

Nationalised banks were seen as the hot favorites of people mostly belonging to the age bracket of 40 years to 75 years. It is observed that most of the respondents had an account in any one of the nationalized banks (65%), followed by Private bank account holders, totaling to 28% and 8% of them having an account in the multinational banks. Most of the respondents had a savings account (75%), followed by salary account (20%) and few of them holding a NRI/NRE account (5%), in the various kinds of banks. The respondents also were mostly aware of the additional facilities provided by the bank and were availing them very often.

The phenomenon has made the customers visit the bank physically only mostly on a weekly or monthly basis. Most of the younger respondents were satisfied utilizing the add-on services of the bank and were visiting the bank only on a need basis, such as to complete any formalities of the account or upgrade or avail other services of the bank. The following pie diagram gives us an idea on the customer's convenience and knowledge of the additional facilities provided with the account in the retail banks.

The majority of the consumers were convinced and readily agreed that add-on services were effective in addressing their banking needs appropriately. The satisfaction of customers was also measured with the help of the below pie diagram, which depicts that all the consumers interviewed were quiet satisfied with most of the features of their account. 65 respondents in 100 were very happy and agreed that they were satisfied, while 15 respondents were very pleased and satisfied with the retail banking services. The other 18 were not very certain of their satisfaction levels and 2 respondents disagreed with the majority.

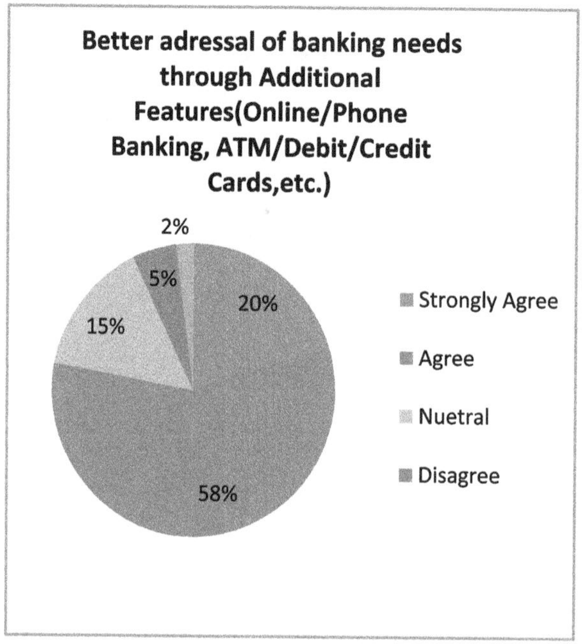

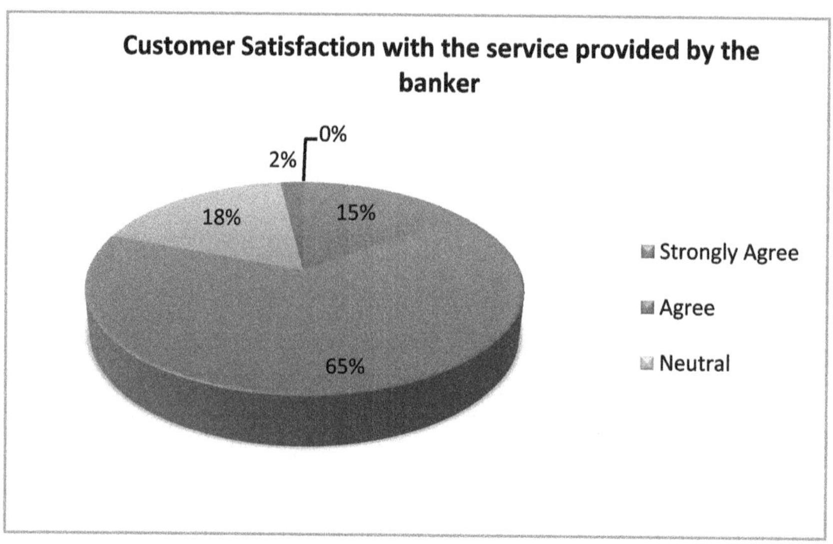

The satisfaction level of customers was also backed by their belief in the grievance re-addresal systems of the retail banks. Almost 75% of the customers were very satisfied by the grievance handling procedure of the banks in case of any mishaps or issues during transactions. Some of the respondents did not require revoking of any such grievances, while 5 of the respondents were very satisfied by the prompt solutions provided by the banks in various instances, like loss of credit/debit cards, bounced cheques, over draft limits, to name a few. The chart below depicts the satisfaction of customers with respect to the grievance re-addressal system of retail banks.

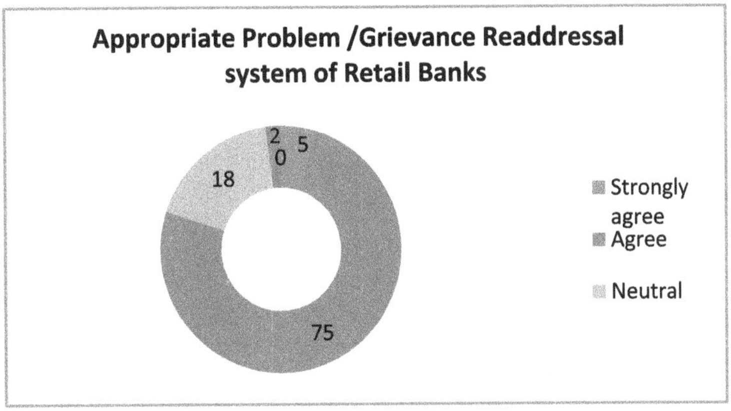

FINDINGS AND SUGGESTIONS

- Any time, anyhow and any where banking is the order of the day and every segment of the market is looking forward to such a service. It is therefore appropriate for the bankers to reach all the "unbanked" sections of the market place in India. Rural areas can be a profitable option to venture into.
- Further customization of services and prompt responses is sought by most of the customers in the survey. It is thus obligatory on the part of retail banks to focus their efforts on creating products for the niche customers. e.g., Feature rich applications with the optimum utilization of internet and mobile phone technologies are still to be enhanced to suit the requirements of various segments of target consumers.
- The effective implementation of automated services requires the customers to gain a technical know-how of the application. This becomes a constraint in few cases, which should be checked by educating the customers on technology usage, which would aid them in utilizing the services effectively.
- Most of the customers were looking at prompt address of transactions during their visit to the banks. The quick disposal of queues at counters and an increase in the number of counters handling customers for their regular transactions, installation of deposit machines with a limit on the deposits, and the like are few of the suggestions given by the customers towards proper customer management.
- An innovative and creative measure in effectively handling consumers is always welcome by the customers. The bank has to take the initiative to make the customer aware of the changes and make sure that the end user is actually happy and comfortable in using the same.
- Properly trained and congenial staff is expected to be serving the customers at banking counters. The bankers need to ascertain that Customer Service Management includes the simplest to the most engaging transaction and that they need to appreciate every effort of the customers to associate with their bank.

- The interest rate on principal amount for fixed deposits should be increased while the minimum balance in case of savings accounts should be decreased, was a popular response in most of the customers surveyed.
- Rotational shift system, banking on Sundays and few optional holidays, prolonging the operational timings of the banks, were few of the proposals expressed by the respondents to enable working class to transact for their banking needs, without compromising on their work schedules.

CONCLUSION

Retail Banking has grown by leaps and bounds since its inception in the early 21st century. The concept of banking at the customer's doorstep with anytime, anyhow and anywhere banking has caught the mindset of the Indian consumers to a great extent. The middle class consumers who used to shy away from the concept of banking are now very comfortable transacting for their personal needs with the advent of retail banking.

A study of the value added services provided by almost all the retail banks in the Indian context has enabled us to understand the concept of customer centric approach of the marketers and has given valid inputs on the working of a retail financial institution towards achieving a competitive advantage in the market.

The data gathered from the interactions with customers of various retail banks has facilitated us in analyzing the highly individualistic nature of their banking needs, in tune with the various services offered by the retail banks. The essence of the suggestions and recommendations of the consumers has been put forth for the retail bankers to act upon, depending on their objectives to achieve customer satisfaction. It has been deduced from the analysis that Retail banking has a great potential in the market and is still in its pre- growth phases. A thorough scrutiny and further employment of the various factors which contribute to the achievement of customer satisfaction shall ensure that the growth phase of Retail banking services yields the expected results and is sustained for a long period of time in the near future.

REFERENCES

1. http://en.wikipedia.org/wiki/Retail_banking
2. http://www.articlesbase.com/banking-articles/retail-banking-in-india-1465022.html
3. The Journal of Sri Krishna Research & Educational Consortium Journal on banking financial services and insurance research (Internationally Indexed & Listed Referred e-Journal) Volume 1, Issue 8 (November, 2011) ISSN 2231-4288.
4. www.iba.org.in/.../IMC-Mrs. Soundara Kumar-SBI.
5. http://www.mckinsey.com/locations/india/mckinseyonindia/pdf/India_Banking_Overview.pdf
6. http://www.investopedia.com/terms/r/retailbanking.asp#ixzz1hFaeN6sy

The Role of Social Banking in Economic Progress: Importance and Challenges

P. Hima Jagathi[1] and M. Madhavi[2]

[1]Associate Professor, Department of Management Studies, Aurora's PG College.

[2]Director, Department of Management Studies, Aurora's PG College.

ABSTRACT

Banking plays a fundamental role in economic progress of a country. It inculcates the habit of savings among people, hence helps in boosting the investment base and speeding up the capital formation. At the same time it also helps out the needy, by providing them timely credit at an affordable cost. But majority of poor rural and semi urban population in India are unable to avail the basic banking facilities. Banks were supposed to concentrate on rendering service to underprivileged people, living below poverty line, and cover more and more unbanked areas rather than just concentrating on their own profitability. Social banking policies were made to shift the focus of commercial banks from selective banking to mass banking. Hence there is a purpose to emphasize the role of Social Banking in Economic Progress.

Keywords: *Banks, Social Banking, Financial Inclusion, Priority Sector lending.*

INTRODUCTION

If the people knew tonight, exactly how the monetary and banking system worked, there would be a revolution before tomorrow morning" - ***Abraham Lincoln***

Banking plays a fundamental role in economic progress of a country. It inculcates the habit of savings among people, hence helps in boosting the investment base and speeding up the capital formation. At the same time it also helps out the needy, by providing them timely credit at an affordable cost. But majority of poor rural and semi urban population in India are unable to avail the basic banking facilities. As a result they are made to rely on private money lenders, charging exorbitant interest rates and are trapped in vicious circle of debt. Since independence, the efforts of the Government have revolved around expanding financial institutions to rural and unbanked areas, so as to increase access to formal credit in rural underdeveloped regions. Banks were supposed to concentrate on rendering service to underprivileged people, living below poverty line, and cover more and more unbanked areas rather than just concentrating on their own profitability. Social banking policies were made to shift the focus of commercial banks from „selective banking□ to „mass banking□. Social banking is rightly defined by Dr Roland Benediktar (2011) as banking with a conscience. Here the bank focuses on investing in community, providing opportunities for the disadvantaged, and supporting social, environmental and ethical agenda. Rather than just concentrating on traditional bottom line i.e., profits, bank emphasizes on achieving triple bottom line of profit, people and planet.

REVIEW OF LITERATURE

Dr (Mrs) Shobana Vasudevan and Prof Aparna Ghaisas (2013) in their research paper entitled, Evolution of social banking in India: Accomplishments and Challenges emphasized that banking sector needs to function with a social conscious apart from business point of view if the economy has to come out of poverty and inequalities. Lot of initiatives has been taken on international level as well as on national front since independence, in India.

According to BI Norwegian Business School, Research Thesis (2012) Social Banks and impact measurement with reference to two banks namely, Charity Bank and Triodos Bank were studied and showed there is a correlation between the Social Initiatives and Performance of banks.

Session Keynote Address delivered by Dr. K. C. Chakrabarty, Deputy Governor, Reserve Bank of India at the 2nd FT-YES Bank International Banking Summit at Mumbai on October 15, (2012) on Social Banking and Finance – Opportunities in Inclusion stated that the impetus for social banking can come from two approaches - one of them being through legal and regulatory requirements. This approach could, however, result in social banking being pursued only from a compliance perspective. The other alternative, which holds greater promise, requires a realisation by market players that social banking could be a viable business proposition.

Robin Burgess and Rohini Pande (2003) studied the importance of expanding rural banks, as an evidence from Indian social banking experiment and stated that the Banking system touches the lives of millions and has to be inspired by a larger social purpose and has to sub serve national priories and objectives such as rapid growth of agriculture, small industries and exports, raising of employment levels, encouragement of new entrepreneurs and development of backward areas.

W. Gary Simpson and Theodor Kohers (2002) their unique contribution of the study is the empirical analysis of a sample of companies from the banking industry and the use of community reinvestment act ratings as a social performance measure. The empirical analysis solidly supports the hypothesis that the link between social and financial performance is positive.

OBJECTIVES OF THE STUDY

1. To understand the concept of social banking
2. To enumerate important Social Banking initiatives taken in India since independence.
3. To understand importance of basic social banking facilities in economic growth of a country.
4. To find out the major landmark programs implemented so far by various banks.
5. To understand various challenges facing by social banking initiatives taken up in India.

RESEARCH DESIGN

The paper is divided into two parts. The first section emphasizes in understanding the concept of Social Banking and Social banking practices in the banking sector. Reviewed various articles on social banking know about the importance and challenges. The second part tries to reflect the importance and Challenges facing in social banking initiatives. It also highlights the social banking practices identified at different banks and implementation of social banking initiatives.

MEANING OF SOCIAL BANKING

Social banking is "a way of value driven banking that has a positive social and ecological impact at its heart, as well as its own economic sustainability"

Social banking has different meanings depending upon the ideology of a particular nation, generally, however, it means that there is an attempt to help the needy and uplift the poor in the society. This implies that banks must lend for a cause rather than for profits. It is banking for poor, rather the poor banking (D. Muraleedharan, 2014).

In 1995, by nationalizing the imperial Bank of India, the Government of India, laid the foundation for social banking. The creation of SBI considerably facilitated extension of credit to people in rural and urban areas. Between nationalization 1955 and liberaliastion in 1992, the Indian Central bank took control in the placement of banks as a means of advancing social objectives. During this period, more than 50,000 new branches were built primarily in unbanked, rural locations. This represented a seven-fold increase in the proportion of rural locations which were banked.

Social banking has three distinct components. Firstly, RBI lowered the cost at which the rural poor had access to credit. Commercial banks interest rates are kept below the average interest rates rural areas and to ensure that commercial banks don't simply use rural deposits to increase urban lending. RBI regulated that a credit-deposit ratio of roughly 60% be satisfied by all rural and semi-urban branches of commercial banks.

Secondly, RBI identified sectors which it felt did not have access to organized lending market or could not afford to pay the interest at the market rate. It then skewed bank lending towards these 'priority' sectors, which included agriculture, small businesses and entrepreneurs.

Finally, the counter piece of social banking is the use of state control of bank placement to reach populations that had previously no access to formal financial institutions. Moreover, branch expansion will be explicitly skewed towards unbanked rural and semi-urban locations.

IMPORTANCE OF SOCIAL BANKING

In the emerging and developing countries, where a significant proportion of the poor remain cut off from access to credit, government intervention in the banking sector is perceived to channelize credit to the needy sectors of the society. Social Banking initiatives are employed by banks serve to distribute resources to the rural poor. The expansion of branches as a part social banking access of the poor, in rural settings can generate significant social returns.

CHALLENGES TO SOCIAL BANKING

The concept of social banking, despite its inherent merits, faces several significant challenges in the process of scaling up. An efficient business delivery model that is capable of delivering banking services to the masses in a cost effective manner is yet to be implemented by banks. While several delivery models have been experimented with, the same has not yet stabilized. Similarly, several alternate technology options are being tried out. However, the alternative that would be able to handle high volume low value transactions, cost efficiently, is yet to be crystallized. Banks also have to refine their pricing practices in order to ensure that the basic goal of social orientation is maintained while ensuring viability and sustainability of social banking initiatives.

Sensitization of bank's manpower on their role in implementing the bank's social banking measures is also a significant challenge as the rationale and guiding spirit behind the initiatives need to be conveyed to the operational staff on the ground. This is of utmost importance as they serve as the frontline contact of the bank with the target groups and hence, are a vital cog in the implementation of bank's social banking initiatives. Besides being technologically conversant with the innovative platforms being adopted by banks, the staff needs to have a behavioural orientation that grooms them to empathies with the vulnerable groups and gain their confidence.

PRACTICES OF SOCIAL BANKING AT SEVERAL BANKS

State Bank of India: Community Services Banking

The state Bank of India is actively involved since 1973 in non-profit activity called Community Services Banking. All branches and administrative offices throughout the country sponsor and participate in large number of welfare activities and social causes.

Apart from the normal banking operations, the Bank, as a responsible and responsive corporate citizen, seeks to reinvest part of its profit in various community welfare projects to improve the quality of life of the poor, neglected, weaker and downtrodden sections of society.

Yes Bank: Inclusive and Social Banking (ISB)

Despite formidable physical outreach and rural footprint of banks, 64% Indians lack access to savings accounts, 87% Indians lack access to ATMs and 73% of the farming sector lacks access to institutional credit. Over the 10 years of its existence, YES BANK has been focusing on 'inclusive' growth of 'emerging India'. For the Bank, financial inclusion is not just a social and regulatory obligation but also a strategic business opportunity. In line with its Responsible Banking vision of mainstreaming sustainability within its core business operations and cognizant of the needs of 'The Next Billion' customers, YES BANK launched a special division, Inclusive & Social Banking (ISB). The genesis of ISB dates back to December 6, 2006 when the bank launched YES SAMPANN, the first-of-its-kind direct micro-finance initiative in technical collaboration with ACCION International. The mandate of ISB is to reach out to un-banked and under-banked population by leveraging our branch network, technology edge and relationship capital in the Public, Private and Social sectors. Working with the guiding principle of Frugal Innovations for Financial Inclusion (FI4FI), ISB has been developing award winning innovative and viable business models, and forging partnerships for seamless implementation of the same.

Bank of Baroda: Baroda R-SETI

Bank of Baroda has always upheld inclusive growth high on its agenda. Bank has established 36 Baroda Swarojgar Vikas Sansthan (Baroda R-SETI) for imparting training to unemployed youth, free of cost for gainful self employment & entrepreneurship skill development and 52 Baroda Gramin Paramarsh Kendra and for knowledge sharing , problem solving and credit counseling for rural masses across the country, as on 31.03.2011. Bank has also established 18 Bank has also established 18 Financial Literacy and Credit Counselling Centres (FLCC) in order to spread awareness among the rural masses on various financial and banking services and to speed up the process of Financial Inclusion, as on 31.03.2011.

ICICI: Social Initiatives Group (SIG)

ICICI Bank's Social Initiatives Group (SIG), a non-profit group set up within ICICI Bank in 2000, pioneered our work on primary health, elementary education and access to finance. ICICI Foundation for Inclusive Growth (ICICI Foundation) was founded in by the ICICI Group in early 2008 to continue building upon the ICICI Group's legacy of promoting inclusive growth. ICICI Foundation works on high impact projects that are sustainable and scalable with pre-defined exits. ICICI Foundation works in partnership with governments leverages the capacities of local NGOs for implementation of its initiatives and adopts a direct intervention model for skill development. ICICI Bank is deeply engaged in human and economic development at the national level through rural self employment training Institute of India.

IDBI: CSR

IDBI designed to make a material, visible and lasting difference to the lives of the disadvantaged sections of society and a dedicated CSR budget carved out of its profits for assorted but deserving CSR initiatives pan-India. IDBI Bank has been progressively ramping up its funding and activity meter in the CSR arena in the last two years, both directly as well as in association with accredited organizations, in order to make a telling impact on targeted strata of society. This encompasses interventions in diversified areas such as promoting education, healthcare, gender equality and socio-economic empowerment, rural development projects, promotion of sports activities etc. IDBI Bank's initiatives in the CSR area continue to be recognized at various for a as apposite public appreciation of the Bank's enhanced stature as a responsible corporate citizen.

CONCLUSION

The architects of social banking experiment in India, in part, to have been justified in stressing social elements in their attempts to use state control banking as an engine for poverty reduction. Commercial banks such as SBI, Yes Bank, ICICI, IDBI and Bank of Baroda appear to be the best equipped to increase the scale Social banking practices. The financial infrastructure, extensive branch network, inherent financial strengths, well established operating procedures, capacity to offer diversified loan, investment deposit services all equipped them to give a trust to Social banking. This also meshes with the philosophy of social banking. The issue then is largely of willingness of commercial banks to come forward and adopt the needs of poor through innovative ways.

REFERENCES

1. Dr. Roland Benedikter "Social Banking and Social Finance, Answers to the Economic Crisis, 2011.
2. Dr. Deepali Pant Joshi, "Social banking, promise, performance and potential", Foundation Books Pvt Ltd., 2006.
3. D. Muraleedharan, "Modern Banking: theory and Practice", 2nd edition, Eastern Economy Edition Publications, 2014.
4. Dr. K. C. Chakrabarty, Deputy Governor, Reserve Bank of India, Session Keynote Address on Social Banking and Finance – Opportunities in Inclusion at the 2nd FT-YES Bank International Banking Summit at Mumbai on October 15, 2015.
5. Robin Burgess and Rohini Pandey, "Do rural banks matter? Evidence from the Indian social banking experiment", discussion paper at Yale University, 2003.
6. Sapna Katara, "A comparative Analysis of CSR of State Bank of India and Bank of Baroda", Internatinal Journal of Multidisciplinary consortium, Vol: 1, No: 1, Sept 2014.
7. W. Gary Simpson and Theodor Kohers, "The link between corporate and social performance: Evidence from Banking Industry", Journal of Business Ethics 35, 2002.

Indian Retail Banking Industry its Opportunities and Challenges in Present Scenario

V. Padmavathi
Associate Professor , Department of Business Management, Auroras PG College.

ABSTRACT

Banks play a vital role in spearheading the economic development of the nation and are the main stimulus of the economic progress. Transactions in retail banking are executed directly with consumers, rather than corporations or other banks. Services offered include savings and transactional accounts, mortgages, personal loans, debit cards, and credit cards. Today, retail banking is being considered as one of the most innovative financial services provided by the various commercial Public Sector Banks (PSBs), private sector and foreign banks. Retail banking has a huge potential considering the growing demand for its products namely, term deposits, consumer durable loans, auto loans, debit card, credit cards, ATM facilities, insurance, online banking, etc. The growing sector of retail lending has contributed significantly to the development of the economy. The higher growth of retail lending in emerging economies can be attributed to the rapid growth of personal wealth, favorable demographic profile, rapid development in information technology, the conducive macroeconomic environment, financial market reforms and small micro-level supply side factors. This development conforms to the liberalization and globalization needs of the Indian economy. As gradual up gradation of skills and technology and restructuring and re-engineering processes are attempted by both foreign and private sector banks, public sector banks in India face new challenges. Further, due to exposure to global trends after information explosion led by internet, customers demand better services from their banks. There is shift from mass banking products to class banking with an introduction of value added and customized products. This paper makes an attempt to ascertain the extent of the customer's awareness and their level of satisfaction regarding retail banking. The study concludes that success rate of retail banking depends on phenomenal opportunities for growth and their challenges and to what extent make use of the opportunities profitably.

Keywords: *Financial Inclusion, Financial Products, Innovation, Mechanization, Urbanization.*

INTRODUCTION: RETAIL BANKING

Retail banking deals transactions directly with consumers, rather than corporations or other banks. Services offered include savings and transactional accounts, mortgages, personal loans, debit cards and credit cards. Retail Banking as a business model is adopted now a days by all the banks in India on account of multiple factors .With the changing paradigm of technology as the driver for retail banking explosion, banks are using different strategies like - redesigning their conventional business methods, re-engineering existing products and inventing products and services, channels of distribution . The objective of retail banking is to provide customers a full range of financial products and banking services.

Hence, they possess some of the following characteristics:

1. Strong credit assessment capability
2. Sound and well developed documentation system

3. Regular follow- up procedure
4. Skilled human resource
5. Technological support

RETAIL BANKING IN INDIA

The origin of retail banking can be traced back to the entry of foreign banks. The conventional banking business by Public Sector Banks (PSBs) was done without any specific demarcation for retail and non retail activities. Foreign banks operating in India set the trend and in the late 1970 and early 1980s and came out with their consumer banking models. Standard Chartered Bank and Grindlays Bank were the pioneers. Citibank created waves in the early 1980s with their credit card products. State Bank of India and some public sector banks like Indian Overseas Bank, Bank of India, Bank of Baroda and Andhra Bank developed and marketed asset products and card products to cater to retail segment. The entry of private sector banks in early 1990s created a new approach to retail banking by banks. With the advantage of technology right from start, these banks had a clear positioning for retail banking and aggressively strategised for creating new markets for the retail segment.

India's banking system has seen some major financial innovations in the past decade as well as steps to promote financial inclusion, schemes that aim to take banking services to yet-to-be-banked areas. The various innovations in banking and financial sector are ECS, RTGS, NEFT, ATM, Retail Banking, Debit & Credit Cards, implementation of standing instructions of customers, payments of utility bills, fund transfers, internet banking, mobile banking, selling insurance products, traveller's cheques and many more value added services. The major impetus for financial innovation has been globalization of financial systems, deregulation, and great advances in technologies.

The retail banking strategies of banks are undergoing a major transformation, as banks are beginning to adopt a mix of strategies like organic growth acquisition and alliance formation.

This has resulted in a paradigm shift in the marketing strategies of the banks. PSBs are adopting aggressive strategies, leveraging their branch network to garner a large share of the retail market. This article attempts to highlight the prospects and the future role of retail banking in India. Retail banking is a very wide term that refers to the dealings of commercial banks with individual customers, both on liabilities and assets side. Mortgages, loans (e.g., personal/housing, auto and educational) on the asset side are the more important products offered by the banks. Related ancillary services include credit cards and depository services.

OBJECTIVES OF THE STUDY

The main objectives of the study are:

1. To study the recent changes in banking sector and identify various factors affecting the growth of Retail banking Business in India.
2. To carry out SWOT analysis of retail banking industry in India.
3. To emphasize on challenges and opportunities of Retail Banking business in India.
4. To give suggestions and to devise strategies to expand Retail Banking in India.

METHODOLOGY

Secondary data has been collected and analysed from various sources such as: books, journals, research papers. Data published by various financial institutions and government agencies like – Reserve bank of India (RBI), national Online International Interdisciplinary Research Journal, {Bi-Monthly}.

FACTORS BEHIND GROWTH OF RETAIL BUSINESS IN INDIA

1. **Increase in Elite Class and Middle Income Groups:** Economic prosperity and the increase in purchasing power has given a fillip to a consumer boom. It is important to note that during the 10 years after 1992, India's economy grew at an average rate of 6.8 percent and continues to grow at the almost the same rate. About 320 million people will be added in the middle-income group in a period of 15 years approximately.
2. **Percentage of Young Population:** Changing consumer demographics indicate vast potential for growth in consumption. 70% of Indian population is below 35 years of age which means that there is tremendous opportunity of 130 million people being added to working population.
3. **Increase in Level of Literacy:** Due to increase in the literacy ratio, people have developed a taste for latest technology and variety of products and services. It has led to greater demand for retail activities specially retail banking activities.
4. **Technological Impact:** Impact of Technological factors played a major role in retail banking. Convenience banking in the form of debit cards, internet and phone-banking, anywhere and anytime banking has attracted many new customers into the banking field.
5. **Change in Consumption Pattern:** Economic prosperity has resulted in the consequent increase in purchasing power of the consumers. During the ten years after 1997, India's economy grew at an average rate of 6.8 percent and continues to grow at the almost the same rate – not many countries in the world match this performance. It means that Indian consumers are now shifting from the tendency of buying more and better quality to new services and products.
6. **Reduction in Interest Rates:** Decline in interest rates has also contributed to the growth of retail credit by generating the demand for such credit for various purposes.

SWOT ANALYSIS OF RETAIL BANKING

STRENGTH

1. **Diversified Asset Portfolio:** Retail banking consists of a wide range of financial product & services. These include deposit product, home loan, loan against equity shares, mortgage loan, auto loan, car loan, payment of bills, credit card, debit card etc. Such a diversified asset portfolios provide banks with higher profit & relatively lower NPA.
2. **Customer Relationship Management (CRM):** The customer Service & Quality implementation through use of CRM tools help banks in acceptance of their banking products and satisfaction of customer that will eventually yield profit for them.

3. **Continuous Innovative Product Development:** In financial services there is an unlimited scope for development & innovation. Banks should approach the customers to find out their financial need & problems and accordingly structure their strategies towards the development of the product & services.

WEAKNESS

1. **High Capital Investment:** Retail banking requires high capital investment. Large amount is spent on managing the diverse range of product & services which further requires large staff & high quality technology. All this reduces the overall banks profitability.
2. **Changes in Technology:** If banks are not able to cope up with the latest technology it may affect their growth. Also the technology requires huge amount of capital investment & if the technology fails then it will affect the bank's reputation and the bank may lose its customers.
3. **High Cost of Marketing:** Retail banking requires strong internal as well as external marketing strategies to be adopted by bank. Under retail banking the management needs those employees who can introduce product properly to their customers. The employees must be aware of the products they are offering to the consumers. Also banks have to spend a lot on its marketing of product to general public. All this increases the expenses of banks in terms of time & cost required to introduce the product.

OPPORTUNITIES AND CHALLENGES

Retail Banking has glorious prospects in an emerging economy like India, where the rising middle class contributes to be the paramount reasons in its growth: India has been identified as the second most fascinating retail destination of 30 emergent markets. The prominent factor promising considerable accession in retail sector is the rising customer purchasing power, following a liberal attitude toward personal debt. As far as acquiring personal debt is concerned, younger generation possesses a great purchasing power as compared to the older generations. The bundling of services and delivery channels has increased of areas the potential conflicts of interest in universal banks financial organization.

1. **Increase in Per Capita Income:** There has been increase in the per capita income over the past few years & is expected to grow in the future also. The purchasing power has also increased due to economic growth and development. Also GDP of India is rising at a very good rate. Currently it is around 8- 9% & is expected to rise in the near future.
2. **Innovation in Financial Products & Services:** This segment has more scope for innovation as banks tries to provide more products & services to their customers as desired by them. Banks can continuously modify its products and services to match the market demand & sustain in this competitive era.
3. **India - Growing Economy:** Retail banking has enormous opportunities in a growing economy like India. A.T. Kearney, a global mgnt. Consulting firm identified India as the '2nd most attractive retail destination' among the 30 emergent markets.

1. The **risk of money laundering** is very important in retail banking. This compels all the banks in the country to consider all the documents with utmost care which they accept in approval of loans to the clients.
2. Rise in **indebtness** is a major concern. There is high degree of uncertainty in consumer credit market.
3. **Outsourcing** has become very important in recent past. Various core activities such as hardware and software maintenance, entire ATM set up and operation (including cash, refilling) etc. are being outsourced by Indian banks. Outsourcing must be done to competent firms only.
4. Another major challenge would be devising appropriate **price mechanism**. Each bank is into a price war and facing competition. This issue is expected to gain importance in future.
5. **Retention of customers** is a major challenge. Banks are expected to take utmost care to retain the ongoing trust of the public by maintaining the secrecy of their personal database. A research by Rich held and Sesser has proved that 5 % rise in customers retention can lead to 35 % rise in profitability in banking business.
6. Customer service should be the end - all in retail banking. Someone has rightly said, "It takes months to find as good customer but only seconds to lose one."Thus, strategy of Knowing Your Customer **(KYC)** is important. KYC issues and money laundering could also be posed as a serious challenge in Retail banking. The venturing of new business can result in the waving of KYC procedures leading to competition for chants. Essential consideration should be taken by the bank, regarding the identification and completion of the documents. Various guidelines have been issued by Reserve Bank in November 2004, on the application of KYC norms.
7. The dependency on **technology** has brought additional responsibilities and challenges in managing, maintaining and optimizing the performance of retail banking networks.

THREATS

1. **Large Default in Loans Repayment:** The increasing competition has made the banks to disburse large number of customer loans, auto loans, home loans, loans on credit cards, educational loans etc. on easy terms without much inquiry. Due to this the no. of case of default in loan repayment has increased. This in turn has increased the bank's bad debts and Non-Performing Assets (NPA).
2. **Customer inconvenience and Privacy Issues:** One of the major problems from customer's point of view is that the customer service representatives of the banks ring up their customers at any time at their places of work, informing them about new products & services. This may cause inconvenience to busy customers. Banks are also responsible for sharing the personal information of the customers with outside agencies like market research groups & other advertisers.
3. **Information Technology:** With the continuous up gradation in technology, number of frauds and scams have increased under the domain of cyber crimes. The unscrupulous

elements have always attacked banks. In many cases these elements have stolen credit card number password & other confidential information relating to customer.

STRATEGIES FOR FUTURE GROWTH OF THE INDIAN RETAIL BANKING

1. **Financial Engineering and Constant Product Innovation:** The time has come when the customer demands a product that is not currently available in the Bankers kitty and the Bank has to literally create customer-specific products. Banker is expected to assume the role of a Financial Engineer. The customer database available with the banks is the best source of their demographic and financial information and can be used by the banks for targeting certain customer segments for new or modified product. The banks should come out with new products in the area of securities, mutual funds and insurance.

2. **Quality Service:** As most of the banks are offering retail products of similar nature, the customers can easily switchover to the one which offers better service at comparatively lower costs, the quality of service that banks offer and the experience that clients have matter the most. Hence, to retain the customers, banks have to come out with competitive products satisfying the desires of the customers.

3. **Introduction of New Channels of Distribution:** Retail customers like to interface with their bank through multiple channels. Therefore, banks should try to give high quality service across all service channels like branches, Internet, ATMs, etc. Banks should leverage effectively on multiple delivery channels (internet, ATMs etc) to reduce the cost of operations. Banks should ensure innovative products to suit the needs and requirements of different types of customers. With the effective usage of the cell phone technology, coupled with web developments, service providers can innovate and offer rich, user-friendly mobile banking applications.

4. **Exploiting Unbanked Areas of Economy:** To enlist the "unbanked" segment of the society by the service providers is a method to expand the retail market. It is this underserved segment should become the focus for the banks This will compensate for the thin margins. The Indian retail banking market still remains largely untapped giving a scope for growth to the banks and financial institutions. With changing psyche of Indian consumers, who are now comfortable with the idea of availing loans for their personal needs, banks have tremendous potential lying in this segment. Marketing departments of the banks be geared up and special training be imparted to them so that banks are successful in grabbing more and more of retail business in the market. Rural or Agricultural credit segment needs to be explored.

5. **Outsourcing:** Outsourcing of requirements would not only save cost and time but would help the banks in concentrating on the core business area. Banks can devote more time for marketing, customer service and brand building. For example, Management of ATMs can be outsourced.

   Infrastructure outsourcing will help in lowering the cost of service channels combined with quality and quickness in delivery.

6. **Efficient and Skilled Management:** For the efficient management of a large and diverse retail portfolio, the most important pre-requisite is the skilled and well–versed employees.

Only experienced man power can withstand the rigour of administering a diverse and complex retail credit portfolio.

7. **Detailed Market Research/Improved Marketing Strategies:** A full fledged marketing department/division would help in evolving a brand strategy, address the issue of alienation from the upwardly mobile, high net worth customer group and improve the recall value of the institution and its products by arresting the trend of getting receded from public memory. Banks may go for detailed market research, which will help them in knowing what their competitors are offering to their clients. This will enable them to have an edge over their competitors and increase their share in retail banking pie by offering better products and services.

8. **Collaborative Arrangements:** Public sector banks can reap the benefit of reaching customers across the country by entering into strategic alliance with other such banks with intensive presence in other regions.

9. The demographic and financial information provided through the customer database can prove highly advantageous to the banks for creating awareness about the innovative products amongst certain customer segments. The new modified and varied products, in the zone of mutual funds, insurance and securities should be introduced by the banks.

10. The eagerly untapped Indian retail banking market has widened the extent of advancements in the banks and financial institutions. Banks have immense scope in this area where the present day customers are now changing their perspectives and switching to the idea of availing loans according to their personal needs .In order to improvise the retail business in the market, banks have introduced marketing departments and special training is also imparted to gratify the needs of the customers.

11. Banks have an extensive network of branches that gives them an edge and provides an opportunity to sell third-party products through these branches.

12. It has turned out to be one of the major cost-effecting and time saving strategy which enables the banks to focus on widened business opportunities. Thus more time can be devoted towards brand building, customer service and marketing, for example, management of ATMs can be outsourced which would save the banks from dealing with complexities of technology.

CONCLUSION

Retail banking requires consistent advancements and modifications. Today entire perspective needs to be changed in banking and financing leading to constant upgrading and revalidation of the banks internal systems, banking are corresponding to retail banking for their growth. This requires product development differentiations, home electronic, mobile banking, cost reduction, cross-selling, innovation etc. Retail banking process has outstanding prospects for growth but its challenges are also appalling. The more the banks would increase their capacity building to meet the challenges, the more will be the growth of banking industry. Advanced technology and customers interest area, the banking sector will continue progressing in coming future also. The analysis lead to the conclusion that banking structure of India is full of potential for growth. Indian banking industry have registered considerable development with significant impact on growth of GDP, a spectacular rise in National income, increase in per capita income and expansion of financial sector of India. For future prospects retail banking has emerged as the showcase of innovation and development, through its various products like personal loan, home loans, educational loans, deposits, credit cards and depository services. Hence there is need of constant innovation of Retail banking. With much scope in the avenues for operations, the true challenge for the banks in the current scenario is to stand out in the midst of hard-hitting regulations of the apex body. Thus the participants, be it a Indian financial player or a foreign entrant in the retail sector have to adopt a different approach in everything viz., products, or services to hold the Indian market share.

REFERENCES

1. Kem, H.J. (2005), "Global Retail Banking" changing paradigms, chartered financial analyst, Icfai Press, Hyderabad, vol. XI no. 10, pp. 56-58.
2. Saurabh Goyal "Retail Banking: An Essence of Present Banking System" Journal of Banking & Finance, Kolkata, Vol – XII, No. 1, Nov, 2007.
3. Manoj kumar Joshi (2007) "Growth Retail Banking in India", ICFAI university press, Hyderabad, pp13-24.
4. Birendra Kumar (2009), "Performance of Retail Banking in India", Asochem Financial Pulse (AFP). India.
5. Avasthi, G.P. and Sharma, M. (2000-01). 'Information Technology in Banking: Challenges for Regulators'. Prajanan. XXIX (4). 17. Website- www.rbi.org.in
7. Bhalla. V.K. (2006) "Management of Financial Services" Discovery Publications, New Delhi.
8. Online International Interdisciplinary Research Journal, {Bi-Monthly}, ISSN 2249- 9598, Volume-V, Issue-II, Mar-Apr 2015 Issue.
9. Hemant. S. Ahuluwalia (2008) "Banking and Financial Services" Adhyayan Publishers, New Delhi.
10. Hajela T.N. (2009) "Banking Reforms" Anne Books Pvt. Ltd., New Delhi
11. Jaiswal, K.S. & Nettu Singh "Retail Banking: Indian Scenario", Indian Journal of Marketing, New Delhi, Vol. XXXVII No.10, Jan, 2008.
12. Reddy, Y. V. 2005. "Banking Sector Reforms in India: An Overview." RBI Bulletin June.

Biometric Innovations in Indian Banking Sector

Nazia Sultana[1] and V. Santhoshi[2]
[1]Assistant Professor and Head, Osmania University College for Women.
[2]Research Scholar, Department of Commerce, Osmania University.

ABSTRACT

Innovation is not new to the banking sector, the banking sector reforms with automation and introduction of ATM and Net banking has proved to be a challenge in the past for both the employees and the customers of the banks. Development of biometric technology has made the use of self-service channels like ATMs viable with respect to the illiterate population. This paper concentrates on how India is preparing itself for this biometric innovation in banking sector and what kind of resistance is faced by the implementers. It also documents the various marketing implications of biometric innovations in banking. The paper also brings forth the initiatives taken up by the government for biometric innovations and compares India with countries that have already implemented biometrics in banking. Most national governments are incorporating biometrics into citizen identity documents or are planning to do so. According to the Acuity Market Intelligence Report (2013), it is said that by 2015, smart card-based citizen IDs — such as passports and national IDs — issued with biometrics will outnumber those without biometrics.

Keywords: *Innovation, Biometrics, Resistance, Marketing, Internet, Technology.*

INTRODUCTION

Banks across the world are already using biometrics in their banking architecture to authenticate employees and customers. Biometrics and other identifiers stored on the documents will elevate the security of a wide range of transaction types. As more citizen credentials and banking processes become biometrics-based, corresponding infrastructures in retail, healthcare, transit and other markets will certainly evolve. Among all banks utilizing biometrics, 52 percent are located in Asia. Japan has more than an estimated 15 million customers using biometric authentication for banking transactions. Banks in Mexico, South America, Africa, and the Middle East are also moving towards the use of biometric identification technology because of its popularity with consumers, and ability to offer more security than traditional personal identification numbers (PINs) and passwords. According to a white paper by Crossmatch, USA (2014), banks in Japan have widely deployed biometrics-enabled ATMs that allow customers to withdraw currency or conduct other transactions after a successful fingerprint scan. There are currently more than 80,000 biometrics-enabled ATMs in Japan and more than 15 M customers using them. Biometric technology is slowly replacing traditional passwords and token-based electronic access, signature-based branch service access, and PIN-based access in mobile banking and at ATMs. Biometrics can be used in branch banking, ATM transactions, internet banking, mobile banking and a single sign on solution for more effective password management. A biometric SSO system will mitigate other security risks and regulatory fines for government compliance. The Indian banking system consists of 26 public sector banks, 20 private sector banks, 43 foreign banks, 56 regional rural banks, 1,589 urban cooperative banks and 93,550 rural cooperative banks, in addition to cooperative credit institutions. Public-sector banks control nearly 80 percent of the market, thereby leaving comparatively much smaller shares for its private peers.

REVIEW OF LITERATURE

There is a limited study done on biometrics in banking and its aid in furthering digital banking. The following section reveals a review of literature on the above mentioned topic.

- Amtul Fatima (2011) opined that the providers of Internet banking services must be more responsive towards security requirements. Biometric based authentication and identification systems are the new solutions to address the issues of security and privacy. In this study, the security threats in Internet banking, its solutions in biometrics and its acceptance in the consumer market are studied using descriptive and exploratory research. The methods of descriptive research are used to obtain information concerning the study.
- Garima Yadav (2013) describe the introduction and adoption of remote banking, after hour services through automatic teller machines (ATMs), phone banking, online services and electronic commerce has changed the nature of financial services, giving people the convenience and the flexibility to do so much more with their time and resources. With remote banking, the channels of transaction move outside the walls of the bank, requiring adequate protection for both bank and customer.
- Moses Okechukwu (2012) described that the growth in electronic transactions has resulted in a greater demand for fast and accurate user identification and authentication. Access codes for buildings, banks accounts and computer systems often use personal identification numbers (PIN's) for identification and security clearances. An embedded fingerprint biometric authentication scheme for automated teller machine (ATM) banking systems has been proposed in this paper. In this scheme, a fingerprint biometric technique is fused with the ATM for person authentication to ameliorate the security level.
- Rana Tassabehji (2012) comments that rising cyber-crimes have heightened existing concerns about e-banking security. However currently the use of biometric technology in the banking sector is not prevalent. The authors developed a biometric system for authenticating e-banking and applied the established System Usability Scale (SUS) to evaluate its effectiveness from the perspective of potential users. The case demonstrated that on the whole users are very favourable towards a biometric banking system and ostensibly found the system developed usable. It was found that when evaluating the biometric system, its different components needed to be considered – namely the biometric technology and the institutional process that supports verification and authentication.
- Sri Shimal Das, Smt. Jhunu Debbarma (2011) in their paper describe Biometrics based authentication as a potential candidate to replace password-based authentication. Among all the biometrics, fingerprint based identification is one of the most mature and proven technique. At the time of transaction fingerprint image is acquired at the ATM terminal using high resolution fingerprint scanner. Security measures at banks can play a critical, contributory role in preventing attacks on customers. These measures are of paramount importance when considering vulnerabilities and causation in civil litigation. This paper focused on vulnerabilities and the increasing wave of criminal activities occurring at

Automated Teller Machines (ATMs) where quick cash is the prime target for criminals rather than at banks themselves.

OBJECTIVES OF THE STUDY

The broad objective of the study is to have an understanding of how biometrics is used in Indian Banking Sector. This objective is further divided into the following sub-objectives:

- To analyze the growth of paperless (electronic and technology enabled) transactions in banking sector.
- To examine the various biometric innovations and their implementation in Indian Banking Sector.
- To gain an insight into the various marketing implications of biometric innovations in banking.

RESEARCH METHODOLOGY: It is a conceptual paper with a few analytical insights, wherein data is analyzed from secondary data that is collected from the reports of RBI, Earnest and Young Report on Banking on Technology (2014), White Paper of Crossmatch USA (2014), Working Paper of Infosys on Digital Transformation (2014), PWC report on Digital Banking (2015) and other secondary sources.

Biometrics in Banking across the World: According to Boukhonine et al., (2005) the main priority of every bank is to provide a safe and secure environment for their clients to perform online banking transactions. Based on the security policy of each bank the main considerations of framing a security policy are accountable, confidentiality, availability, integrity and non-repudiation are the primary concerns. Therefore the banks implement the access controls based on the concerns mentioned above by making use of physical devices such as the support access cards, and other automated monitoring system which has the ability to accept and deny the usage of any particular object in the system. Technology Adoption Model (TAM) was the basic model being used in most of the research papers related to the acceptance of technology where the core constructs of the study being perceived ease of use (PEU) , Perceive usefulness related to the intention of sue of technology. Biometric ATMs are being filed for a new patent application by Bank of America. This patent application outlines a system for authenticating users with a combination of a pin-code and fingerprint biometrics. Poland's Bank Zachodni WBK is piloting a biometric signature solution using Hitachi's finger vein readers throughout its branch network. Bank Zachodni WBK has been offering the service to customers in Lubin.

Table 1 Usage of biometrics in Banks across Different Countries

Country	Usage (%)
USA	32
Europe	9
Africa	6
Australia	1
Asia	52

(Source: John Trader 2014, Impact of Biometrics in Banking, www.blog2sys.com, adapted from Text Road Publication Report)

Several major banks around the world have recently announced they are deploying various biometric technologies to improve the authorization security of their mobile banking apps. Most banks have utilized mobile devices for biometrics that will help to provide the first level of security. Such type of control is called traditional access control. Voice biometrics is also been used by banks (on a pilot basis) such as ING Direct Canada and ANZ. If voice biometrics gain success, Bank of America will patent for authenticating mobile transactions through voice biometrics and this may soon be seen as replacing OTP/Pins. Wells Fargo is currently working on integrating both facial and voice recognition technology into its mobile banking app to improve security checks. There are many software companies that are closely working with banks for face and voice authentication technologies. Wells Fargo is one such bank that is working with SpeechPro to develop the application and it has invited 100 customers to test the face and voice authentication technology. Using their iPhone's built in camera and microphone; Wells Fargo customers scan their face and voice. Customers can then verify their face and voice by matching it against the unique profile they have previously set up, enabling them to proceed with their banking. Wells Fargo said the entire authentication process takes about 23 seconds to complete. The bank intends to launch the bi-modal authentication service to the general public by next year after it resolves some minor issues and further develops the app to suit newer technologies. Wells Fargo is also looking to install iris recognition capabilities for its mobile

India's Preparation for Biometric Innovation in Banking: Data from RBI, Planning Commission, Ministry of Finance and PWC Report on Indian Banking sector suggests that there were 11.2 billion e-transactions annually, out of which 74% of transactions by debit and credit cards and 6.88 billion (83%) transactions are carried out through ATM. As more and more Indians are using banking services, it becomes imperative for banks to innovate and include biometrics in their architecture. Over a period of three years there has been an almost two-fold increase in the number of adults having access to bank accounts. In the year 2011, there were 296.1 million adults accessing bank accounts while in 2014 the figure has gone up to 425 million adults accessing bank accounts. The following section deals with an understanding of use of technology in banking.

Table 1 Government Initiatives

Digital Connectivity	3G Connectivity	Smartphone Penetration	Rural banking
2014 - 15% access	2012 - 23 million	2012 - 29 million	42300 villages to be provided with universal mobile access by 2018
2034 - 80% access	2016 - 266 million	2016 - 382 million	320 billion INR for establishing rural broadband in 2.5 lakh villages by March 2017.

(Source: www.rbi.gov.in, RBI, Ministry of Finance and PWC analysis)

Indian government has been taking various initiatives to facilitate innovation in Indian banking sector. Some of the initiatives include a) Digital Connectivity b) 3G Connectivity c) Smartphone Penetration d) Universal mobile access and establishment of rural broadband. There has also been a steady increase in the number of electronic transactions that gives an impetus to innovation in banking in India as shown in the following figure.

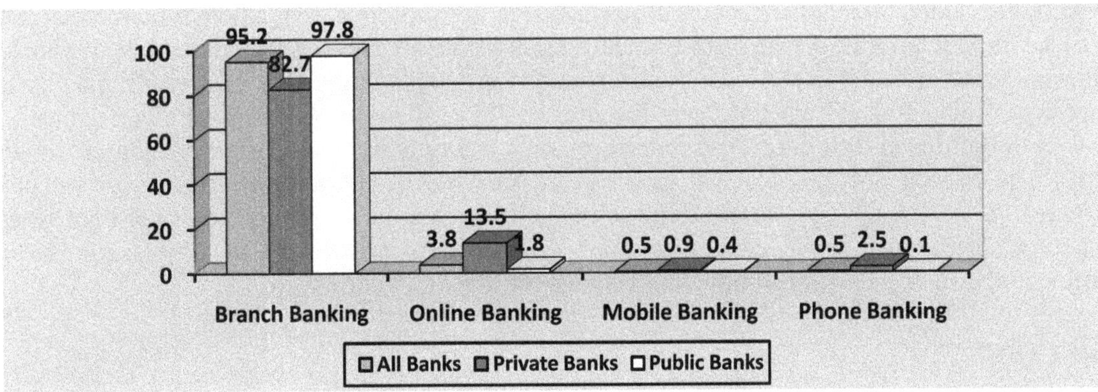

(Source: Earnest & Young and Indian Bankers Association Report Banking on Technology January 2014)

Figure 1 Numbers of Requests Processed

Government of India Initiative for Introduction of Biometrics in Indian Banking: The Indian government has geared up for fingerprint or eye scan enabled ATMs to leverage the biometric-based Aadhaar number, which establishes uniqueness of every individual on the basis of demographic and biometric information. HDFC Bank has already deployed the biometric technology across 60 two-wheeler dealerships and 200 car dealerships, and is planning to expand the service to 400-500 two-wheeler dealerships and 300-400 car dealerships over the course of the current financial year. Unique Customer Identification (UCI) across banking system can be of paramount importance. It is observed that, while some of the Indian banks have established a unique customer identification process, there is no unique identification across the banking system based on a shared database. This could enable borrowers to circumvent the risk profiling guidelines and obtain multiple facilities across banks. UCI could eventually graduate to a Legal Entity Identifier (LEI). LEIs are a unique ID associated with a single corporate entity which assists in easy identification of the entity across multiple financial market utilities and aids in tracking settlement activity and exposures. A large private bank has been asked to carry out a pilot project for biometric authentication while making payments through PoS (point of sales) terminals with merchant establishments. Today, they are faced with an equally formidable phenomenon: a nationalistic fervor wrapped around a 'Make in India' credo that backs local technology (like the biometric authentication) and no profit local payments entity (like the National Payments Corporation of India). While officials from the Indian Banks' Association insist that banks are "on the same page" with the government on Aadhaar, senior bankers, speaking on condition of anonymity, convey a different message. This would mean dual technology and dual cost - linking with the Aadhaar server for KYC as well as bank server for the fund source. It would mean reconfiguring the software and equipping all banks, branches, ATM and PoS terminals with biometric readers.

CONCLUSION

This paper has focused on how biometrics helps to lead a technology enabled banking sector. It can be concluded that Indian banking sector has seen the appropriate initiation of biometrics and is awaiting the arrival of many government initiatives given the increase in number of people having access to banking services, use of internet and mobile applications for availing banking services. Many Indian banks are entering into strategic alliances with software companies to adopt biometrics in their banking architecture. India basically has biometric introduction limited to access control operations of network and treasury and ATM transactions and epayments. There is a large scope for biometric innovations to be introduced in other banking operations such as branch banking, internet banking, Mobile banking, document processing, fraud detection, loan origination and other banking operations.

REFERENCES

1. Amtul Fatima (2011). E-Banking Security Issues – Is There A Solution in Biometrics? *Journal of Internet Banking and Commerce, August 2011, vol. 16, no.2.*
2. Garima Yadav (2013). Application of Biometrics in Secure Bank Transactions. *International Journal of Information Technology and Knowledge Management IJITKM,* Volume 7 Number 1 pp. 124-127.
3. Moses Okechukwu Onyesolu (2012). ATM Security Using Fingerprint Biometric Identifier: An Investigative Study. *International Journal of Advanced Computer Science and Applications*, Vol. 3, No.4, 68.
4. Rana Tassabehji (2012). Evaluating biometrics for online banking: The case for usability. *International journal of Information Management*-32.
5. Sri Shimal Das, Smt. Jhunu Debbarma (2011). Designing a Biometric Strategy (Fingerprint) Measure for Enhancing ATM Security in Indian E-Banking System.. *International Journal of Information and Communication Technology Research,* Volume 1 No. 5.
6. Acuity Market Intelligence, 2013 Report.
7. White Paper "Biometrics in Banking" January 2014, CrossMatch, USA. White Paper "Revival of Biometrics in Banking: Heralding a New Era in mpayments- Biplav Panda, TCS Financial Solutions, retrieved from www.tcs.com/resources/whitepapers/pages/biometrics-in-banking.aspx
8. John Trader, "Impact of Biometrics in Banking" July 2014, retrieved from www.blog2sys.com/financial-services/impact-biometrics-banking
9. Justin Lee, "Banks around the world deploy biometric authentication technologies", June 2015, retrieved from www.biometricupdate.com/201506
10. "Logging into digital banking- Creating access, transforming lives", April 2015, retrieved from www.pwc.in/assets/pdfs/publications, , ASSOCHAM, India.

Mobile Banking
A Study on Growth of Mobile Banking

M. Radhakrishna
Asst Professor, Bharat Institute of Engineering & Technology (BIET).

ABSTRACT

Mobile banking is an advanced technological feature offered to customers to execute banking transactions more accurately and effectively. This service effectively used by the customers who are using Smart phones. Today most of the customers are looking the alternatives for executing the transactions from their office or house. This application mostly attracted by the educated people.

The present paper studies the services provided by the bank to customers through mobile banking. This paper also focuses on what are the measurements need to be taken by the customers and banks while executing the services by using mobile banking applications.

This present study also notified the pros and cons of the mobile banking services.

Keywords: *Mobile banking, Technology, customers, transactions and services.*

INTRODUCTION

Mobile banking is a facility in banking system that allows the customers of a bank or financial institution to execute the financial transactions through a mobile device such as a mobile phone or tablet.

Mobile banking refers the service provided for customers by the banks and financial services with the help of telecommunication devices. Mobile banking has given the traditional banking a newer look Any where Banking. With this banking facility customers don't need Personal computer or Laptop to execute the banking operations just they need a cell phone to avail banking services.

The advantage of Mobile banking is that it helps to cut down the costs and it is more economical than tale-banking. Mobile banking services will become more popular once the availability of the smart phones with larger screens and bigger memory size.

Online banking has given more freedom to customers to deal with their accounts without requiring them to actually step into a branch of bank which they have account. The goal of Mobile banking is to expand the freedom to customers even more by making customer is not even required to have personal computer or laptop. Mobile banking application allows the user to view account balances, make transfers and pay bills. Mobile banking comes into the picture to address the basic limitation of Internet banking. If we only consider Asian development countries, the availability of mobile connectivity is really huge. When one may not find out a landline telephone or an internet connection, but still in those remote places getting mobile connectivity is not a major issue today.

Mobile banking is sometimes referred to as M-banking. It makes it possible for you to access your financial accounts and conduct transactions wirelessly, using you mobile device. It's no longer impossible to deposit a check while sitting on a beach or to pay the electric bill while sightseeing halfway around the world.

HISTORY OF MOBILE BANKING

In Present days the Internet is commonly available distribution channel, the services of Internet made available to rural areas. In last two decades the users of Internet is drastically increased. Before the entry of Internet if any customer need any banking service it is mandatory to visit any of branches of the bank. With the help of internet services the burden on customer is reduced to some extent, when cell phones turned into smart phones, and began to mimic the power found in most computers, banks have been able to provide customers with powerful mobile banking apps that allow completing you banking from whereever you are. This includes making deposits depending on the bank and its mobile applications checking funds, making bill payments, transferring or spending money. Mobile banking differs from the payment futures available on many of today's smart phones, as it provides a sign on link to your individual checking or savings accounts by an app you download from your banks website.

Once smart phones took over from cell phones, and the size and capabilities of mobile devices increased, so did the effectiveness of mobile banking. Banks introduced mobile banking apps that accommodated more types of cell phones, but smart phone users and advanced apps gave mobile banking the boost that made it a safe and viable choice. Consumers preferred the easier navigation and improved images and graphics offered by these updated, technologically advanced apps.

Banks faced mobile banking challenges in the early part of the decade until the first smart phones hit the market in 2007. Consumers found it difficult to view their financial information on the small cell phone screens that were common at the turn of the 21st century. By 2008, even smaller banks began to offer mobile banking services and apps. By then, larger banks and their customers were using these services regularly.

Banks, the consumer community and mobile network operators are the major stakeholders in mobile banking. The integration of telecommunications and information technology enable services must address the needs of the end users and bank customers.

LITERATURE REVIEW

Internet banking and mobile banking are both electronic banking systems. The only difference is, the customers using Internet banking are using computers that are connected to Internet, while customers using mobile banking are using wireless devices to do transactions.

There are a number of studies exploring the mobile banking revolution either by providing case studies or by discussing broader application for financial systems.

Rotchanakitumnuai & Speece (2003) in their report stated that, corporate customers do not accept electronic form of banking, which can assist banks to implement this self-service technology more efficiently. Further they suggested that security of the channels is a major factor inhibiting wider adoption. Those already using electronic form of banking seem to have more confidence that the system is reliable, whereas non-users are much more service conscious, and do not trust financial transaction made via e- channels. Garrett (2011) referred that mobile banking is the future but that security is a concern for wireless.

Vaithilingam, Nair & Guru (2013) investigated the adoption of mobile services in Malaysia and found trust and security have a significant impact on the adoption of mobile banking. As is the case with online banking, consumers are asking these questions, "Whether the bank will store the user id and passwords in the database?" "Will the mobile banking encrypt the transaction?" To minimize the customers concern about mobile security, one banking strategy is to provide more description about the mobile security such as encryptions and authentication methods.

Steadman (2011) advocates that technology is the enabling factor that allowed mobile banking to emerge. "Always –on" connectivity demand by customers coupled with the fact the internet has evolved from fixed wired through wireless to mobile connection, meant that financial institutions had to pursue alternative channels to provide their services in order to meet customers' expectations.

Jonathan Morduch (2009) summed up the excitement around mobile banking in this way. "Fast, convenient and easy, the holy trinity of marketing adjectives. Any product or service that can legitimately claim to be all three should sell itself.

Mankiw (2000) referred it is also advisable to be mindful that monetary policy and its transmission mechanisms are subject to the influence of external factors such as, currency exchange rate consideration and existing liquidity rules.

OJBECTIVES OF STUDY

- To Study the growth of the Mobile banking
- To know the Impact of the Mobile banking on customer services
- To analyse the problems in using Mobile banking
- To suggest Necessary measurements to Mobile banking customers

ANALYSIS ON MOBILE BANKING USERS

Table 1 Analysis on Age group of Mobile banking users

Age/year	2011	2012	2013	2014
18-29	45	48	50	51
30-44	38	40	41	43
45-59	12	9	5	4
60 and above	5	3	4	2

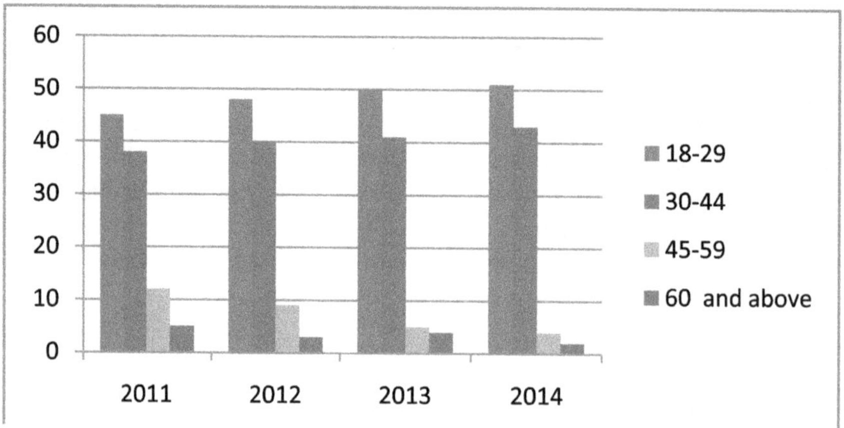

Figure 1 Analysis on Age group of Mobile banking users

From the above table it is clearly depicting that the age group of between 18 -29 are using mobile banking services compare with other age group customers, the reason is these young people technically more advance to compare to other age group mobile banking users. It is also found that the working professionals who is age group is between 30-44 is also using these mobile banking services efficiently.

Table 2 Geographical Analysis on Mobile banking users

Places/year	2011	2012	2013	2014
Metro	75	72	73	70
Non - Metro	22	15	17	18
Not - Remote	2	11	8	9
Not remote	1	2	2	3

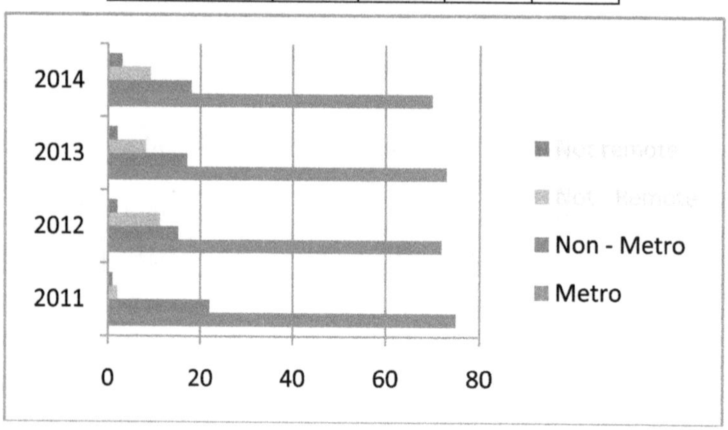

Figure 2 Geographical Analysis on Mobile banking users

From the above analysis we can interpret that the Mobile banking users are Metros are higher than Non-metro, Remote and other areas. It is clearly indicated that the working professionals in metros are familiar with the mobile banking services. It is also indicating the mobile banking users are increasing in Non metros from the year 2011 to 2014.

CONCULISION

Mobile banking users are increasing since last five years, the rapid growth of the smart phones created significant impact on growth of the mobile banking. The present research study found the conclusion that these services are effectively utilizing the professionally qualified persons who are living in metros and other urban areas. In rural and semi urban people are concern about security while executing the financial transactions. These users are not familiar with the mobile banking applications. The research report suggests the banks or financial services who are offering mobile banking services need to conduct some awareness programmes to promote mobile banking services.

Electronic Banking in India-Opportunities and Challenges

Sunindita Pan
Lecturer in Economics, Loyola Academy Degree & P.G.College.

ABSTRACT

A sound and effective banking system is the backbone of an economy. The present and future of any economy depends upon the success and development of banking. The economy can function smoothly if banking system is capable of meeting new challenges posed by the technology. The earlier brick and mortar branch is no longer sufficient. Today Indian banking industry is in the midst of an Information technology revolution. The technology holds the key to the future success of Indian Banks. The technology is now taking banks to the homes or offices, 24 hours a day, 365 days a year through ATMs, mobile banking and PC banking. The existence of electronic banking has become inevitable due to the standards required to be matched at the international level. There is no denying the fact that information technology has been the most rapidly changing industry in India. Information revolution led to the evolution of internet, which lead to e-commerce continued by evolution of e-banking. With the development of e-business, e-banking became essential. All types of e-transaction require the services of e-banking. The aim of this paper is to analyse the meaning of electronic banking and to present all the alternative banking products and services. This paper also analyses the various barriers in the process of e-banking in India.

Keywords: *economy, technology, electronic-banking, ATMs.*

INTRODUCTION

Information technology has become an important tool in today's organizations. Today banks operate in a highly globalised and in competitive environment. Banks have traditionally been in the forefront of harnessing technology to improve their products, services and efficiency. In India, e-banking is in a nascent stage. Finland is the first country in the world to take a lead in e-banking. In India ICICI bank which initiated e-banking early in 1997 under the brand name Infinity. E-banking refers to electronic banking. It is also called as virtual banking or online banking. The traditional model for banking has been through branch banking. Only in the early 1990s there has been start of non-branch banking services. Development has been taking place in many areas of Information technology. These changes have affected the functioning of banks and financial institutions. Quotation of Bill Gates, the world leader in expanding IT and related possibilities for not only business but also education, research and services, "We need banking, do we really need banks"? Is worth mentioning here.

E-banking is fast becoming a norm in the developed world and is being implemented by many banks in developing economies. E-banking came into being mainly due to development in information and communication technologies besides globalization, increasingly demanding customers and de-regulation of the industry. It is helping to re-define the role of branch banking and moving branches away from transactional banking to become customer service centres. E-banking is defined as the delivery of new as well as traditional banking products and services to customers through electronic, interactive communication channels. It includes the system that enables financial institution customers, individuals or businesses to access accounts, transact business or obtain information on financial products and services through a public or private network.

In general, e-banking uses the technology that allows customers to enjoy banking and financial services electronically. In today's context e-banking implies on-line banking or net-banking because a large share of banking activities is conducted using internet technology. E-banking means electronic banking where all the banking services are offered through different electronic media such as telephone network, TV technology, computers, ATM, internet technology etc,. Banking is trading in money and credit. For this purpose banks accept deposits and lend loans as their primary functions. To support primary functions, banks developed several associated services called agency services and general utility services. E-banking is offering all these services through electronic media, especially through internet.

OBJECTIVES OF THE STUDY

- To understand the experience in offering banking transactions and services through electronic delivery channels and functions of e-banking in India.
- To study the e-banking challenges and opportunities in India.

RESEARCH METHODOLOGY

The study is based on secondary data and is analytical in nature. The sources of data are report on trends and progress of Indian banking published by reserve Bank of India.

SALIENT FEATURES OF ELECTRONIC BANKING

Today banking is known as innovative banking, information technology has given rise to innovations in the product designing and their delivery in the banking and finance industry. The main goal is better customer services, customer satisfaction and customer retention. Presently, banking sector has come up with lot of initiatives in providing a better customer services with help of new technologies. In present scenario, banks all over the world are making their business strategies in view of new opportunities offered by e-banking. It has encouraged real banking behavior closer to the neoclassical economies theories of market functioning.

- Introduction of Magnetic Ink character recognition (MICR)
- Electronic Funds transfer system
- Cheques truncation technology
- Personal computer power
- 24 hours banking service, 7 days a week
- The interactive voice response system
- Shopping products like credit, sales, direct debits, computerized retail sales
- Development of plastic card
- Funds transfer

Important e-banking products and services

Today's banks are offering various delivery channels to provide products and services to their customers. The IT has helped banks in increasing the range of their products and services and also in marketing them more effectively. E-banking is nothing but online banking. It is a congregation of different components which are associated services to the primary banking services. The major channels are:

- Automated Teller Machines (ATM): These are the cash dispensing machines which are frequently seen at banks and other locations such as shopping centre's or building societies. The aim is to allow customer to draw cash at any time and to provide banking services. To obtain money from the machine customer need special ATM card and notified personal identification number. The card is issued free of charge. The card must be inserted into the machine and personal number typed in. With such systems security is a permanent concern. The first ATM was installed in India by HSBC in 1987.
- Smart Cards: a smart card usually contain a kind of computer chip. The microprocessor is under a contact pad on one side of the card. The host computer and card reader talk to the microprocessor. The microprocessor enforces access to the data on the card. The chips in these cards are capable of many kinds of transactions. It uses sophisticated encryption to protect value as it passes from one card to another.
- Electronic Funds Transfer System (EFT): It is another e-banking product that facilitates transfer of funds from any branch of a bank to any other branch of any bank in the shortest time. The participants of the scheme are individual customer through their banks/branches, service branches of the banks and RBI. There is no intermediation of paper based system. It is a system of processing and communication of payment through electronic methods. It assumes greater significance in Indian banking system as RBI also encourages the commercial banks to adopt this. Inter and intra-bank transfers of funds are made through this mechanism.
- Electronic clearing services:
  1. Electronic credit clearing services: It is simple, reliable and cost effective solution for bulk and repetitive transactions like salary, pension, dividend through banks. Under this system, organizations that have to make bulk payment to large number of beneficiaries prepare the credit instructions on the magnetic media and submit the same to RBI through their bankers. The bank gets the instruction on a magnetic media and according to the agreement, payments are made automatically. RBI coordinates and processes the programme. The clearing house settles the accounts.
  2. Electronic debit clearing services: It covers the payment to utility organizations like telephone and electricity bills etc. It was introduced in India in March 1996. This service deals with the payments by a large group of people to a single institution. Under this facility, the receiving organization enters into an agreement with e-bank and clearing house settles the accounts.
- Mobile banking: It works on the text Messaging facility also called the SMS that is available on mobile phones. This allows one to send a short text message form mobile phone and sent it out to a particular number. Mobile banking alert facility informs one promptly of all the transactions in his accounts. It keeps him updated wherever he goes.

- Internet banking: India can be said to be on the threshold of a major banking revolution with net banking having been already unveiled. It is a medium of delivery of banking services and a tool for business development. It is largely used as marketing tool. It is generally used for information on deposit products and downloading application form. It can be used to receive loans at local branch by filling up applications on internet. It provides detail about account holding and transactions. It handle receipt and payment of bills online
- Telebanking: By dialing the given telebanking number through mobile or landline from anywhere, the customer can access his account and by following the user-friendly menu, entire banking can be done through Interactive voice Response (IVR) system. The system provides balance inquiry and transaction inquiry, statement of account by e-mail, cheque book request, utility bill payment and voice out of last five transactions. It is fast becoming one of the most popular products. The usage of tele-banking is limited and cannot be extended for cash transactions.
- Electronic Data Interchange: It refers to the electronic exchange of structure information using telecommunication like payment order, debit, credits, and statement of accounts. As part of EDI, satellite communication network has also entered the banks. Using computer network banks can transfer financial information. By using this facility, banks can reduce the cost of transferring data and information.

Benefits of e-banking

E-banking services whether delivered online or through other mechanism, have spread quickly in recent years. Many inventions and revolutions have taken place in the history of banking but no such things have changed the business of banking as fast as the e-banking revolution. E-banking has facilitated banks to scare borders, change strategic behavior and bring out new possibilities.

1. **Benefits to the Customer**: Customers are the ultimate targets for all banking innovations. Bank automation, computerization and online banking are introduced for the convenience of customers. Bank customers are broadly divided into two categories general public and merchants or traders.
   - It provides anywhere banking and anytime banking to the customers.
   - It facilitates cash withdrawal from any branch/ATM.
   - It brings down costs of banking to the customer over a period of time.
   - It is very convenient and easy to operate without much effort or waste of time.
   - E-banking expands the domain of access to banking services like payment of utility bill, manage all accounts in one place, apply for loan or credit card, order traveler's cheeques, increase overdraft, order a cheque book, track payment history, integrate the data with personal finance programs, change contact details, get alerts, railway pass.
   - It makes possible to manage several transactions within a limited time and thus reduces operating costs.
   - Customers enjoy high standard quality services.

- It provides complete information about various doubts of customers. Customers get quick response.

2. **Benefits to the Bank**
   - Reduces customer visits to the branch and thereby intervention of customer.
   - Inter-branch reconciliation is immediate thereby reducing chances of fraud and misappropriation.
   - Innovative, secure, competitive.
   - By connecting all the branches through Wide Area Network, anywhere banking facility can be provided.
   - Scope and potential for better profitability.
   - Helps in establishing better customer relationship and retaining and attracting customers.
   - Banks are able to use the time more productively and are able to introduce more innovative services to the customers.
   - Bank employees are free from tension of heavy rush during peak hours
   - It facilitates to create and develop large variety of value added services.
   - Due to unlimited business, less transaction costs, revenue of banks improved significantly.
   - Banks can now offer international banking services.
3. **To Traders and Merchants**
   - Less need for traders to provide credit facility to their customers.
   - Increase in business due to increased purchasing power of the credit card holders and ease with purchasing.
   - Globalizing the trade with market expansion of traders.
   - Avoid risk involved in handling cash.
   - Provides internationally standardized services at low transaction cost.
   - It facilitates immediate settlement of payments.
   - It is easy for the traders to verify the status of customers.
4. **To Economy or Government**
   - Globalizing trade through e-commerce.
   - Providing national products and services a global market.
   - Promote exports and increased inflow of foreign exchange.
   - Eliminate risk of carrying heavy cash.
   - Transparency in transactions.

Challenges

1. **Infrastructural Barrier:**

- Weak telecommunication like satellite networks and communication bandwidth
- Hardware available is not sufficient in the country
- Flaws in design and implementation of bank's system.

2. **Knowledge Barrier:**
   - Limited trained human resources
   - Improper use of technology
   - Lack of technical knowledge
   - Flaws in design, implementation and monitoring of bank's information system
3. **Legal and Security Issues:**
   - Limitation of law and regulation
   - Potential of fraud
   - Denial of e-documents in courts
   - Weak security measures.
4. **Economic Barrier:**
   - Heavy investment for new infrastructure
   - High cost of internet penetration
   - Low ability to achieve communication equipment by people in India.
5. **Social Cultural Barrier:**
   - Less awareness and familiarity regarding new technology
   - Illiteracy
   - Charging fees
   - Perception of e-banking is a threat to the bank's employees
   - Some clients tend to bank to communicate with the bank's staff
   - Barrier of English language.
6. **Management Barrier:**
   - Managerial risks for bank management
   - Resistance of employees for new technologies
   - Lack of adequate coordination, interaction and cooperation between banks and other decision makers
   - Lack of strategic management
   - Change of managers.

Opportunities through e-Banking

- Untapped rural markets: Majority of India's population lives in rural areas and is largely untapped market for banking sector. In all urban areas banking services entered but only few big villages' only banks have entered. There is a vast untapped rural market for e-banking. Through e-banking banks can enter new markets.

- Multiple channels: Banks offer various channels to access their banking products and services such as ATM, telephone/mobile banking, video banking etc. to increase the banking business. E-banking provides scope for new businesses.
- Better customer service: Every engagement with customer is an opportunity to develop customer's trust on the banks. Due to increased competition, customer services have become the base for judging the performance of banks. Better customer services are the best mode to grow banking business. E-banking provides opportunity to deliver high level of customer services and improve efficiency.
- Online finance: There will be increasing convergence in product offerings, banking services, share trading, insurance, loans based on the data warehousing and data mining technologies. Anytime anywhere banking will become common. E-banking provides opportunities to develop new ways of working.
- Retail lending: It has become a focus area in respect of financing of consumer durables, housing, automobiles etc. It has helped in risk diversification and in enhancing the earnings of banks with better recovery rates.

CONCLUSION

The challenge for the financial institutions is to find satisfactory answers to business issues and satisfy banks and customers. Banks must adapt to the electronics age. Consumers demand it. Economics drives it. Banks must provide it. It is suggested that banks must provide the best mix of online and offline conveniences at competitive rates and deliver it at an affordable price. This will help banks to improve their service and gain competitive advantage by retaining and attracting their customers. In e-banking, the core security areas must be paid utmost attention– confidentiality, integrity and availability. Banks are required to restructure, reinvent and reengineer themselves to meet the necessary criteria, offer better products and acquire the competitive edge. The shift in the banks from traditional to modern e-banking services has been welcomed due to its advantages but Indian banks are taking time to get rooted. If e-banking is handles in the right manner by banks and customers, then it would take the economy to great heights.

REFERENCES

1. Dr. Miryala, Ramesh Kumar and Reddy, M.Venkat Ramana (2015) - trends, challenges and Innovations in Management.
2. Pradhan, Rudra Prakash (2009) - "Forecasting Financial Markets in India", p 76-85.
3. Tripathy, Nalini Prava (2007) "Financial services", pg 201.
4. Sharma, K.C. (2007) - "Modern Banking in India", page 239.

Role of RRB in Socio Economic Development: A Case Study of Prathama Bank

Ila Chaturvedi
Amity University, Noida.

ABSTRACT

Regional Rural Banks in India are an integral part of the rural credit structure of the country. Since the very beginning, when the RRBs were established on October 2, 1975, these banks played a pivotal role in the economic development of the rural India. The Prathama Bank has developed its own model of micro finance i.e. ***Prathama Model****. It has been widely appreciated and acknowledged by NABARD, GOI and other international forums. The Bank has promoted largest number of SHGs, JLGs and Farmers' Clubs in the state of UP. Prathama Model is successful in belying the common myth that Banking with poor is a risky venture. PRATHAMA BANK is more aggressive in innovation and it is position ahead in terms of services. So the banks must create and sustain an environment that promotes creativity.*

Keywords: *RRB, Prathama Bank.*

Regional Rural Banks in India are an integral part of the rural credit structure of the country. Since the very beginning, when the RRBs were established on October 2, 1975, these banks played a pivotal role in the economic development of the rural India. The primary objective of establishing Gramin Bank in India was to provide credit to the rural masses who were economically weak, particularly the small and marginal farmers, artisans, agricultural laborers and even small entrepreneurs.

HISTORY OF REGIONAL RURAL BANK

The history of RRBs in India dates back 1975. It is the Narsimham Committee that conceptualized the foundation of Gramin Bank in India. The committee felt the requirement of 'regionally oriented rural banks' that would address the dilemmas and demands of rural masses with local feel, yet the same degree of professionalism of commercial banks.

Five Gramin Banks were set up on October 2 with a total authorized capital of Rs 1 crore, which later augmented to Rs 5 crore. There were five commercial banks viz. Punjab National Bank, State Bank of India, Syndicate Bank, United Bank of India and United Commercial Bank which sponsored the Gramin Banks. The equities of Gramin Banks were divided in a proportion of 50:35:15 among the Central Government, the Sponsor Bank and the concerned State Government.

REVIEW OF LITERATURE

According to Nathan, Swami (2002), policies of current phase of financial liberalization have had an immediate, direct and dramatic effect on rural credit. There has been a contraction in rural banking in general and in priority sector ending and preferential lending to the poor in particular. Chavan and Pallavi (2004) have examined the growth and regional distribution of rural banking over the period 1975-2002. Chavan's paper documents the gains made by historical underprivileged region of east, northeast and central part of India during the period of social and development banking. These gains were reversed in the 1990s: cutbacks in rural branches in rural credit deposits ratios were the steepest in the eastern and northeastern states of India. Policies of financial liberalization have unmistakably worsened regional inequalities in rural banking in India. Professor Dilip Khankhoje and Dr. Milind Sathye (2008) have analyzed to measure the variation in the performance in terms of productive efficiency of RRBs in India and to assess if the efficiency of these institutions has increased post-restructuring in 1993-94 or not.

Dr. M. Syed Ibrahim (2010) carried out a study on the topic "Performance Evaluation of Regional Rural Banks in India". In this study, it was concluded that RRBs in India showed a remarkable performance in the post-merger period

OBJECTIVE OF STUDY

(i) To identify and analyse the innovation initiative of selected bank, in special reference to PRATHAMA BANK

(ii) To analyze the affect of these innovation on the rural area

RESEARCH DESIGN

The present study is empirical in character based on the analytical method. The study is exclusively based on secondary data which is collected, compiled mainly from annual reports of the Prathama Bank, NABARD and RBI. Other relevant information was collected from journals, conference Proceedings and different websites.

PRATHMA BANK: A SNAP SHOT

Prathama Bank is the first Gramin Bank of India, sponsored by Syndicate Bank established on 2nd October, 1975, with its Head Office at Moradabad in accordance with Regional Rural Bank Ordinance 1975 issued on 26th September, 1975 (Replaced later by Regional Rural Bank Act, 1976(2) of 1976 of Government of India).

Prathama Bank is a Scheduled Bank placed under the IInd schedule of Reserve bank of India. Ownership of the Bank is lies with the Central Government 50 %, Syndicate Bank 35 % and the Uttar Pradesh Government 15 %. The Bank is functioning in 4 districts namely Moradabad, Rampur, Amroha and a newly formed Sambhal district with a network of 301 branches.

The Bank has developed its own model of micro finance i.e. ***Prathama Model***. It has been widely appreciated and acknowledged by NABARD, GOI and other international forums. The Bank has promoted largest number of SHGs, JLGs and Farmers' Clubs in the state of UP.

UNIQUE FEATURES

- Strong Financial Base with Reserves of 730 crore and Net Worth of 739 Crore
- Total Business Rs.8141 Crore as on 31.03.2014
- CD Ratio - 83 % among the highest in the state of UP

- CRAR – 18.48 %
- All branches on CBS with facility of RTGS/ NEFT

PRATHMA MODEL

Realizing the obvious need for being close to the rural society ,the bank took the initiative for the success of micro credit development through people's participatory program i.e. SHGs and a innovative tool named as "Prathama Model" was developed and implemented on the basis of Bank's past experiences of rural development, field work and research. This low cost model is a synergic blend of "Bank Officers" and "members of farmers club".

SELECT VILLAGES AND THEIR PROGRESS REPORT

	Taharpur	Chhapna	Papsara	Moonda pandey	Bilaspur	Fatehpur chhitra	Sarkara kamal	Fatehpur vishnoi
Number of villages attached to branch	15	14	10	08	12	10	09	10
No. of SHGs formed by branch	679	471	388	354	496	311	398	130
No.of SHGs credit linked	549	372	272	289	423	273	358	122
Total no. of SHG members covered by the branch	6893	4889	4752	3847	5368	3234	4153	1344
Total population in villages								
1991	32721	27446	10172	35622	5421	16063	9577	9000
2001	38971	32137	13274	43571	7353	18110	12224	13800
2010	27821	40234	18254	67891	15789	22103	14656	18360
Household below poverty line								
2001	1370	3089	618	205	1029	350	468	300

Contd...

2008	528	1535	325	104	441	150	168	420
2014	417	2568	498	578	278	214	186	732
Total deposits of branch								
2001	2.52 crore	2.15 crore	2.74 crore	2.70 crore	300 lakh	2.91 crore	3.30crore	4.89 crore
2008	6.25 crore	9.24 crore	5.46 crore	8.61 crore	1945 lakh	6.14crore	7.45 crore	9.49 crore
2014	12.30 crore	12.98 crore	11.28 crore	24.23 crore	2931 lakh	12.85 crore	14.16 crore	16.70 Crore
Literacy level								
2001	25%	37%	39%	23%	46%	75%	72%	35%
2008	48%	45%	61%	62%	62%	80%	85%	51%
2014	70 %	70%	73%	70%	86%	86%	95%	70%
Women entrepreneurs								
2001	152	85	52	25	36	50	172	125
2008	557	332	536	389	379	421	477	278
2014	863	456	738	873	487	519	630	460

GRAPHICAL ANALYSIS OF DATA

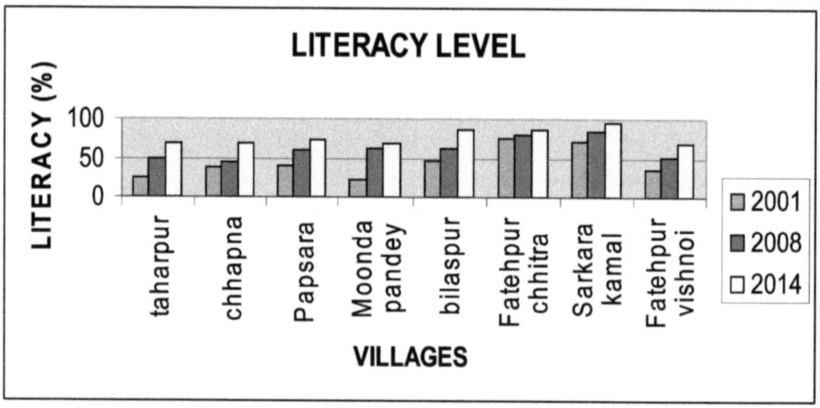

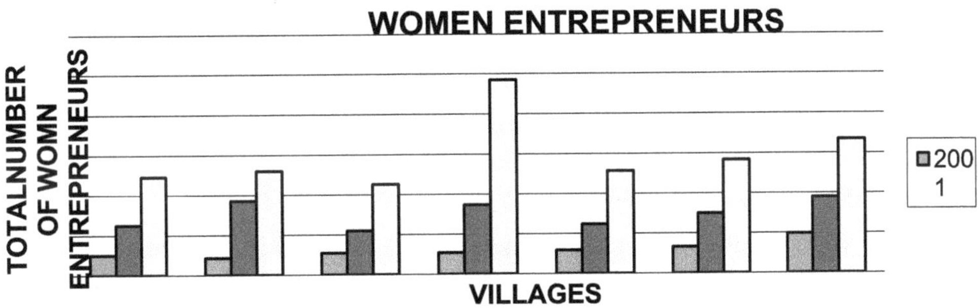

Village names

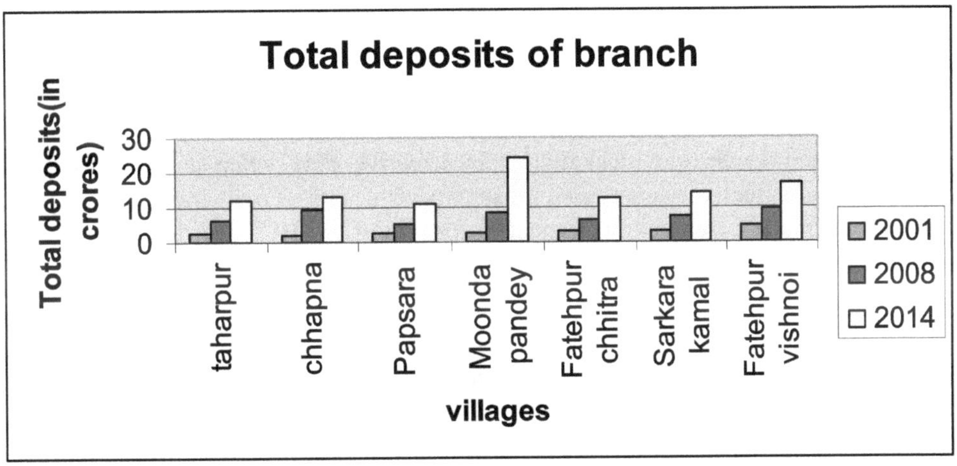

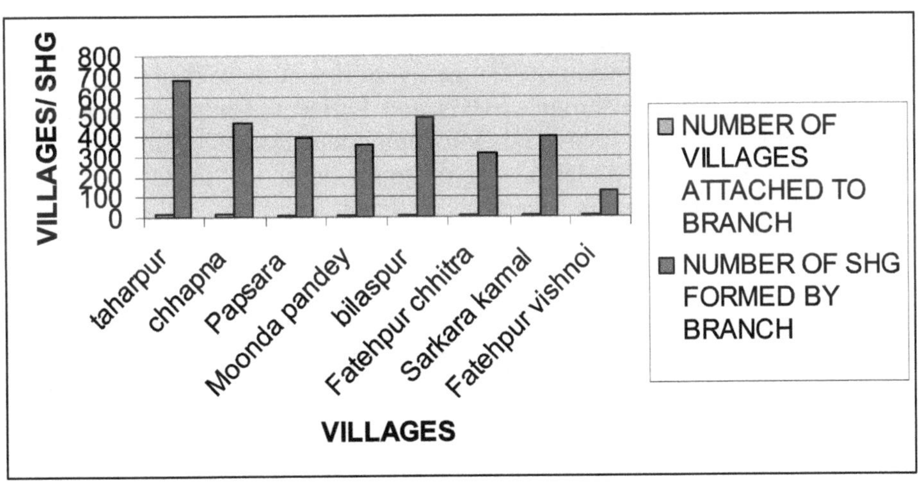

ANALYSIS

1. A total of 88 villages were linked to different branches which itself is commendable.
2. The highest number of SHGs were formed in Taharpur followed.
3. Number of total deposits has increased six times in most cases. Moonda Pandey has shown a remarkable rise in the increase in the total deposits of branch.
4. Literacy level has also gone up in all the villages
5. Number of women entrepreneurs have also gone up remarkably. Moonda Pandey again top this list .The number of women entrepreneurs have increased 34 times in Moonda pande. Papsara comes second as it shows an increase by 14 times from 2001 to 2014.

Bank's Strategy: Prathama Model in pictographic form is shown below:

Bank + FCs' member = A magic in rural development

Credibility + Motivation + Field work Acceptability + Ground level touch + People's participation through SHGs + Missionary Zeal

This ground level touch and local dialect is effective only when it is backed by Bank's credibility. Bank has effectively combined these two virtues of its own and member of Farmers' Clubs and this has made a tremendous impact in formation of SHGs and their financial linkages with Bank.

Prathama Model's Achievement: This low cost model has added new dimensions in the field of rural development, mainly through creating awareness amongst them and through microfinance. Bank is making dedicated efforts for socio-economic awareness of rural population in its service area and more than 1600 such programs were organized during the last fourteen years and during the year 2013-2014, 127 such developmental programs have been organized. All these efforts have made it possible to encompass more than 341689 members in the ambit of Self Help Group Scheme thus developing in them the habit of "savings for future".

Prathama Model – A Business Strategy: Prathama Model is successful in the common myth that Banking with poor is a risky venture. The recovery rate is more than 94% in this scheme. Moreover due to social pressure through SHGs and Farmers' Clubs, some hard core NPA accounts have become regular or recovered. Most important feature of this model is that cost involve is very low. Prathama Model has given great boost to "IMAGE" of the Bank in particular and "Growth" in business in general.

CONCLUSION

After detail study of policies and strategies of PRATHAMA BANK, it can be concluded that this bank is providing very innovative services. This bank has focused on the backward side of the society. The CSR policy of the bank is really very innovative. It is observed that banks in India moving towards sustainability through innovative service operations and offerings. The sample considered here for analysis has proved this point very clearly. The rate at which innovation are adopted by firm constitute an important part of the process of technological change. PRATHAMA BANK is more aggressive in innovation and it is position ahead in terms of services. So the banks must create and sustain an environment that promotes creativity.

REFERENCES

1. Satish P. Goyal, "Performance Analysis of Top 5 Banks in India HDFC, SBI, ICICI, AXIS, IDBI", Pune 2010.
2. Blau, P. M. & Schoenherr, R. (1971). The Structure of Organization, New York, Basic Books.
3. Boudreaux, D. O., Payne, B. C. & Rumore, N. C. (1995). Bank stock repurchases: A multivariate analysis', The Journal of Bank Cost & Management Accounting, vol. 8, pp. 40-48.
4. Bryant, M. S. 1997, 'A case-based reasoning approach to bankruptcy prediction modeling', Journal of Intelligent Systems in Accounting, Finance and Management, vol. 6, pp.195-214.

Websites:- www.rbi.org.in

www.moneycontrol.com

www.investmentz.com

http://www.allbankingsolutions.com/camels.html

www.prathamabank.org

A Premerger Risk Analysis of Kotak Bank Ltd through Camels: 2011 – 2015

Dr. M. Jayasree[1] and CS Pavana Jyothi

[1]Research Guide, Assistant Professor, HBS.
[2]Research Scholar, GITAM University.

ABSTRACT

Due to the huge competition in the banking industry, government policies, changing socio economic conditions, banks in India are initiating strategic processes to sustain competition and grow. One such move initiated by Kotak bank is merger of IngVysya Bank from 1st April 2015. I wanted to understand whether this is really a strategic move for the inorganic growth or a strategic move to bailout a weak bank by taking over another bank. In the process I used CAMEL approach to study the health and performance of the bank and found that the bank is performing well. For the purpose of this study I used five years data i.e from 2010-11 to 2014-15.

Keywords: *Merger, CAMEL, Kotak Bank.*

INTRODUCTION

Merger is generally combining of two similarly sized business entities to form a new company. The combining of two or more business sntities, generally by offering the stockholders of one company securities in the acquiring company in exchange for the surrender of their stock is called a merger.

Mergers and acquisitions are strategic decisions taken for maximisation of a company's growth by enhancing its production and marketing operations. Mergers are not uncommon in Banking Sector and Indian banking sector is no exception to that. Banking sector in order to gain strength, expand the customer base, cut competition or enter into a new market .There are many examples of bank mergers in India and to say a few " Bank of Rajasthan vs. ICICI bank, Bharath Overseas Bank vs IOB, HDFC Bank vs Centurion Bank etc.,"

There are various types of Mergers:

- Horizontal merger: This kind of merger exists between two companies who compete in the same industry segment. For example, combining of two banking companies.
- Vertical merger: Vertical merger is a kind in which two or more companies in the same industry but in different fields combine together in business. For example, a steel manufacturing company acquiring a coal supply company.
- Conglomerate merger: is a kind of venture in which two or more companies belonging to different industrial sectors combine their operations. For example, merging of software Company with a manufacturing company.

Merger and Acquisition in the banking sector it has the capacity to ensure efficiency, profitability and synergy and Deregulation (LPG) in the financial market , market liberalization and a number of other factors have played important function behind the growth of mergers and acquisitions in the banking sector

However in the process of a merger or acquisition or takeover the share holders of either entity shouldn't be put to loss, the merger should help both the entities. It shouldn't be a bailout operation of a sick company. There are so many factors, which need to be taken care while differentiating good banks from bad ones. However *t*o examine sickness in a bank **CAMEL** approach is highly used. **CAMELS** measures the performance of banks from each of the important parameter like Capital Adequacy, Assets Quality, Management Efficiency, Earning Quality and Liquidity.

LITERATURE REVIEW

MERGERS AND ACQUISITIONS

There are many factors, which have been considered as significant in managing Mergers and Acquisitions effectively like the factors considered in a marriage. It is said that a Merger or Acquisition is like a marriage between two corporate or business entities.

Ivancevich, Schweiger and Power (1987): The aspects of communication should be expected to focus on employees' concern like layoffs, changes in work rules, compensation, and pension etc.

Cartwright and Cooper (1990): Studied the wave of merger activity and they found the positive relationship in combination of people and the fusion of organizational cultures. They reported from a sample of 157 middle managers involved in the merger of two U.K. Building Societies. Post-merger measures of mental health and suggested merger to be a stressful life event, even when there is a high degree of cultural compatibility between the partnering organizations.

Appelbaum, Gandell, Yortis, Proper, and Jobin (2000): Examined the multiple organizational factors, which directly affect a merger as well as the merger process. They addressed the issue of communication and its importance throughout the merger and acquisition (M&A) process.

Schuler and Jackson (2001): proposed a three-stage model of mergers and acquisitions that systematically identified several human resources issues and activities.

Paul (2003): studied the merger of Bank of Madura with ICICI Bank. He also attempted to study the suitability of the merger between the 57 year old Bank of Madura with its traditional focus on mass banking strategies based on social objectives, and ICICI Bank, a six year old 'new age' organisation, which had been emphasising parameters like profitability in the interests of shareholders.

Zollo & Singh (2004): studied the knowledge-based view of corporate acquisitions and tested the post acquisition consequences on performance of various functions and parameters. They used a sample of 228 acquisitions in the U.S. banking industry and found that knowledge codification strongly and positively influences acquisition performance, while experience accumulation does not. Furthermore, increasing levels of post-acquisition integration strengthen the positive effect of codification.

Saraswathi (2007): Studied the merger of Global Trust Bank and Oriental Bank of Commerce. It was found by the author that this merger paved the way to several things in the transition period and pre merger strategy.

Murthy (2007): Studied the case of five bank mergers in India viz. Punjab National Bank and New Bank of India, ICICI Bank and Bank of Madura, ICICI Ltd. and ICICI Bank, Global Trust Bank and Oriental Bank of Commerce and Centurion Bank with Bank of Punjab. It was concluded by the author that consolidation is necessary due to stronger financial and operational structure, higher resources, wider branch network, huge customer base, technological advantage, focus on priority sector, and penetration in rural market.

Maire and Collerette (2011): Studied the case of an international post-merger integration project in the private banking sector. This experience suggest that successful integration management mainly rests upon capabilities in communication, organization, and change management.

CAMEL

In the process of continuous evaluation of the bank's financial performance both in public sector and private sector, the academicians, scholars and administrators have made several studies on the CAMEL model but in different perspectives and in different periods.

Kwan and Eisenbeis (1997) observed that Asset Quality is commonly used as a risk indicator for financial institutions, which also determines the reliability of capital ratios. Their study indicated that capitalization affects the operation of financial capitalization affects the operation of financial institution. More the capital, higher is the efficiency.

Godlewski (2003) tested the validity of the CAMEL rating typology for bank's default modelisation in emerging markets. He focused explicitly on using a logical model applied to a Database of defaulted banks in emerging markets.

Prasuna (2003) analyzed the performance of Indian banks by adopting the CAMEL Model. The Performance of 65 banks was studied for the period 2003-04. The author concluded that the Competition was tough and consumers benefited from better services quality, innovative products and better bargains.

Sarker (2005) scrutinized the CAMEL model for regulation and supervision of Islamic banks by the central bank in Bangladesh. The study enabled the regulators and supervisors to get a Shariah benchmark to supervise and inspect Islamic banks and financial institutions from an Islamic perspective.

Derviz *et al.* (2008) investigated the determinants of the movements in the long term Standard & Poor's and CAMEL bank ratings in the Czech Republic during the period when the three biggest banks, representing approximately 60% of the Czech banking sector's total assets, were privatized (i.e., the time span 1998-2001).

Siva and Natarajan (2011) empirically tested the applicability of CAMEL norms and its consequential impact on the performance of SBI Groups. The study concluded that annual CAMEL scanning helps the commercial bank to diagnose its financial health and alert the bank to take preventive steps for its sustainability.

Chaudhry and Singh (2012) analyzed the impact of the financial reforms on the soundness of Indian Banking through its impact on the asset quality. The study identified the key players as risk management, NPA levels, effective cost management and financial inclusion.

BRIEF PROFILE OF THE BANK

Kotak Mahindra group established in 1985 by Mr.Uday Kotak. It is one of India's leading financial services conglomerates. In February 2003, Kotak Mahindra Finance Ltd. (KMFL), the Group's flagship company, received a banking license from the Reserve Bank of India (RBI). With this, KMFL became the first non-banking finance company in India to be converted into a bank – Kotak Mahindra Bank Limited (KMBL).

In a study by Brand Finance Banking 500 published in February2014 by the Bankers magazine (from The Financial Times Stable), KMBL was ranked 245th among the world's top 500 banks with brand valuation of around half a billion dollars ($481million) and brand rating of AA*.

KMBL is also ranked among the top 5 Best Ranked Companies for Corporate Government in IR Global Ranking. ING Vysya Bank has merged with Kotak Mahindra Bank with effect from April 1, 2015.

RESEARCH METODOLOGY

RESEARCH DESIGN

CAMEL is a ratio-based model used to evaluate the performance of banks with the help of different criteria, viz. Capital Adequacy, Asset Quality, Management Quality, Earnings and Liquidity. The present study is a descriptive research study based on analytical research design

OBJECTIVES OF THE STUDY

The main objective of the study is to analyze the financial position and performance of The Kotak Bank Ltd, as a premerger risk analysis by using CAMEL model

DATA COLLECTION AND ANALYSIS

Entire study is depending on the secondary data of the bank under study. All the required data is collected from the annual reports from the company's website. Study period is from 2010 to 2014 i.e., 5 Years.

DATA ANALYSIS

For the purpose of data analysis, a simple average is calculated basing on the five years data, on each parameter i.e., Capital Adequacy, Asset Quality, Management Efficiency, Earnings Quality and Liquidity.

The CAMEL Framework

Regulators, analysts and investors have to periodically assess the financial condition of each bank. Banks are rated on various parameters, based on financial and non-financial performance. One of the popularly used assessments goes by the acronym CAMEL, where each letter refers to a specific category of performance.

C- Capital Adequacy: This indices the bank's capacity to maintain capital commensurate with the nature and extent of all types of risks, as also the ability of the bank's managers to identify, measure, control, monitor and control these risks.

A-Asset Quality: This measure reflects the magnitude of credit risk prevailing in the bank due to its composition and quality of loans, advances, investments and off-balance sheet activities.

M-Management Quality: Signaling the ability of the board of directors and senior managers to identify, measure, monitor and control risks associated with banking, this qualitative measure uses risk management policies and processes as indicators of sound management.

E-Earnings Quality: This indicator shows not only the amount of and the trend in earnings, but also analyses the robustness of expected earnings growth in future.

L-Liquidity: This measure takes into account the adequacy of the bank's current and potential sources of liquidity, including the strength of its funds management practices.

The components of the CAMEL rating system comprise of both objective and subjective parameters.

Internationally, and in India, these ratings are used by regulators to determine in supervision policies for individual banks. Ratings are assigned for each component on a scale of 1 to 5.

Banks with ratings of 1 to 2 are considered to present few, if any, supervisory concerns, while banks with ratings 3, 4, or 5 present moderate to extreme degrees of supervisory concern.

The rating analysis and interpretation are typically done along the following lines:

Rating analysis	Rating analysis interpretation
1.0-1.4	Strong:-Sound in every respect, no supervisory responses required.
1.6-2.4	Satisfactory:-Fundamentally sound with modest correctable weakness.
2.6-3.4	Fair (watch Category):- Combination of weakness if not redressed will become severe. Watch Category- requires more than normal supervision.
3.6-4.4	Marginal (some risk of failure):- Immoderate weakness unless properly addressed could impair future viability of the bank. Needs close supervision.
4.6-5.0	Unsatisfactory (high degree of failure evident):- High risk of failure in the near term. Under constant supervision/cease and desist order.

DATA ANALYSIS AND INTERPRETATION

CAPITAL ADEQUACY RATIO

Capital base of a financial institution facilitates depositors to understand the actual risk and their own perception about the organization. Also, it is a significant control on the financial managers to maintain adequate levels of capital. Capital adequacy is very useful for a bank to conserve & protect stakeholders confidence and prevent the bank from bankruptcy. Reserve Bank of India prescribes banks to maintain a minimum Capital to risk-weighted Assets Ratio (CRAR) of 9 % with regard to credit risk. However for Market risk and Operational Risks RBI prescribed different levels of capital requirements,

$$\text{CAR} = \frac{Tier\ 1\ Capital + Tier\ 2\ Capital}{Risk\ Weighted\ Assets} \times 100$$

Period	2010-11	2011-12	2012-13	2013-14	2014-15	Weighted Avg
CAR	19.92	17.52	16.05	18.83	17.17	17.897

As per RBI Guidelines every bank is supposed to maintain CRAR of 9%, to manage the Credit Risk. In the case of Kotak Bank, during the study period the weighted average of CRAR is 17.897%, which is highly satisfactory.

ASSET QUALITY

Asset quality determines the healthiness of financial institutions against loss of value in the assets as asset impairment risks the solvency of the financial institutions. The weakening value of assets has a spill over effect, as losses are eventually written-off against capital, which eventually expose the earning capacity of the institution. With this framework, the asset quality is assessed with respect to the level and severity of nonperforming assets, adequacy of provisions, distribution of assets etc.

Average Gross NPA's in the industry is between 4% to 5% , and this helps in comparing the bank's asset quality and performance in the asset management.

$$\text{AQ} = \frac{Gross\ NPA's}{Net\ Advances} \times 100$$

Period	2010-11	2011-12	2012-13	2013-14	2014-15	Weighted Avg
AQ	2.00	1.60	1.60	2.00	1.90	1.820

Kotak Bank is able to maintain average gross NPA's at 1.820% (during the study period), which a very low level comparing to the average industry level. This shows the bank is maintaining good quality in assets and the loan disbursement as well as recovery management is good.

MANAGEMENT QUALITY

Management efficiency, another indispensable component of the CAMEL framework, means adherence to set norms approved by the board. It proves that the bank is proactive in the dynamic environment and proves the employees quality of the bank.

$$MQ = \frac{Net\ profit}{Total\ Number\ of\ Employees} \times 100$$

Period	2010-11	2011-12	2012-13	2013-14	2014-15
MQ	2.80	3.70	4.60	5.00	6.00

Net profit to total employees is increasing every year and it is as high as 6% during the year 2014 -15. Bank is able to maintain a very good per employee profit ratio inspite of increase in the total number of employees, This indicates the employee quality and in turn the quality of the management.

EARNINGS QUALITY

To study the earnings quality the following **FIVE** important parameters are included.

(a) Operating Profit to Average Working Funds **OP to WF**

(b) Interest Income to Interest expenses **II to IE**

Period	2010-11	2011-12	2012-13	2013-14	2014-15	Weighted Avg
OP to WF	15.44	18.24	18.71	17.70	17.50	17.52
II to IE	2.00	1.68	1.66	1.73	1.76	1.77

Operating Profit to working funds indicates the effective usage of the working funds and the efficiency of the banks is measured through the ratio. The bank is able to use the working funds very effectively and could generate a weighted average Operating profit of 17.52%, which indicates a very high efficiency of usage of working funds.

Interest Income to Interest Expenses is another important parameter wherein the ratio indicates that capacity of the bank to meet Interest Expenses (on deposits) from the Interest Income (Loans and Advances). Weighted average of the ratio is 1.77% or 1.77, which indicates that the bank is able to generate more by 1.77 times than the Interest Expenses , which is a good indication that the bank is maintaining a good spread on advances.

From the above ratios it can be concluded that the banks earnings quality is good.

LIQUIDITY RATIO

Liquidity ratio indicates the capacity of the bank to meet its current liabilities on time. The efficiency of the operations is studied from this ratio. The ratio can neither be too high nor too low. If the ratio is too high it indicates that the bank is not deploying the working funds properly and on the contrary, if the ratio is too low it indicates the illiquidity in the operations and may have to face challenges in meeting the obligations.

To study the liquidity efficiency the following ratios are used.

(a) Liquid Asset to Total Assets **LA to TA**

(b) Liquid Assets to Total Demand Deposits **LA to DD**

Period	2010-11	2011-12	2012-13	2013-14	2014-15	Weighted Avg
LA to TA	0.40	0.40	0.40	0.60	0.50	0.46
LA to DD	2.06	2.50	2.50	2.50	2.60	2.43

The bank is maintaining both the ratio's very satisfactorily and efficiently. Liquid Assets to Total Assets at a weighted average ratio of only 0.46 indicates a very low ratio and at the same time it is maintaining a ratio 2.43 against total demand deposits, which is very good and efficiently managed.

FINDINGS AND CONCLUSION

Due to the increasing competition, government policies, emergence of new banks on the Indian Banking canvas, it is becoming inevitable for the existing banks, to consolidate and compete. Therefore the Kotak Banks move in the present merger is highly strategic, since the ING Vysya is an old generation private bank, with lots of special characters like, specific community supported bank, with concentration in south India. It helps the Kotak bank to expand in the south also and helps for a very fast growth and development.

1. Kotak Bank's performance on the lines of CAMEL is satisfactory.
2. Proposed merger of The IngVysya Bank Ltd, with the Kotak Bank is not a bailout package, but a strategic move for the Kotak Bank for the Inorganic growth.

References

1. Bhattacharyya, A and Sahay, P (1997), "The impact of liberalization on the productive efficiency of Indian commercial banks" European Journal of Operational Research, vol. 98.
2. Ivancevich, Schweiger and Power, Mergers and Acquisitions, the role of stake holders.
3. Cartwright and Cooper, The Psychological Impact of Merger and Acquisition on the Individual: A Study of Building Society Managers , Sage Journal.
4. Justin Paul , Bank of Madura Merger with ICICI Bank, an analysis, SSRN, Sep 2003.
5. Saraswathi, K.V. (2007). Crucial HR Management Issues in Bank Consolidation: Some Cases. In Bose, J. (Ed.), Bank Mergers: The Indian Scenario. (226-243). Hyderabad: The ICFAI University Press.
6. Arora, S and Kaur, S (2008), "Diversification by Banks in India: What are the Internal Determinants?"The Indian Banker.
7. Schraeder, M., and Self, D.R. (2003). Enhancing the Success of Mergers and Acquisitions: Schuler, R. and Jackson, S. (2001). HR issues and activities in mergers and acquisitions. European Management Journal. 19(3), 239-253. doi:10.1016/S0263-2373(01)00021-4.
8. Weber, Y., & Fried, Y. (2011). Guest Editors' Note: The role of HR practices in managing culture clash during the post merger integration process. Human Resource Management, 50(5), 565- 570.
9. Zollo, M., & Singh, H. (2004). Deliberate learning in corporate acquisitions: post-acquisition strategies and integration capability in U.S. Bank mergers. Strategic Management Journal,
10. Bodla, B.S. and Verma, R. (2006), "Evaluating Performance of Banks through CAMEL Model: A Case Study of SBI and ICICI". The ICFAI Journal of Bank Management, Vol.5(3).

11. Hirtle and Lopez (2008), "ABA Banking Journal, Banks performance evaluation by camel model". Finance Trade Publications, Vol. 4(4).
12. Chaudhry, et.al (2012): "Impact of Reforms on the Asset Quality in Indian Banking", International Journal of Multidisciplinary Vol. 5(2).
13. Gupta, et.al (2008) "Dynamics of Productive Efficiency of Indian Banks". International Journal of Operations Research, Vol.5(2).
14. Prasad K.V.N.G. Ravinder and D. Maheshwari Reddy (2011), "A CAMEL Model Analysis of Public and Private Sector Banks in India". Journal of Banking Financial Services and Insurance Research, Vol1(5).
15. Prasuna, D G (2004), "Performance Snapshot 2003-04". Chartered Financial Analyst, Vol. X(11).

Websites Used:

1. www.kotak.com
2. www.moneycontrol.com
3. www.rbi.org.in

Emerging Trends Reforms and Policies in Banking Industry – A Road Map to Financial Inclusion

K. Prasad[1] and Venu Kesireddy[2]

[1&2]Assistant Professor, Vaagdevi College of Engineering (Autonomous)

ABSTRACT

A sea change has been taken place in the banking environment since the initiation, to teach the financial literacy, saving mobility, financial assistance and remittance of Government benefits, grants, loans and subsidy. Despite various measures for financial inclusion, poverty and exclusion continue to dominate socio-economic and political discourse in India even after six decades of post economic independence era. Though economy has shown impressive growth during post liberalization era of 1991, impact is yet to percolate to all sections of the society and therefore, India is still home of 1/3 of world's poor. A vast segment of India's population exists on the margins of India's financial systems. There is growing concern about people being 'under-banked'. Financial inclusion is important priority of the country in terms of economic growth and development of society. It enables to reduce the gap between rich and poor. It helps to channelize money-flow to the economy; it ensures people who are unable to access financial system so far can access it with ease. The paper discusses the various reforms policies and trends in persuasion of financial inclusion in India.

Keywords: *Financial Inclusion, Access to Financial Services, Prandhan Mantri Jan-Dhan Yojana, Insurance, RuPay Debit card.*

INTRODUCTION

The term financial inclusion refers to delivery of financial services at an affordable cost in a fair and transparent terms and conditions to vast sections of disadvantages, weaker and low income groups including household enterprise, small medium enterprise and traders. It not only enhances overall financial intensity of agriculture but also help in increasing rural nonfarm activities which lead to development of rural economy and improve economic condition of people. Financial inclusion include micro credit, branchless banking, no- frills bank accounts, saving products, pension for old age, microfinance, self help group, entrepreneurial credit etc. In short.

Financial Inclusion is: NFA + Banks + OFIs + MFI + IT = Financial Inclusion

where, NFA - No frills bank account, OFIs - Other financial Institutions MFI - Micro financial Institutions, IT – Information Technology.

Thus, financial inclusion needed for equal opportunities to all section of people in country, inclusive growth, economic development, social development and business opportunity.

Statement of the Problem

The developments in the banking sector were witnessed only in the field of expansion and spread of bank branches, generation of huge employment and mobilization of savings rather than improvement in the efficiency that counts a lot. Besides these, still out of 125 crores of Indian population majority people were not have the financial literacy, financial inclusion and bank accounts to access Government benefits, insurance coverage, saving mobility etc.

REVIEW OF LITERATURE

Sustained growth of the nation and its continued prosperity depend critically on universal financial services covering all people. Further, empirical evidence shows that inclusive financial system significantly raises growth, alleviate poverty and expand economic opportunity.

Dr. Joji chandran, (2008). Financial inclusion means the provision of affordable financial services, viz., access to payments and remittance facilities, savings, loans and insurance services by the formal financial system to those who tend to be excluded.

Thorat, (2006). Financial inclusion is delivery of banking services at an affordable cost to the vast sections of disadvantaged and low income groups. Unrestrained access to public goods and services is the sine qua non of an open and efficient society. As banking services are in the nature of public good, it is essential that availability of banking and payment services to the entire population without discrimination is the prime objective of the public policy.

According to Dr. C. Rangarajan, Chairman of the Committee on Financial inclusion, 2008 - "Financial Inclusion can be defined as the process whereby it is ensured that viable financial services & products are provided to the weaker sections at prices that are affordable, through a transparent and just Institution".

"Financial inclusion may be defined as the process of ensuring access to financial services and timely and adequate credit where needed by vulnerable groups such as weaker sections and low income groups at an affordable cost."

According to Former UN Secretary – General Kofi Annan:- "The stark reality is that the poor people in the world still lack access to sustainable financial services, whether it is savings, credit or insurance. The great challenge before us is to address the constraints that exclude people from full participation in the financial sector. Together, we can and must build inclusive financial sectors that help people improve their lives".

According to Mahatma Gandhi:- "Real India Lives in Villages", and village economy is the backbone of Indian economy. The existing extensive formal banking structure is still not sufficient to meet the growing demand of rural credit. Financial inclusion is delivery of financial services more especially the banking services at an affordable cost to vast sections of disadvantaged and low income groups.

OBJECTIVE OF THE STUDY

To study the vital important reforms in India created substantial change in economy, discuss the various emerging methods enhance policies of financial inclusion and to draw conclusions emerged from the study.

RESEARCH METHODOLOGY

The methodology to be adopted for collection of the data and analysis of data and interpretation of data as discussed below.

COLLECTION OF DATA

For the purpose of the study secondary data was collected from the Newspapers, RBI bulletin, various reports on Indian banks, publications of Indian Banks, Indian Institute of Bankers, National Institute of Bank Management and various journals on Banking etc.

SCOPE OF THE STUDY

Scope of the Study confined to reforms of important committees, new licencing policies financial services like availability of basic savings bank account, access to need based credit, remittances facility, insurance and pension to the excluded sections i.e., weaker sections & low income groups.

Recommendations of Narasimham Committee Report I - 1991

Narsimham Committee was set up in order to study the problems of the Indian financial system and to suggest some recommendations for improvement in the efficiency and productivity of the financial institution.

The committee has given the following major recommendations:

(a) **Reduction in the SLR and CRR:** The committee recommended the reduction of the higher proportion of the Statutory Liquidity Ratio 'SLR' and the Cash Reserve Ratio 'CRR'. Both of these ratios were very high at that time. The SLR then was 38.5% and CRR was 15%. This high amount of SLR and CRR meant locking the bank resources for Government uses. It was hindrance in the productivity of the bank thus the committee recommended their gradual reduction. SLR was recommended to reduce from 38.5% to 25% and CRR from 15% to 3 to 5%.

(b) **Phasing out Directed Credit Programme:** In India, since nationalization, directed credit programmes were adopted by the government. The committee recommended phasing out of this programme. This programme compelled banks to earmark their financial resources for the needy and poor sectors at confessional rates of interest. It was reducing the profitability of banks and thus the committee recommended the stopping of this programme.

(c) **Interest Rate Determination:** The committee felt that the interest rates in India are regulated and controlled by the authorities. The determination of the interest rate should be on the grounds of market forces such as the demand for and the supply of fund. Hence the committee recommended eliminating government controls on interest rate and phasing out the concessional interest rates for the priority sector.

(d) **Structural Reorganizations of the Banking Sector:** The committee recommended that the actual numbers of public sector banks need to be reduced. Three to four big banks including SBI should be developed as international banks. Eight to Ten Banks having nationwide presence should concentrate on the national and universal banking services. Local banks should concentrate on region specific banking. Regarding the RRBs (Regional Rural Banks), it recommended that they should focus on agriculture and rural financing. They recommended that the government should assure that henceforth there won't be any nationalization and private and foreign banks should be allowed liberal entry in India.

(e) **Establishment of the ARF Tribunal:** The proportion of bad debts and Non-performing asset (NPA) of the public sector Banks and Development Financial Institute was very alarming in those days. The committee recommended the establishment of an Asset Reconstruction Fund (ARF). This fund will take over the proportion of the bad and doubtful debts from the banks and financial institutes. It would help banks to get rid of bad debts.

(f) **Removal of Dual Control:** Those days' banks were under the dual control of the Reserve Bank of India (RBI) and the Banking Division of the Ministry of Finance (Government of India). The committee recommended the stepping of this system. It considered and recommended that the RBI should be the only main agency to regulate banking in India.

(g) **Banking Autonomy:** The committee recommended that the public sector banks should be free and autonomous. In order to pursue competitiveness and efficiency, banks must enjoy autonomy so that they can reform the work culture and banking technology up-gradation will thus be easy. Some of these recommendations were later accepted by the Government of India and became banking reforms.

Committee on Comprehensive Financial Services for Small Businesses and Low Income House Holds - Dr. Nachiket Mor (2013).

A committee appointed by RBI to make recommendations to reach financial service to every nook and corner of India and make 100 per cent financial inclusion headed by Dr. Nachiket Mor gave following guidelines. They are:

1. **Universal Electronic Bank Account (UEBA):** By Jan 1, 2016 each Indian resident, above the age of eighteen years, would have an individual, full-service, safe, and secure electronic bank account.
2. **Ubiquitous Access to Payment Services and Deposit Products at Reasonable Charges:** By Jan 1, 2016, the number and distribution of electronic payment access points would be such that every single resident would be within a fifteen minute walking distance from such a point anywhere in the country. Each such point would allow residents to deposit and withdraw cash to and from their bank accounts and transfer balances from one bank account to another, in a secure environment, for both very small

and very large amounts, and pay reasonable charges for all of these services. At least one of the deposit products accessible to every resident through the payment access points would offer a positive real rate of return over the consumer price index.

3. **Sufficient Access to Affordable Formal Credit:** By Jan 1, 2016, each low-income household and small-business would have convenient access to formally regulated lenders that have the ability to assess and meet their credit needs, and offer them a full-range of suitable credit products, at an affordable price. By that date, each District and every significant sector (and sub-sector) of the economy would have a Credit to GDP ratio of at least 10 per cent. This ratio would increase every year by 10 per cent with the goal that it reaches 50 per cent by January 1, 2020.
4. **Universal Access to a Range of Deposit and Investment Products at Reasonable Charges:** By Jan 1, 2016, each low-income household and small-business would have convenient access to providers that have the ability to offer them suitable investment and deposit products, and pay reasonable charges for their services. By that date, each District would have a Total Deposits and Investments to GDP ratio of at least 15 per cent. This ratio would increase every year by 12.5 per cent with the goal that it reaches 65 per cent by January 1, 2020.
5. **Universal Access to a Range of Insurance and Risk Management Products at Reasonable Charges:** By Jan 1, 2016, each low-income household and small business would have convenient access to providers that have the ability to offer them suitable insurance and risk management products which, at a minimum allow them to manage risks related to: (a) commodity price movements. (b) Longevity, disability, and death of human beings. (c) Death of livestock. (d) Rainfall. And (e) damage to property, and pay reasonable charges for their services. By that date, each District would have a Total Term Life Insurance Sum Assured to GDP ratio of at least 30 per cent. This ratio would increase every year by 12.5 per cent with the goal that it reaches 80 per cent by January 1, 2020.
6. **Right to Suitability:** Each low-income household and small-business would have a legally protected right to be offered only suitable financial services. While the customer will be required to give informed consent she/he will have the right to seek legal redress if she/he feels that due process to establish Suitability was not followed or that there was gross negligence.

ATMs in Kirana Shops

ATMs have fast become an integral part of Indian banking population, cutting across all areas – rural, semi urban, urban and metro, banks particularly the Public Sector Banks (PSBs) are to be credited with this remarkable accomplishment although some foreign banks and new private banks were early entrants. It would not be exaggerated to say that PSBs put the ATMs on a 'mass revolution' mode. ATMs benefit both customers and banks.

ATMs on Site and Off Site

Bank Group	2005 (Per cent)		2014 (Per cent)	
	On-site ATM	Off-site ATMS	On-site ATM	Off-site ATMS
SBG	30	70	56	44
NBs	67	33	63	37
OPBs	64	36	50	50
NBPs	34	66	32	68
FBs	27	73	22	78
SCBs	43	57	52	48

Source: Indian Bankers Association.

ATM centers need 24 hours security, CC cameras, Air Condition to maintain its services to customers. Each transaction costs Rs.20 to the customers by the bank. Banks are planning to establish ATMs Kirana shops where it has 150 to 200 transaction per day. The amount paid to the agencies for dispensing money in ATMs centre for security employee salary, AC expenses, electricity charges & CC cameras expenses all together becomes above Rs.50000 Per Month (PM) as maintenances expenses.

If these ATMs are established in Kirana shops the above expenses will be saved by Banks. They need to pay Rs.2,000 to Rs.10,000 PM to Kirana shop holders for maintenance charges.

New Guidelines to Issue Licence to Banks

The Standing Committee on Finance presided as Chairperson: Mr. Yashwant Sinha presented his report on "Policy on New Licences in the Banking Sector" on October 18, 2013. It reviewed the performance of new banks and the guidelines for setting up of new banks while keeping in mind the objective of financial inclusion. The key observations and recommendations are mentioned below:

The final guidelines pave the way for corporate houses like Anil Dhirubhai Ambani Group, Larsen & Toubro, Tatas, Mahindra and Mahindra, Life Insurance Corporation and Aditya Birla Group to enter the banking business.

1. Entities or groups should have a past record of sound credentials and integrity, be financially sound with a successful track record of 10 years.
2. The Committee recommended raising the minimum paid-up capital requirement for new banks from the current Rs 500 crore to Rs 1000 crore. It opined that starting a bank with Rs 500 crore as capital could limit operations of the bank and that increasing the minimum requirement would also screen out less serious players.
3. As per norms notified by RBI, on receipt of licence, promoter has to start operations within one year and list the company within three years of commencement of the business and new banks should open at least 25 per cent of branches in unbanked (population up to 9,999 as per the latest census) rural centres.
4. Before granting licences, RBI would seek feedback about applicants from other regulators, enforcement, investigative agencies like IT Department, CBI, ED, as deemed appropriate.

5. Following the grant of licence, the promoter group, which could be a Public Sector Entity as well, will be required to set up a wholly-owned Non-Operative Financial Holding Company (NOFHC).
6. Existing Non-banking Financial Company (NBFC) will be eligible to apply for a bank licence, if considered eligible, NBFCs may be permitted to promote a new bank or convert themselves into banks.
7. The new entity will have to comply with the priority sector lending targets and sub-targets as applicable to the existing domestic banks.
8. Banks promoted by groups having 40 per cent or more income from non-financial business will require RBI's prior approval for raising paid-up voting equity capital beyond Rs 1,000 crore for every block of Rs 500 crore.
9. According to RBI norms, the NOFHC will initially hold a minimum of 40 per cent of the paid-up voting equity capital of the bank which shall be locked in for a period of five years and which shall be brought down to 15 per cent within 12 years.
10. With regard to corporate governance, the new guidelines instructed that, at least 50 per cent of directors of the NOFHC should be independent directors.
11. As regards procedure for grant of bank licence, RBI said applications will be screened by the central bank itself before being forwarded to the high level advisory committee for further scrutiny.
12. Entities or Groups in the private sector that are 'owned and controlled by residents' as defined in Department of Industrial Policy and Promotion (DIPP) Press Note 2, 3 and 4 of 2009 / FEMA Regulations as amended from time to time and entities in Public Sector shall be eligible to promote a bank through a wholly-owned Non-Operative Financial Holding Company (NOFHC).
13. The capital requirements for the regulated financial services entities held by the NOFHC shall be as prescribed by the respective sectorial regulators. The bank shall be required to maintain a minimum capital adequacy ratio of 13 per cent of its risk weighted assets (RWA) for a minimum period of 3 years after the commencement of its operations subject to any higher percentage as may be prescribed by RBI from time to time. On a consolidated basis, the NOFHC and the entities held by it shall maintain a minimum capital adequacy of 13 per cent of its consolidated RWA for a minimum period of 3 years.
14. The bank shall get its shares listed on the stock exchanges within three years of the commencement of business by the bank.

Hon'ble Prime Minister Narendra Modi on 15 August, 2014 announced "Pradhan Mantri Jan-Dhan Yojana (PMJDY)" which is a National Mission for Financial Inclusion. The task is gigantic and is a National Priority. This National Mission on Financial Inclusion has an ambitious objective of covering all households in the country with banking facilities and having a bank account for each household. It has been emphasised by the Hon'ble PM that this is important for including people left-out into the mainstream of the financial system. Prime Minister's People Money Scheme is a scheme for comprehensive financial inclusion launched by the Prime Minister of India, Narendra Modi on 28 August 2014· He had announced this scheme on his first Independence Day speech on 15

August 2014. Run by Department of Financial Services, Ministry of Finance, on the inauguration day, 1.5 Crore (15 million) bank accounts were opened under this scheme. By 28 January 2015, 12.58 crore accounts were opened, with around ₹10590 crore (US$1.7 billion) were deposited under the scheme, which also has an option for opening new bank accounts with zero balance.

The scheme has been started with a target to provide 'universal access to banking facilities' starting with "Basic Banking Accounts" with overdraft facility of Rs.5000after six months and RuPay Debit card with inbuilt accident insurance cover of Rs. 1 lakh and RuPay Kisan Card. In next phase, micro insurance & pension etc. will also be added.

Under the Scheme

1. Account holders will be provided zero-balance bank account with RuPay debit card, in addition to accidental insurance cover of Rs 1 lakh (to be given by 'HDFC Ergo').
2. Those who open accounts by January 26, 2015 over and above the 1 lakh accident, they will be given life insurance cover of 30,000 (to be given by LIC).
3. After Six months of opening of the bank account, holders can avail 5,000 overdraft from the bank.
4. With the introduction of new technology introduced by National Payments Corporation of India (NPCI), a person can transfer funds, check balance through a normal phone which was earlier limited only to smart phones so far.
5. Mobile banking for the poor would be available through National Unified USSD Platform (NUUP) for which all banks and mobile companies have come together

Financial Inclusion: Current Status – India

Despite various measures for financial inclusion, poverty and exclusion continue to dominate socio-economic and political discourse in India even after six decades of post economic independence era. Though economy has shown impressive growth during post liberalization era of 1991, impact is yet to percolate to all sections of the society and therefore, India is still home of 1/3 of world's poor .

- Census, 2011 estimates that only 58.7% of the households have access to banking services.
- The present banking network of the country (as on 31.03.2014) comprises of a bank branch network of 1,15,082 and an ATM network of 1,60,055. Of these, 43,962 branches (38.2%) and 23,3341 ATMs (14.58%) are in rural areas.

The statistics show that there is substantial progress towards opening of accounts, providing basic banking services during the recent years as indicated above. However , it is essential that all the sections be financially included in order to have financial stability and sustainability of the economic and social order.

According to World Bank Findex Survy (2012) only 35% of Indian adults had access to a formal bank account and 8% borrowed from a formal financial institution in last 12 months. The miniscule number suggests an urgent need to further push the financial inclusion agenda to ensure that people at the bottom of the pyramid join the mainstream of the formal financial system.

Recent Important Guidelines on Financial Inclusion

- 2006: In January, banks were allowed to enlist non-profit Bank Mitr (Business Correspondent) as agents for delivery of financial services, acting in the capacity of 'last-mile infrastructure'.
- 2008: In April, it was determined that BCs should be located not more than 15 kilometers from the nearest bank branch, so as to ensure their adequate supervision.
- This was a very restrictive rule that severely limited the expansion of this model.
- 2008: The RBI issued operative guidelines for mobile banking and amended the same
- in December 2009 to ease the various transaction limits and security norms.
- 2009: Individual for profits were allowed to participate as BCs, and this category included kirana store, gas stations, PCOs etc. Further , BCs were al l owed to operate up t o 30 kilometers from t he nearest bank branches.
- 2009: Banks were allowed to apply ' reasonable' service charges from customers to ensure viability of the BC model, and to pay a ' reasonable' commission/fee to the BCs to incentivize them.
- 2010: In June the RBI and TRAI were able to reach an initial agreement regarding the rollout of mobile banking, whereby TRAI would deal with all interconnection issues and RBI would handle the banking aspects such as KYC checks, transaction limits etc.
- 2010: In September, all companies listed under the Companies Act (1956) were allowed to act as BCs, with the exception of non-bank financial companies.
- 2010: The same directive determined that the distance rule was open to and optional relaxation in certain cases, based on the decision of the State Level Bankers' Committees. However, document verification falls under the domain of the banks, to ensure adherence to KYC norms. This does slow down the account opening process.
- 2011: In January, TRAI announced its intent to fix mobile tariffs for financial services as against their current market pricing, with a view to ensuring affordability .
- 2011: RBI issued guidelines for opening Aadhaar Enabled Bank Accounts to facilitate routing of MGNREGA wages and other social benefits in to the accounts using EBT .
- 2012: RBI permitted Aadhaar letter as a proof of both Identity & Address for the purpose of opening of bank Accounts.
- 2012: GoI introduced Sub Service Area (SSA) approach for opening of banking outlet and for Direct Cash Transfer.
- 2012: Aadhaar Payment Bridge System (APBS) was introduced for centralized credit of Social Benefits.
- Guidelines on Direct Benefit Transfer issued by GOI.
- 2013: To ease the account opening process RBI permitted to use e-KYC.

- TRAI issued guidelines on USSD based mobile banking services for FI.
- 2014: RBI issues guidelines for scaling up of Business Correspondent model.

Financial Inclusion - Summary progress of all Banks including Regional Rural Banks (RRBs), during five years period are as under: India, which is home to 21 per cent of the world's unbanked adults, faces a significant challenge in catching up with the rest of the world in universalising banking access, reveals global financial figures released recently by the World Bank.

The World Bank paper, "The Global Findex Database 2014 - Measuring Financial Inclusion around the World," says that three countries - India, China and Indonesia - accounted for 38 per cent of the world's unbanked adults, of which China accounts for 12 percent and Indonesia 6 per cent.

"Both China and India saw strong growth in account ownership between 2011 and 2014; in China account penetration increased from 64 percent to 79 percent, and in India from 35 percent to 53 percent. Translated into absolute numbers, this growth means that 180 million adults in China and 175 million in India became account holders with the two countries together accounting for about half the 700 million new account holders globally," the paper said. In comparison, 94 percent of adults had accounts in high-income OECD economies.

World Bank Chief Praises Prime Minister Modi's Jan Dhan Yojana

The World Bank chief Jim Yong Kim today said that the "strong visionary leadership" of Prime Minister Narendra Modi has resulted in "extraordinary effort" by India on financial inclusion of its people. The World Bank in a report released this week said by January 2015, 125 million bank accounts had been opened under the Pradhan Mantri Jan Dhan Yojana launched in August 2014 for comprehensive financial inclusion with the goal of opening a bank account for every household in India. As a point of comparison, a 2013 survey had found that fewer than 400 million people in the country had an account, the World Bank said in a report.

"This is an extraordinary Indian effort," Dr Kim said at a panel discussion here organised on the sidelines of the annual spring meeting of the International Monetary Fund and the World Bank. Dr Kim attributed this to the "strong visionary leadership" of Prime Minister Modi and the Reserve Bank of India Governor Dr Raghuram Rajan. Dr Kim also said access to financial services can serve as a bridge out of poverty.

"We have set a hugely ambitious goal - universal financial access by 2020 - and now we have evidence that we're making major progress," he said." This effort will require many partners - credit card companies, banks, micro credit institutions, the United Nations, foundations, and community leaders. But we can do it, and the payoff will be millions of people lifted out of poverty," he added. Participating in the panel discussion along with Master Card CEO Ajay Banga, State Bank of India (SBI) Chairman Arundhati Bhattacharya briefed the audience on the successful efforts of the SBI in implementing the Jan Dhan Yojana."Forty-nine per cent of the accounts under Jan Dhan Yojana are being held by women," Ms Bhattacharya said.

The World Bank Group and a broad coalition partners including multilateral agencies, banks, credit unions, card networks, micro finance institutions and telecommunications companies today issued numeric commitment that would help promote financial inclusion and achieve universal financial access by the year 2020.

Pradhan Manthri Jan dhan Yojana accounts opened up to 31-3-2015

S. No	Bank Name	No. of accounts opened (Lakh)			No of Rupay Debit cards	Balance in accounts (Rs.lakhs)	No of Zero balance accounts
		Rural	Urban	Total			
1	PSB	625.35	529.09	1154.44	1081.10	1218505.25	661.82
2	RRB	217.11	390.08	256.11	178.22	257711.10	156.16
3	PRSB	359.87	250.79	61.06	55.49	90813.06	34.13
	Total	878.44	593.18	1471.63	1314.82	1567029.41	852.13

Source: Newspapers.

Under Pradhan Manthri Jan Dhan Yojana is a key success factor by opening number accounts by Public Sector Banks (PSB), Regional Rural Banks (RRB), Private Sector Banks (PRSB) has 1471.63 lakhs. The number of Rupay debit cards issued under this scheme was 1314.82 lakhs. Really it is a great achievement to create path for the financial literacy, inclusion, insurance benefit, access government benefits.

FDI Indian Banks

A foreign bank or its wholly owned subsidiary regulated by a financial sector regulator in the host country can now invest up to 100% in an Indian private sector bank. This option of 100% FDI will be only available to a regulated wholly owned subsidiary of a foreign bank and not any investment companies. Other foreign investors can invest up to 74% in an Indian private sector bank, through direct or portfolio investment. The Government has also permitted foreign banks to set up wholly owned subsidiaries in India. The government, however, has not taken any decision on raising voting rights beyond the present 10% cap to the extent of shareholding.

The new FDI norms will not apply to PSU banks, where the FDI ceiling is still capped at 20%. Foreign investment in private banks with a joint venture or subsidiary in the insurance sector will be monitored by RBI and the IRDA to ensure that the 26 per cent equity cap applicable for the insurance sector is not breached.

All entities making FDI in private sector banks will be mandatorily required to have credit rating. The increase in foreign investment limit in the banking sector to 74% includes portfolio investment [i.e., foreign institutional investors (FIIs) and non-resident Indians (NRIs)], IPOs, private placement, ADRs or GDRs and acquisition of shares from the existing shareholders. This will be the cap for any increase through an investment subsidiary route as in the case of HSBC-UTI deal. In real terms, the sectoral cap has come down from 98% to 74% as the earlier limit of 49% did not include the 49% stake that FII investors are allowed to hold. That was allowed through the portfolio route as the sector cap for FII investment in the banking sector is was 49%.

Criticism

The scheme has been criticized by many experts from the banking sector as an effort to please voters that has created unnecessary work-burden on the public-sector banks. The opposition party Congress alleged that Mr. Modi was trying to take credit of the financial inclusion scheme started by UPA government and the new yojana had got nothing new. According to the experts, temptations presented by the Prime Minister like zero balance, free insurance and overdraft facility would result in duplication. Many individuals who already have bank accounts may have had accounts created for themselves, lured by the insurance covers and overdraft facilities. As per the scheme, a very few people are eligible to get the life insurance worth Rs.30,000 with a validity of just five years. However, these 'secret' conditions were not shown in the TV advertisements of the scheme. The claimed overdraft facility has been completely left upon the banks. As per the government notice, only those people would get the overdraft facility whose transaction record is satisfactory as per the banks. It is quite unlikely that many people would get this facility as the banks would avoid potential NPAs. The claimed accidental insurance has also proved to be a non-existing scheme as the Rupay card holders have got no legal paper for any such accidental insurance.

CONCLUSION

Financial inclusion not one time efforts, it is an ongoing process. It is a huge project which requires concerted and team efforts from all the stakeholders – the Government, financial institutions, the regulators, the private sector and the community at large. From the sporadic attempts of today dispersed across the nation, it should gather momentum and grow in geometric proportions and develop into a focused and effective movement. If this is to be achieved, it requires the passionate involvement, dedication and commitment of all stake holders. It requires a major mindset change in the minds of every individual involved –citizen, banker, bureaucrat, regulator etc., all, and, therefore, creating awareness at all levels. At the same time, the role of technology in the whole scenario cannot be undermined either. It has to be admitted that today, more than even before, technology plays a vital role in bringing about integration in society of all social and economic classes. Accessibility, affordability, appropriateness and benefits determine how deep financial inclusion penetrates the social fabric of the village. Financial inclusion can empower even the poorest person and bring about a dramatic change in his fate. As observed by expert economists the basic ingredient of overcoming poverty is packed inside each poor person. All we need to do is to help this person to unleash this energy and creativity.... Only place in the world where poverty will exist will be in the museums and no longer in human society." With combined efforts of all the stakeholders, viz., politicians, economists, policy makers, regulators, banks, NGOs and other similar entities, this can be made possible.

REFERENCES

1. Press Information Bureau, Govt. of India. 27 August 2014. Retrieved 28 August 2014."Prime Minister to Launch Pradhan Mantri Jan Dhan Yojana Tomorrow".
2. The Economic Times. Retrieved 28 August 2014. "PM 'Jan Dhan' Yojana launched; aims to open 1.5 crore bank accounts on first day".

3. ET Bureau (28 August 2014) "Modi: Banking for all to end "financial untouchability".
4. www.pmjdy.gov.in/account-statistics-country.aspx.
5. http://www.licindia.in/pages/PMJDY_Guidelines&Features.pdf.
6. http://timesofindia.indiatimes.com/city/pune/Jan-Dhan-Yojana-didnt-add-to-PSU-banks-profits-Union/articleshow/46081367.cms

Off-Site Monitoring and Surveillance (OSMOS) in Banking – A Technological Perspective

D. Maheswara Reddy
Professor of Management, Dr YSR National Institute of Tourism and Hospitality Management.

ABSTRACT

The on-site financial inspection for domestic and foreign banks is based on CAMELS. But after introducing Basel II, the banking supervision was focused much on market discipline, higher levels of transparency. Off-site monitoring and surveillance for banks was instituted by RBI in 1995 and used as a part of crisis management.

As banks are growing in the volume and value across the globe, its supervision and surveillance much matters for their respective central banks. In this context, an attempt is made to understand the integration of off-site monitoring and surveillance (OSMOS) in banking system with technology. This paper focuses on the central bank's supervisory capabilities and its technology. Further it also examines the practices of supervision on the banking system both in terms of on-site and off-sit monitoring and surveillance. It captures some information about the functioning of OSMOS in different countries and explained about different supervisory agencies.

Keywords: *Off-site monitoring, surveillance, on-site inspection, Lotus Notes, early warning system, CAMELS, NPAs, data quality.*

INTRODUCTION

For effective and efficient supervision of banks, the central bank requires both on-site and off-site periodic information. The on-site financial inspection for domestic and foreign banks is based on CAMELS. But after introducing Basel II, the banking supervision was focused much on market discipline, higher levels of transparency. Off-site monitoring and surveillance for banks was instituted by RBI in 1995 and used as a part of crisis management.

The main objective of the any central bank's supervision is to protect the interest of depositors, proper use of technology with efficient system and practices. To achieve these objectives the guidelines are keep on changing in tune with ever changing monetary policies of the central banking. And thereby the banks are forced to move from reactive risk management practices to proactive risk management practices.

OBJECTIVES OF THE STUDY

1. To understand on-site and off-site monitoring of banking system by RBI as supervisor.
2. To understand off-site monitoring of banking system by Central bank in different countries.
3. To know the benefits of off-site monitoring and surveillance (OSMOS) to the banks and RBI.
4. To examine the up gradation of technology in off-site monitoring and surveillance (OSMOS).

ON-SITE AND OFF-SITE MONITORING OF RBI

RBI has the responsibility to supervise over the banks in order to assess their financial and operational conditions and the quality of management. On-site inspection and off-site monitoring are the two important methods to monitoring the entire banking system in the country. On-site inspection is carried out on an annual basis where as off-site monitoring is done normally between two periods of on-site inspection. The main objective of off-site surveillance is to monitor the financial health of the banks.

In USA, on-site monitoring and in New Zealand, off-site monitoring considered as most important.

The Narasimham Committee recommended the setting up of off-site monitoring system to strengthen the financial sector supervision.

BFS was setup to implement the off-site monitoring; to make available the ongoing information about the health of the banks, to capture systematic trends in banking policy initiatives, to better focus on supervisory effort and to identify the banks financial deterioration and act as an early warning system (EWS).

OFF-SITE MONITORING OF CENTRAL BANK IN DIFFERENT COUNTRIES

Off-site surveillance in different countries has evolved over a period of time, depending on the country's financial system and its level of growth and development. Currently the UK, US, France, Singapore and Hong Kong are considered to understand trends in the off-site monitoring.

United States: In the United States FED, Office of the Comptroller of the Currency (OCC) and FDIC are important agencies which monitor and surveillance the banking system.

Office of the Comptroller of the Currency (OCC): The OCC charters, regulates, and supervises all national banks and federal savings associations as well as federal branches and agencies of foreign banks. The OCC is an independent bureau of the U.S. Department of the Treasury. In regulating national banks and federal thrifts, the OCC has the power to:

- Examine the national banks and federal thrifts.
- Approve or deny applications for new charters, branches, capital, or other changes in corporate or banking structure.
- Take supervisory actions against national banks and federal thrifts that do not comply with laws and regulations or that otherwise engage in unsound practices. Remove officers and directors, negotiate agreements to change banking practices, and issue cease and desist orders as well as civil money penalties.
- Issue rules and regulations, legal interpretations, and corporate decisions governing investments, lending, and other practices.

Its mission is to ensure that national banks and federal savings associations operate in a safe and sound manner, provide fair access to financial services, treat customers fairly, and comply with applicable laws and regulations.

In US the supervision is very strong on-site examination. Off-site surveillance process is called The Financial Institutions Monitoring System (FIMS) which supplements the supervision. FIMS is used to track the financial conditions of individual banks and banking organizations between on-site examinations. FIMS also cover the operations of supervision like capital adequacy, asset quality, earnings etc.

FED prepares Uniform Bank Performance Report. This report generated quarterly and covers the important supervisory indicators.

United Kingdoms: In UK the financial system is supervised by the Finical Services Authority and is done mostly with off-site monitoring. On-site work is done by reporting accountants who are specialized in bank audit. The supervisory process is found in three phases; risk assessment phase, tools of supervision phase and risk evaluation phase. Of which the risk based supervisory is dynamic, in that the analyst receives new information throughout the process.

France: In France the off-site monitoring system involves prudential regulation of banks on five parameters like minimum capital and reserves, liquidity, large exposures ratio, solvency ratio and capital adequacy ratio. The supervisory agency is Commission Bancaire which supervises the entire banking system in the France. The bank's compliance with the prescribed guidelines is monitored quarterly and violations are dealt accordingly. The off-site information is supplemented by on-site inspection reports. Actions under off-site surveillance are preventive measures like advising bank management, resorting to on-site inspection and other measures and disciplinary sanctions.

Singapore: Banks supervision in Singapore is the responsibility of Monetary Authority of Singapore (MAS). It has adopted off-site monitoring for continuous banks supervision in the Singapore. Under this system it has prescribed set of returns which are suppose to send to the MAS by all banks monthly, quarterly and annual. Those returns cover; capital adequacy, asset quality, statutory liquidity, connected lending, call money borrowings, negotiable certificates of deposit, balance sheet, large borrowers, profit and loss account, foreign exchange business transacted and loan syndication.

Hong Kong: The Hong Kong Monetary Authority (HKMA) has the responsibility to promote general stability and effective working of the banking system in the Hong Kong. A member of off-site team is supervising a portfolio of banks as a Case Officer. It collects monthly/quarterly prudential off-site returns covering assets and liabilities, profit and loss, capital adequacy, liquidity, large exposures, loan classification, maturity profile of assets and liabilities, foreign exchange position, interest rate risk, country risk, market risks and a certificate of compliance with various requirements under the law. There is a CAMEL rating system in place to trigger discretionary supervision.

OFF-SITE MONITORING AND SURVEILLANCE (OSMOS)

In the efficiency of off-site mentoring, technology played a greater role. As such RBI has introduced OSMOS, the computerized off-site system to monitor banks in 1995. This technology helped the Reserve Bank of India (RBI) to enhance its capability of supervisory role. When OSMOS was set up the technology was 'Lotus Notes'.

Prior to the operational stabilization of OSMOS, the supervisory process of RBI was on financial health of banks dominated by on-site examination this is not given enough information on the financial health of the banks. With the introduction of OSMOS, its process is mixture of both on-site and off-site and has provided the benefits to both banks and RBI.

It helps in proper management information system (MIS), which means sending in prudential reports to RBI. Now-a-days the chairman of a bank carries a set of latest DSB returns to all the meetings and discussions. It helps the banks to compare their performance in lines of CAMELS (i.e. capital adequacy ratio, asset quality, managerial excellence, earnings quality, quality of liquidity and systems) and try to improve on such aspects where they lag behind.

It helps the bank in understanding the report, on will money borrowings, interest charges on advances and paid on deposits, non-performing assets (NPAs), Non-statutory liquidity ratios (SLR) investments of banks, expense ratios of banks periodically.

Benefits to Reserve Bank of India (RBI)

OSMOS act as an early warning signal to the supervisor as the data available on frequent basis it helps in reviewing banking system on a half-yearly basis in the basis of off-side data. It supports policy making.

It provides data for IMF, world bank and other international Rating agencies it help in various of Macro prudential Indicators (MPI) on a half yearly basis. Recently, the furs shifted and from Macro prudential Indicators (MPI) and towards more broad based financial sound indicators (FSI).

Upgradation of Technology

In the year 1995, Department of internal development (DFID) of UK is in need of keeping best international practices in supervision of banking system. As such it appointed Price Water House Coopers, London to conduct or the system requirement study, while SRS study made by UK the RBI agreed to outsource the software for the same.

Benefits derived on amount of the upgraded software which include; Ensure validation of returns with data quality coupled with simple loading process, 150 standard reports enabling bank monitoring division to analyze financial position of banks, Data warehousing component feature was added and using VSAT, the OSMOS data was available to major regional offices to view the data and use the information for holding meaningful discussions with banks.

REFERENCES

1. www.rbi.org
2. http://www.occ.gov

Mobile Banking in India: Challenges and Prospects

K. Aruna and M. Saritha
Assistant Professors, Vaagdevi College of Engineering (Autonomous).

ABSTRACT

Mobile banking certainly seems to be one of the biggest innovations along with CBS (Core Business System) and ATM in the field of banking and this will have a long lasting effect on how banking business is conducted. Automation of some routine work processes in banks in the mid-80's has moved on and resulted in business process re-engineering culminating in making banking services branchless, anytime and anywhere ,facilitated new product development and enabled near real time service delivery. CBS and ATMs have enabled banks to provide banking services 24 × 7 × 365 *but not really helped in expanding their reach to the unbanked or reach to the customer wherever she/he. At the end of January* 2012 *the total wireless subscriber base was* 936 *million out of which,* 313 *million subscribers were from rural areas. Even ATM and Internet banking have their limitations when it comes to penetration in rural areas. Mobile as a technology, which is low cost, ubiquitous and efficient with a potential to enable achievement the goal of deeper financial inclusion, has been recognized across the world. Any system has certain minimum features to attract customers and keep them engaged in the long run, such features are easy of use , safety and security, accessibility and affordability. Mobile Banking meets all these requirements but still the usage is nowhere near its potential.*

Keywords: *Mobile Banking, Information and Communication Technology (ICT), Mobile Network Operation (MNO), Core Banking System (CBS).*

INTRODUCTION

Mobile banking is simply performing bank transactions such as balance checks, account transactions, payment with help of mobile phone. It can also be understood as availing banking and financial services with the help of mobile telecommunication device. The scope of services offered in mobile banking may include getting account information, transferring funds, sending checkbook request managing deposits, taking quick check of transactions and so on. Mobile banking today is most often performed by SMS (Short Message Service) so that is also known as SMS banking. The very feature of mobile banking 'Anytime- Anywhere Banking' is making it very popular among all the categories.

In India traditional branch-based banking remains the most widely adopted method of conducting banking transaction, at same time commercial banks are undergoing a rapid change by the information & telecommunication (ITC) technology. ICICI bank pioneered in mobile banking services in India. Among public banks, Union Bank of India was first to introduce mobile banking (Ali et al. 2010). Today many commercial banks have launched mobile banking using ITC technology and now they can reach out to customers and provide them with not only general information about its services but also the opportunity of performing interactive retail banking transactions anytime, anywhere. Mobile Banking refers to provision and availment of banking and financial services with the help of mobile telecommunication devices. The offered services may include facilities to conduct bank transactions, to administer accounts and to access customized information. In the broader sense mobile banking as that type of execution of financial services in the course of which - within an electronic procedure - the customer uses mobile communication techniques in conjunction with mobile devices (Pousttchi and Schurig2004). Around 1.72 crore people are using mobile banking services in the country and private bank HDFC Bank has the largest number of such customers. As on October 2012, nearly 1.72 crore customers are utilising the Mobile Banking Services among the 42 banks which provide the facility, Finance Minister P. Chidambaram said in a written reply to the Lok Sabha. According to the list, private sector bank HDFC tops with 88.88 lakh customers are using mobile banking services.

OBJECTIVE OF THE STUDY

1. To study the need for mobile banking services in India.
2. To discuss the customised mobile banking products in India.
3. To analysis the current issues in the mobile banking landscape.
4. To draw conclusions from the study of mobile banking services in our country.

In olden day getting draft for outstation payment is cumbersome and clearing used to take a lot of time, outstation cheques would take all the more time, reconciliation and maintaining books by the bank branches would require additional manpower and customers were never satisfied. During the last one decade, things have changed at a rapid pace and all because of technology. The initial steps of tapping technology came in the form of adoption of the core banking systems (CBS) which led to near collapse of geographical location of parent branch. Today most of the customers tapping the technology led internet banking and interconnected ATM network to transact the business desktop PCs became our anytime bank branches. Then came the next revolution – mobile banking which added anywhere to the truly anytime banking. Weaning the customer from physical banking and building customer awareness and confidence in these non face-to-face modes of banking has been a herculean task for the banking industry. In this exciting and challenging journey, the Reserve Bank, as a pro-active regulator, has defined enabling policies and, at times, has goaded the industry in achieving the desired results. The Governments, both at the central and the state levels, have also been taking measures in encouraging electronic payments and receipts, such as, electronic money transfers and e-mode of transactions for their receipts and payments.

NEED FOR MOBILE BANKING

Technology adoption has changed the face of banking in India. What started as a mere automation of some routine work processes in banks in the mid 80's has moved on and resulted in business process re-engineering is making banking services branchless, anytime and anywhere, facilitated new product development and enabled near real time service delivery. Technology helped banks to reach the doorsteps of the customer by overcoming the limitations on geographical/physical reach in branch banking and easing the resource and volume constraints mobile banking will as an important part of the business but also rapidly evolving channel to deliver better customer service, expand product range, retain market-share, enhance revenue, drastically reduce operating expenses and above all remain socially relevant without sacrificing sustainability in ICT based financial inclusion plans.

Mobile banking occupy an important place in banking and in a very short time and is expected to provide much needed platform for taking banking to the unbanked masses. Mobile banking certainly seems to be one of the biggest innovations along with CBS and ATMs in the field of banking and this will have a long lasting effect on how banking business is conducted. CBS and ATMs provided banks the much needed technological fill up to break the shackles of branch banking architecture. CBS and ATMs have enabled banks to provide banking services 24 × 7 × 365 but have not really helped in expanding their reach to the unbanked or reach to the customer wherever he/she is. One tends to concur with the view of many academicians and practioners that this limitation can be overcome to a large extent by leveraging the mobile phone enabled banking or mobile banking. We must see it as the *giant leap* of the banking industry – leveraging technology to promote anytime and anywhere banking and more deeper and sustainable financial inclusion.

GUIDELINES ISSUED BY RBI

Recognizing the potential of mobile banking, Reserve Bank of India issued the first set of guidelines in October 2008. The guidelines defined mobile banking as undertaking banking transactions using mobile phones by bank customers that would involve credit/debits to their accounts. This definition in a sense provided larger canvas to mobile payments which in a narrow sense involved only payment made for a product or service using the mobile phone either remotely or at the point of sale (PoS). These guidelines, which were very broad-based, laid down the technology and security standards pertaining to safety, confidentiality, integrity, authenticity and non-repudiability. As this was a nascent technology and, to build up customer confidence in terms of minimizing frauds, the Reserve Bank mandated that all transactions should be encrypted irrespective of the value. The Reserve Bank also made inter-operability a cornerstone of its policy. After the initial set of guidelines, several policy relaxations have been made to further encourage the use of mobile banking taking into account changing economic environment and feedback of the industry and customers.

Restricted Financial Institutions: The guidelines state that only existing financial institutions and banks are allowed to offer mobile banking. Although the guidelines cover Microfinance Institutions (MFIs). Significient economies of scale cannot be achieved by these due to existing large fixed costs. For a very inexpensive solution, it would have been more effective to allow non-profit organisations or evangelical organizations to build their own MFI without being encumbered by large existing infrastructure.

Rupee Transactions: All transactions must be done only in India's national currency, the rupee. While this may not be a threat in the beginning, this may pose a constraint for interoperability between Indian mobile payments and the world. Also it excludes providers from the lurcative remittance market in India and limits areas from which mobile operators can be profitable.

Existing Account Holders: The guidelines also states that only those have valid account would be allowed mobile banking to the large number of unbanked customers in India.

The growth in mobile banking is rapid but yet to reach the critical mass. It should provide payment services at a cheaper, secure and seamless manner to the existing and potential customers. It is becoming the next wave of financial and technological innovation in banking by universalizing access to banking service without jeopardizing prudential and regulatory framework of the financial sector.

GROWTH OF MOBILE BANKING

In India where a majority of population still lives in rural areas that do not have presence of formal banking and providing banking facility has been a major challenge. Of the 0.6 million villages in India, the total number of villages with banking services through brick and mortar branches and alternate banking channels stands at approximately 0.14 million villages as at end March 2012. India has the highest number of households (approximately 145 million) who are excluded from banking. However, with the growing reach of the mobile, it has now become possible to provide the banking facilities to people who were not able to enjoy this facility so far. At the end of January 2012, the total wireless subscriber base was 936 million out of which, 313 million subscribers were from rural areas. Use of mobile banking services among this huge base of subscribers is, however, very low. Even amongst the existing bank customers less than one percent of them are covered under the mobile banking services. Notwithstanding the existing low base of customers, the growth in mobile banking transactions has shown increasing trend. For example, in the month of June 2012, 3.43 million transactions amounting to `3067.10 million were processed as compared to 1.41 million transactions amounting to `984.66 million processed in June 2011 - an increase of about 143 per cent in volume and approximately 211 per cent in value terms. It is, however, evident that the potential of mobile banking technology is yet to be fully exploited.

State Bank of India (SBI) has witnessed a 46% surge in the mobile-banking space in the 2014, said the bank in a press release on Tuesday. SBI saw 1.25 crore customers transacting via mobile phones in 2014 compared with 85.78 lakh in 2013, said the release.

According to RBI data, fiscal 2012-13 saw 22.5 million mobile banking users, witnessing a growth of 73.69% compared with 2011-2012. The volume in 2012-13 also rose 108.53% y-o-y. State Bank of India chairman Arundhati Bhattacharya said, “India has just witnessed the launch of message-banking. We are confident once this is understood by the people, there will be an explosion of banking activities in the mobile space. This is what the future of banking holds.”

In 2014, SBI saw about 70% of the customers from non-metro cities, according to the release. The average transaction per customer was Rs 7,052, which emphasises that more retail customers are using the mobile banking facility, it added.

“At present, customers can access the bank through State Bank Anywhere — the bank’s smart phone app which is integrated with internet banking. The service which is expected to be used by the masses is State Bank Freedom, which can be accessed by all phones,” the release noted. “Mobile banking will also play a larger role in the yet-to-be-launched payment banks with which SBI plans to have tie-ups,” Bhattacharya said.

Mobile banking is considered a significant step towards furthering financial inclusion given the vast telecom network in the country. At a recent banking retreat held in Pune, bankers had discussed digitising top 30 processes and also deepening the mobile banking penetration.

MODELS OF MOBILE BANKING

Models of branchless banking can be classified into three categories. They are explained as follows.

1. Bank-focused model: The bank-focused model emerges when a traditional bank uses non-traditional low cost delivery channels to provide banking services to its existing customers.
2. Bank-led model: The bank-led model offers a distinct alternative to conventional branch-based banking in that customer conducts financial transactions at a whole range of retail agents (or through mobile phone) instead of at bank branches or through bank employees.
3. Non Bank-led model: The non bank-led model is where a bank does not come into the picture (except possibly as a safe-keeper of surplus funds) and the non-bank (e.g. Telco) Performs.

Why a Bank Led Model?

Mobile as a technology, which is low-cost, ubiquitous and efficient with a potential to enable achievement the goal of deeper financial inclusion, has been recognized across the world. Different countries are following different mobile banking models depending upon their requirements and availability of infrastructure. Vision of financial inclusion, provision of payment services is one amongst the four services that we have clubbed under financial inclusion viz., a deposit product, a credit product, a micro-insurance product and a remittance product. Given this orientation, we would all agree that only banks can provide these services while adhering to the KYC/AML requirements. Accordingly, the Reserve Bank of India has consciously adopted the bank-led mobile banking model. The bank led model has also been endorsed by the Inter-Ministerial Group of the Government of India constituted in November, 2009. There are, however, counter-views within the country and internationally as well suggesting that the non-bank led mobile banking model that have been found to be very successful elsewhere should be tried out here. It is often not appreciated when citing these success stories that only one service, i.e., a remittance product, is being offered and not the complete bouquet of financial services envisaged. The other three products identified under financial inclusion can obviously not be offered by a non-bank. Moreover, particular environments in a few countries enabled the non-bank led model to be successful viz. presence of a monopoly operator, very poor banking infrastructure and availability of a national identification number. Is it not surprising that the same success story has not been repeated by the same service operator in a neighbouring country?

Cross Border Remittance through Mobile Banking

Reserve Bank has allowed only few banks and authorized entities to undertake such cross-border transactions. To obviate any operational difficulty in remitting and receiving funds, bank account-to-bank account cross-boarder remittance has been permitted under the money transfer service scheme (MTSS). Realizing the need for facilitating hassle-free withdrawal of funds at the beneficiary end, Reserve Bank has also permitted transfer of funds to the beneficiary's account or to a pre-paid instrument (PPI) issued by banks which could be m-wallet also. The underlying rationale is to ensure flow of cross boarder funds through the banking channel only irrespective of the media, (which could also be mobile sets) opted for undertaking the transactions.

Grievance Redressal Mechanism

The most often faced problem in mobile banking is as to who owns the customer – the mobile network operator (MNO) or the bank? Whom shall the customer contact in case of any service related grievance? Who is required to resolve the issue? Since India has accepted the bank-led mobile banking model, the customers of the banks get full protection for effecting transactions through this delivery channel as in the case of any other banking transaction. Reserve Bank lays particular emphasis on its continuing pursuit of customer satisfaction and protection and timely resolution of complaints. Accordingly, the customers using mobile banking have recourse to the Banking Ombudsman's customer complaint redressal machinery.

Role of MNOs as Technology Service Provider (TSP)

The MNOs are expected to play the role of a technology service provider while banks are expected to provide banking services. Both the stakeholders should work together to take banking through the medium of the mobile to the masses. The customer vetting including compliance with KYC norms, customer protection, etc., should remain within the domain of the banking sector. It is heartening to note that this unique approach is taking roots with a couple of successful collaborations between banks and MNOs.

Role of MNOs as TSP–cum-BC

You may all be aware that 'for-profit' companies can now be engaged as BCs by banks. This provides another avenue to the MNOs for tapping their reach in taking banking to the masses. MNOs are particularly well placed to make use of this opportunity to become the BCs of banks keeping in view the fact that mobile phones have become ubiquitous. It is glad to note that a few MNOs have indeed become BCs of some banks. It is sure that the nascent strides being taken in this regard are likely to fructify into major achievements soon. Such collaborations between the banks and the MNOs enables each of them to exclusively perform their respective designated roles – as bankers and service providers. Reserve Bank expects that these experiments get up scaled and across the spectrum and result in a win-win partnership for both the parties, leveraging their respective capabilities and reach.

Tapping USSD to Expand access to Mobile Banking Services

The common USSD platform is offered by all MNOs, the same is expected to lead to an exponential growth of transactions in the IMPS. Simultaneously, the IMPS platform for person-to-business (P2B) transactions (i.e., in the merchant transactions) has now been enabled. Along with it, person-to-person (P2P) remittances can now be made to beneficiaries based on their bank account number or *Aadhaar* number which is mapped to the mobile number of the beneficiary. The requirement of MMID at the beneficiary end, therefore, becomes optional. Further, the non-bank entities like the Pre-Paid Instruments (PPI) issuers have been permitted to join the IMPS network through a sponsor bank for facilitating domestic money transfers. All these measures should lead to an increase in transactions and should significantly contribute to the revenue streams of the MNOs also. With this enabling technology within reach of the stakeholders, they need to work together in a co-operative and collaborative manner to promote and popularize this unique product.

Permitting Cash-out in Mobile Wallets

The mobile wallet is a pre-paid instrument (PPI) issued in electronic form which resides on the mobile phone. The potential of PPIs including mobile wallets, Reserve Bank of India has laid down an enabling regulatory framework for such instruments. Simply put, the mobile wallets being issued in India are e-money products and can be used for purchase of goods & services. Mobile wallets can also be used for funds transfers where the holder has been subjected to a fully compliant KYC. The only difference in mobile wallets issued by non-banks in India and other countries is that cash-out is not permitted in India as it is akin to acceptance of demand deposit. The rationale behind the decision is based on the fact that non-banks are not permitted to accept deposits for maturity less than one year.

Security and Acceptability Issues

Any system has to have certain minimum features to attract customers and keep them engaged in the long run, such features are: ease of use, safety and security, accessibility and affordability. Mobile banking meets all these requirements but still the usage is nowhere near its potential. In the case of mobile banking, which is a novel product, the customer needs to be assured that it would provide her with the same kind of comfort levels that any other payment mechanism currently makes available. Comfort can be derived by the customers when they are able to put through transactions with ease with a zero-fail rate and not have any concerns regarding security issues. Customers should also be made aware as to whom they should approach in case of a failed transaction and how speedily their grievances are redressed. This is where a lot of work needs to be done to make the public aware of customer friendly as also safety features of mobile banking and engage the customers for a long term relationship. It would also like to inform that recently, the Institute for Development & Research in Banking Technology (IDRBT), established by the Reserve Bank of India launched the Mobile Banking Security Lab (MBSL). The Lab aims at exploring and providing solutions to the much needed safety, security, reliability and inter-operability, for both on low end and high-end mobile sets. The Lab will also provide the benefit of a common technical centre for all banks and financial institutions. The testing platform of the Lab would help the banks to test their security applications in mobile banking. The Lab will also help in providing education services on security related matters in all Indian language enabling awareness creation amongst the users.

Quality of Service – Issue of Sustainable Excellence

TRAI has come out with the "Mobile Banking (Quality of Service) Regulations 2012" specifying the standards for MNOs while facilitating mobile banking which will go a long way in further improving the mobile banking services in the country. The MNOs should strive towards meeting these service standards to the banks to enable the customers to enjoy customer friendly banking services.

Engaged Employees

Role of employees in driving any business to reach a critical mass is the most important but the least understood issue. The role of BCs or agents, who are being deployed by banks to expand their reach, is, equally important as they represent the banks to the common man and are going to lay down the foundation of bank-customer relationship. It is being assumed that technology will take care of every aspect of banking as most of the processes are being automated. While this is true to a certain extent, it is the combination of frontline human-resources and front-end of technology which acts as the catalyst for service delivery in a nation like India. Employees are expected to help customers to move from being 'assisted' initially to becoming 'self-reliant' in use of banking related technologies including mobile banking. For the employees to hand-hold the customers, they themselves should be fully conversant with the product. Thus, for mobile banking to grow, the employees would have to strive towards improving customer service, enhancing customer satisfaction and removing any apprehensions regarding the safety and security of mobile banking transactions.

CHALLENGES OF MOBILE BANKING

Security Problem

The security mechanism adopted by the banks face many security issues like being attacked by un-authorized users is of highest prets stolen, proirity in terms of security. If the device gets stolen them un-authorized persons may find the password fovour saved files. Many customers save their password in their mobile. Uneducated persons are less aware of these issues and thus leading to loss of trust by customers

Virus attacks in Mobile Banking

There are 50,000 different types of computer viruses and trojans safe targeted mobile users. Zrus is commonly used to steal mobile transactions no of password.

Confidential Information

The biggest challenge for mobile banking services is security. In the past survays the same has been generalized as the biggest challenges for internet banking also. Security gere simply means that nobody else can know the confidential information of customer's bank account.

Performance

Mobile banking is anytime and anywhere so that needs to ensure that their systems remain ready for the same. As customers will find mobile banking more and more useful, their expectations will increase. If the banks will be unable to meet the performance and they may lose customer confidence.

Official Language

India has 18 official languages which are spoken across the country. The state governments also are dictated to correspond in their regional language for official purposes. Additionally two thirds of the population in India is illiterate, creating difficulties in deployment of mobile banking solutions. For Indian mobile banking, this will be cumbersome to overcome.

Valid Bank Account

The guidelines of RBI states that only those having a valid bank account would be allowed mobile banking. This limits the full potential of mobile banking to extend micro credit and bring banking to the large number of unbanked customers in India.

PROSPECTS OF MOBILE BANKING

1. Round the clock availability and ease of transactions attracts customers to Mobile Banking in India.
2. Through Mobile messaging and other such interfaces, banks provide value added services to the customer at marginal costs.
3. The main characteristics of mobile banking is anywhere/any time banking.
4. In India 60% of mobile banking transactions account balances, this is a significant step in building consumer trust.
5. According to the study by SBI maintaining a conventional rural bank branch cost Rs.5,00,000 per year in salaries alone which would need about Rs.20 million in deposits to sustain that at a break even point. A typical Indian village with population of 2000 can't support a conventional bank branch. Mobile banking may be the only viable method to extend banking services to rural areas in India.

SERVICES OFFERED BY MOBILE BANKING

1. Mobile banking services includes account information of mini statement and checking of account history, alerts on account activity or passing of set thresholds, monitoring of term deposits, access to loan statements, access to card statements, mutual funds/equity statements, insurance policy management and pension plan management.
2. Payments & Transfers includes domestic and international fund transfers, micro-payment handling, mobile complaint submission and recharging, commercial payment processing and bill payment processing.
3. Investments include portfolio management services, real-stock quotes and bill payment processing.
4. Supporting service includes status of requests for credit, including mortgage approval, insurance coverage, cheque book and card requests, exchange of data messages and email, including tracking, credit card balance.
5. Content services are general information such as weather updates news, loyalty-related offers and location based services.
6. Push based mobile banking services includes credit/debit alerts, minimum balance alerts and bill payment alerts. Pull based mobile banking services of transaction based are fund transfer, bill payment and other financial services like shares trading and enquiry based services includes account balance enquiry, account statement enquiry, cheque book requests and recent transaction history.

CONCLUSIONS

The future Mobile banking depends on efforts of all concerned parties – the service providers, service facilitators, regulatory system and customers. In India 52 banks have started mobile banking for their customers and, of them, only a few have achieved sufficient traction in mobile banking transactions. This need to be reviewed by each individual bank at the corporate level and strategy should be worked out to operationalise mobile banking to reap all its benefits. Banks need also have to be proactive in up scaling their mobile banking products and services if they have to safeguard their traditional advantage in the payment system and leverage it to expand their customer base including the tech-savvy, Educating users and potential users, particularly through engaged employees, remains a challenge in the sphere of mobile banking which is true for any new technology based service offering. All the stakeholders need to put in concerted and sustained efforts in spreading awareness about the benefits of mobile banking. Reserve Bank would be happy to collaborate with banks and the Indian Banks' Association (IBA) as part of its e-BAT (electronic Banking Awareness and Training) initiatives to spread retail e-payment awareness. Simulation/training camps, town-hall events and reaching out to schools and colleges across the nation to 'catch them young.' It is expected that these initiatives will bring awareness of the various technology payment products including the mobile banking and the ease with which they can be used to encourage the use of non-cash payment products. Mobile banking has a great potential. But it is at the initial stage of this development. It should be the earnest endeavor of all the stakeholders - banks, MNOs, technology vendors, NPCI, Reserve Bank, Government of India, IBA, industry associations like the FICCI, and, of course, the customers to make mobile banking as ubiquitous as the mobile itself. It is for us to harness this potential to achieve the objective of reaching to the customer wherever he/she is, deepening the financial inclusion supported by low cost, secured ICT based mobile banking model and moving towards a less-cash society.

REFERENCES

1. Address delivered by Shri Harun R. Khan, Deputy Governor, Reserve Bank of India, at the FICCI-IBA (FIBAC) 2012 Conference.
2. Banzal S. (2010), "Mobile Banking & M–Commerce and Related Issues".
3. Barnes, S.J., Corbitt, B. (2003), "Mobile banking: concept and potential", *International Journal of Mobile Communications*, 1 (3), 273-288.
4. Black, N. J., Lockett, A., Ennew, C., Winklhofer, H. & McKechnie, S. (2002), "Modelling consumer choice of distribution channels: an illustration from financial services", *International Journal of Bank Marketing*, 20 (4), 161-173.

A Study on Revolution in Indian Banking Industry Transforming Life of Millions

Balki Vani
Assistant Professor
CUK

ABSTRACT

Banking in India is as old as its trade and commerce. It had developed good social organization. Manu, the great Hindu law-giver of ancient India had dealt with law relating to deposits and money lending. The operations of the then bankers comprised of accepting deposits, advancing money against pledge of goods, securities as well as mortgages, granting personal loans, acting as bankers for King or the Government, as custodian for valuables and sometimes even managing currency of State.

The banks play an important role in the economic life of the country. At present, their importance can be understood by the fact that the failure of one big bank can shake the roots of the whole global economy, and can bring in major recession in the world. As in 2008, the collapse of Lehman Brothers, caused the recession worldwide. Its consequences are still not over.

In the pre-banking era, the people used to depend upon the money lenders to serve their needs of money and were often exploited by them. When the banks came into existence, it facilitated the exchange of money and trade and promoted the welfare of society. In traditional banking, much of the operations of the banking industry were manually operated. There was large amount of human intervention. Manual registers and pages using dot matrix printer were used for storing record. As it is said "To err is human", so the system was prone to error. It was prone to manual errors.

As the systems were not unified, integration of data across the nation was also an issue. So the data collected at HO level was not consistent, which also affected their decision making ability. Earlier the customer was restricted to his branch. The customer had to face restrictions on operations of his account even with same bank but at different branch. So in a way customer was disabled. Different processes were followed at different branches of the same bank. It lacked standardization of procedures.

Keywords: *Banking System, Human Intervention, Economic Life.*

OBJECTIVES OF THE STUDY

1. To study the situations of pre-banking era.
2. To anlyse the growth and importance of Banking sector.
3. To understand the impact of banking sector on Economic system.
4. To suggest better methods for future growth of banking sector.

LITERATURE REVIEW

Even if the bank wanted to introduce a change in a particular process, then to implement it at a national level it was very difficult. With such banking technology data analysis or business intelligence was very limited. Neither the bank could gather right information nor was it able to make optimal use of existing data. This severely hampered the banking business as a whole. Going to bank was like an item of agenda for people. Even for deposit or withdrawal of money, a lot of customer's time was spent.

Then came the Liberalization era in the early 1990s, the then Narasimha Rao government embarked on a policy of liberalisation and gave licences to a small number of private banks, which came to be known as New Generation tech-savvy banks. With IT revolution around the globe, it entered into banking domain as well. Banking is the lifeblood of any country's financial system. With the traditional system in place, need of the hour was to infuse technology in banking.

However, it will be a little while before small businesses and households can access their services as these 11 payments banks are expected to take off by only by February 2017. A major advantage is that payments banks will lead to elimination of cash transactions among low-income households. "Currently 90 per cent of transactions are in cash and are estimated to be of multiple trillions, we believe there is a huge opportunity for payments banks to power these transactions electronically," said Rishi Gupta, MD and CEO, Fino PayTech.

Nachiket Mor panel which proposed the concept of payments banks said this design is functionally equivalent to a recently introduced class of companies called pre-paid instrument providers (PPIs) that are permitted to receive cash deposits from customers, store them in a digital "wallet", and allow customers to pay for goods and services from their digital "wallet". The financial sector is witnessing a revolution in the mobile wallet segment and over three dozen companies are operating in India.

While such PPI companies are currently permitted to accept a maximum amount of Rs 50,000 in their "wallet" from their customers and are required to maintain an escrow account with a scheduled commercial bank where these aggregate amounts received from customers are credited immediately upon receipt, payments banks can do all these services at their level. Given significant concerns with the current PPI model with respect to the know your customer (KYC) aspect, inability to pay interest on balances, and contagion risk; and taking into account the need to urgently provide access to payment services and deposit products to millions of individuals, the committee recommends that a set of payments banks may be licensed under the Banking Regulation Act.

FACTORS PROMOTING GROWTH OF BANKING AND FINANCIAL SERVICES

The Banking Laws (Amendment) Bill that was passed by the Parliament in 2012 allowed the Reserve Bank of India (RBI) to make final guidelines on issuing new bank licenses. Moreover, the role of the Indian Government in expanding the banking sector is noteworthy. It is expected that the new guidelines issued by RBI will curb practices of impish borrowers and streamline the loan system in the country. In the coming time, India could see a rise in the number of banks in the country, a shift in the style of operation, which could also evolve by incorporating modern technology in the industry.

Another emerging trend witnessed by the banking sector is the use of social media platform like Facebook to attract customers. In September 2013 ICICI bank launched a Facebook bill payment and fund transfer service called 'Pockets' for customer convenience.

According to a report by Zinnov, a Globalization and Market Expansion firm, 'IT adoption in BSFI sector in India', the Information Technology Industry spend in BFSI vertical is expected to reach USD 3.5 billion by Financial Year 2014. The study also highlighted 'the growing maturity of Indian BFSI organizations in IT adoption, as technology is seen as a driver of business value. Technology firms have great potential to explore in the BFSI sector, which contributes to eight per cent of India's Gross Domestic Product.'

A NEW ERA

IT in Banking

Remember the days when people used to stand in long lines to withdraw money or when a cheque deposited took a week to get credited to your account. The banking industry has traveled a long way from there and all this has been possible due to use of information technology in banks. Information and communication technology has brought a transformational change in banking operations and payment systems in banks.

Banks have benefited a lot by this in terms of reduction in operational costs and efficiency improvement. But the primary beneficiaries of this have been the bank's customers. Some of the transformations brought about by inclusion of IT and how it has benefited the bank's customers are depicted below:-

(a) Core Banking Solution (CBS): A comprehensive, integrated-yet-modular core banking solution, can cater to bank's needs and multiple business segments. With Core Banking Solution, banks can effectively meet challenges of reducing operational cost and establishing customer intimacy. It can enable bank to reduce the time to market for new products, thereby staying ahead in the competition, and fulfilling compliance mandates. Banks can also manage higher transaction volumes and increased customer expectations, with ease.

CBS integration completely revolutionized the way banks operate. It has automated all core banking operations such as recording of transactions, passbook maintenance, interest calculations on loans and deposits, customer records, balance of payments and withdrawal. Customers can deposit or withdraw money from any of the bank branch all over the country. This saves a lot of time and cost for both the bank and the customer.

(b) Automated teller Machines: Earlier people had to visit branches to withdraw money or at the time of emergency at night or holidays, they had to rely on others for money. But now with the huge network of ATMs there is no need for the customers to visit the bank branches and stand in long queues to withdraw or deposit money. They just have to visit any nearby ATM (of any bank), swipe their card and withdraw money within seconds.

(c) Smart Cards: It is popularly known as plastic money. These pocket sized integrated circuit embedded cards have eliminated the need for paper money. People need not to carry loads of cash in their pocket, they can shop by swiping their card and the money automatically gets debited from their account.

(d) Internet Banking: It has eliminated the need to visit bank branch to a great extent. Just sit in the comfort of your house and customers can perform any banking transaction they want to perform. Checking account statements, transferring money, paying bills etc everything has been made possible at a click of a mouse.

MICR and automated cheque clearing - Magnetic ink character recognition (MICR) allows computers to read the number printed on the cheque. This expedited cheque clearing process to a great extent and also eliminated human errors. Now with the introduction of automated cheque clearing and cheque truncation system (CTS) the need for physical cheques is completely eliminated. Cheques can be scanned and converted to electronic form. This saved the time required to transfer cheques from one city to other and reduced the cheque clearing time from 3 days to 1 day.

(e) Mobile banking: This has further increased the ease for a bank's customer. Now the customer does not require a pc or laptop to get in connection with his bank. He can perform all banking transactions via a mobile device kept in his pocket.

(f) Banking the unbanked: Information technology is also playing a key role in financial inclusion. Financial institutions such as FINO make use of technology for acquiring customers in rural areas. Fino's banking correspondents move with hand held devices in rural areas and enable transactions at customer doorstep. This proves to be a lot of ease for customer and also reduces cost of transaction for bank, a transaction that costs $1 at a bank branch costs only 40 cents using FINO's banking correspondent model. Technology has also helped in improving the operational efficiencies in government facilities such as PDS, NREGA and RSBY.

(g) RFID in Banks: The latest trend in the banking industry is the usage of RFID technology for the better customer relationship management. New tech savvy banks like YES bank, use this technology for its customers so that it can give a personal touch to its customers when they enter its premises.

The RFID enabled chips in mobiles of customers help them to pay at shopping centres just by waving their mobiles in front of contactless readers. The money is directly debited from their accounts.

RESEARCH DATA

(a) With the potential to become the fifth largest banking industry in the world by 2020 and third largest by 2025 according to KPMG-CII report, India's banking and financial sector is expanding rapidly. The Indian Banking industry is currently worth Rs. 81 trillion (US $ 1.31 trillion) and banks are now utilizing the latest technologies like internet and mobile devices to carry out transactions and communicate with the masses.

The Indian banking sector consists of 26 public sector banks, 20 private sector banks and 43 foreign banks along with 61 regional rural banks (RRBs) and more than 90,000 credit cooperatives.

(b) **Recruitment Trends in BSFI Industry:** The Banking and Financial Services Industry is expected to recruit about 8.4 million people as per the growth rate each year. BSFI workforce requirement between 2008 and 2022 is expected to be about 4.2 million and sector may create up to 20 lakh new jobs in the next 5-10 years.

Advantaged by issuance of new licences and efforts being made by the RBI and the Government to expand financial services into rural areas, the hiring trend may further get a boost from the public sector banks. Since most banking workforce is scheduled to retire in the times to come, they would be in dire need of fresh talent. According Randstad India, global HR service provider in India, the banking sector will generate 7-10 lakh jobs in the coming decade and the sector would be the among top job creators in 2014.

According to Human Resource and Skill Requirements in the Banking, Financial Services & Insurance Sector (2022) report, apart from the on-rolls employment there is significant contractual employment across all the above segments through various financial positions such as Direct Selling Agents (DSA's), Insurance agents, Mutual Fund Advisors, etc.

(c) **Challenges in BFSI:** The major challenge faced by the Indian Banking and Financial sector is that the level of financial exclusion in India is alarming and there is an urgent need to find a plausible solution to the same. The IBA–BCG survey of banks revealed that the level of confidence in finding profitable solutions for financial inclusion is not very high. Financial inclusion has solely been the responsibility of public banks up until now, but by using inclusive growth as one of the criteria for new licences (new banks have to open 25 per cent of their branches in rural areas); the RBI will have made the new private sector banks responsible as well. Currently, public sector banks have more branches than any other bank group in the rural and semi-urban areas.

The RBI has encouraged voluntary consolidation in the past but to no avail. India critically needs at least 3 to 4 large banks that are globally competitive and can meet the growing demands for cross-border acquisitions by the Indian corporate and take on larger ticket risks on their balance sheets without hitting limits ceilings. As per The Banker in 2012, there is no Indian bank in the top 10 amongst the list of top 1000 banks of the world, whereas China has 4 banks in the top 10 list.

In fact, Chinese banking giant–ICBC, occupies the third rank on the top 1000 banks of the world, while Indian banking giant–State Bank of India ranks at a low 60. Given the fact that over 70 percent of the market is dominated by PSBs, the Government of India and the RBI will have to drive consolidation amongst the large PSBs to create 'large banks' by mandating the merger of identified banks. This will be a significant departure from the previously stated non-interventionist policy of the finance ministry and the RBI, and as expected, will require great political will power and many levels of dispute resolution models.

The banking and insurance industry is challenged by competitive pressures, changes in customer loyalty, stringent regulatory environment and entry of new players, all of which are pressuring the organizations to adopt new business models, streamline operations and improve processes.

ROAD AHEAD

An IBA-FICCI-BCG report suggests that India's gross domestic product (GDP) growth will make the Indian banking industry the third largest in the world by 2025. According to the report, the domestic banking industry is set for an exponential growth in coming years with its assets size poised to touch USD 28,500 billion by the turn of the 2025. With the deposits growing at a CAGR of 21.2 per cent (in terms of INR) in the period FY 06–13, there has been evident growth in the overall industry.

This growth can be attributed to banks shifting focus to client servicing. Public as well as private sector banks are underlining the importance of technology infrastructure, in order to improve customer experience and gain a competitive edge. Utilizing the popularity of internet and mobile banking, banks are increasingly adopting an integrated approach for asset–liability match, credit and derivatives risk management.

*By **Resham Ber***

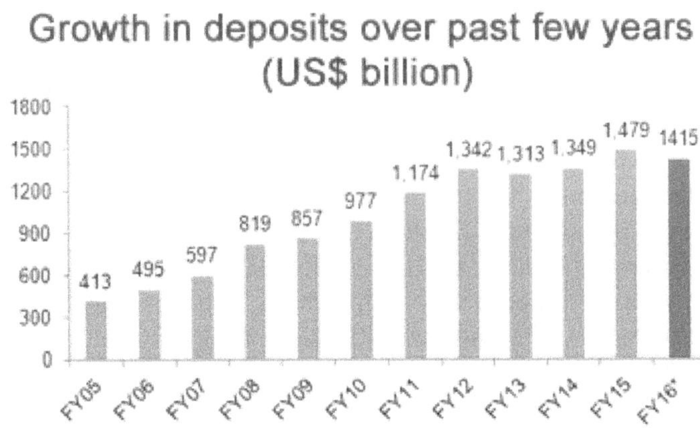

Source: Reserve Bank of India (RBI), TechSci Research ,
FY16*- till May 29

Raising capital for public sector banks (PSBs) — Yes, it could be a problem in the future!

As per KPMG in India's analysis, capital requirements of public sector banks in the future will be based on three assumptions:

- GDP growth rate of 6-7 percent that will require credit growth of 20 percent
- Basel III norms applicable to higher risk assets that banks will have to develop in the future (Micro small and medium enterprises (MSME), retail)
- Government ownership in the range of 50-60 percent. Assuming an annual credit growth rate from FY12-FY21 at 20 percent and the annual risk weighted asset growth rate at 22 percent, we expect the Tier-I capital requirement for public sector banks for the same period to be in the range of INR 9,60,000 crore1. Given our current fiscal deficit, government may not be able to infuse additional capital in public sector banks.

Also, the government's intent to not dilute their stake leaves them with few options:

- The Government could consider creating a holding company (Holdco) and transfer its stake in the PSBs to this company. The Holdco can raise long term debt from domestic and international markets to infuse equity in the PSBs and act as an investment company for the Government of India.
- The Government could consider diluting its stake in PSBs through issuance of Differential Voting Rights (DVR) such that the economic stake dilution is also kept to the minimum. The Government could avoid any dilution in its voting rights by first infusing money into the banks through issuance of normal shares to itself, which would raise its stake during the interim period, and follow this up with DVR issuance to the extent that its effective (voting rights) holding remains unchanged. The money can be infused either through preferential allotment of equity shares or through allotment of warrants.
- The Government may consider in the future on having a Golden share in each of the PSBs under which while the Government's economic and voting stake may fall below 51 percent, it will always have the right to control the respective PSBs due to the possession of this Golden share.

M&A in PSBs will be a reality only when the Reserve Bank of India (RBI) intervenes Expect competition from foreign banks as they acquire 'near national treatment'. Can two healthy public sector banks voluntarily merge to create a large bank? Considering the past record, no! Most of the mergers in the past have been either through the acquisition of a small or regional bank by a large private bank (such as the acquisition of Centurion Bank of Punjab by HDFC Bank 2 or the Bank of Madura by ICICI Bank 3), or through the RBI managed process of a forced amalgamation of a potentially failing bank into a strong bank (such as the post-moratorium amalgamation of GTB Bank with Oriental Bank of Commerce4 or the acquisition of Bank of Rajasthan by ICICI Bank5).

One of the most critical challenges of any mandated merger will be linked to the integration of the two teams in the merged entity. Efficiency gains will only accrue if the branch and skills overlaps of banks being merged are resolved amicably – both of which will severely test the relationship with strong trade unions and the working environment with bank staff competing to retain their jobs. Thus to achieve any consolidation, the Government and the RBI will have to strengthen their resolve to manage these tricky and politically sensitive issues. The RBI announcement of a roadmap for seeking the conversion of systemically important foreign banks to 'Wholly-Owned Subsidiary (WOS)' was to have a better regulatory control over such banks, separation of ownership and management, clear and simple resolution in the event of bankruptcy and ring fencing of the capital within the country.

In simple terms, the overall idea was to protect the tax-payer's money being used as bail-out as was witnessed post-2008 when some of the foreign banks withdrew funds from India. The foreign banks operating in India with large networks would be keen to convert to WOS if they get national treatment in terms of opening branches in metros and tier-II cities and not just to expand branch network within the context of RBI regulations. Foreign banks are also circumspect about adopting this route as the RBI has insisted that foreign banks should meet the priority sector lending (PSL) norms including the sub-targets (not portfolio buys) in direct agriculture and small scale enterprises (SSE) lending.

The 'rising middle class' will account for close to one third of the population in the next 20 years Middle class consumers are prominent drivers of growth and consumption in India due to their increasing disposable income. A report by National Council for Applied Economic Research's (NCAER) Centre for Macro Consumer Research indicates that by 2015-16, India will be a country of 53.3 million middle class households, translating into 267 million people. NCAER defines Indian middle class as the one with income level between INR 3.4 lakh-17 lakh at 2009-10 level.

Investment in banking products may not be the default choice for the middle class While a rise in consumption is a given, all savings and investments going to banks is not. Banks would have to strive hard to attract deposits in the future as the rising segment opens up to other avenues for savings and investments such as mutual funds, insurance, real-estate and commodities. Statistics by the Reserve Bank of India (RBI) indicate that the share of claims on the government, which largely reflects small savings, that had picked up over the years, particularly during the first half of 2000s, declined during the second half largely in response to the unchanged (administered) interest rates on small savings since 2003-04. In fact, households disinvested their holdings of Small Savings during 2007-08 and 2008-09.

DATA INTREPRETATION

Global growth did not recover as expected across most major developed and rapid-growth economies in 2013-14. During the year gone by, the central bankers across the globe took decisive steps to restore confidence in markets and broader economy. In Europe, the banking situation improved in part due to the long-term refinancing operations of the European Central Bank (ECB), which helped ensure there was plenty of liquidity in the system. In the US, the picture was more upbeat but still mixed. And although businesses and consumers started to borrow again, credit growth remained tepid. The global economic environment broadly strengthened, and is expected to improve further, with much of the growth impetus emanating from advanced economies. There was acute financial volatility in emerging market economies, and increases in the cost of capital which dampened investments and weighed on growth.

- The banking sector, being the barometer of the economy, is reflective of the macro-economic variables. While the Indian economy is yet to catch strength, the Indian banking system continues to deal with improvement in asset quality, execution of prudent risk management practices and capital adequacy.
- The Reserve Bank of India (RBI) maintained a status quo in interest rate since January 2014. However, despite the retail inflation softening in recent periods, it'll be a little while before the Central Bank would opt for rate cut.
- Indian banking industry, with total asset size of Rs 81 trillion (USD 1.34 trillion), is expanding continuously but on a cautious note. The fact that the industry is plagued by bad loans, the lenders have chosen to go slow in terms of credit off take. Fiscal 2014 saw a combination of various external and internal events that kept markets turbulent, interest rates high and investor confidence low, resulting in shrinking investment and GDP growth.

KEY POINTS

Supply	Liquidity is controlled by the Reserve Bank of India (RBI).
Demand	India is a growing economy and demand for credit is high though it could be cyclical.
Barriers to entry	Licensing requirement, investment in technology and branch network, capital and regulatory requirements.
Bargaining power of suppliers	High during periods of tight liquidity. Trade unions in public sector banks can be anti reforms and orchestrate strikes. Depositors may invest elsewhere if interest rates fall.
Bargaining power of customers	For good creditworthy borrowers bargaining power is high due to the availability of large number of banks.
Competition	High- There are public sector banks, private sector and foreign banks along with non banking finance companies competing in similar business segments. Plus the RBI is all set to issue new banking licenses soon.

PROSPECTS

While the medium term prospects point towards an improving growth scenario, given the improved macroeconomic fundamentals it is highly likely that there will only be a modest economic recovery in FY15.

- That said, the Indian economy is now on the threshold of a major transformation, with expectations of policy initiatives by the change in guard at the Centre. Positive business sentiments, improved consumer confidence and more controlled inflation should help boost the economic growth. With a new and stable Government in place now, a clear revival in the investment climate is sure to come. Higher spending on infrastructure, speedy implementation of projects and continuation of reforms will provide further impetus to growth. A moderate recovery is likely to be seen in FY15 and the real GDP is expected to grow by 5.3%-5.5%. While the CPI inflation is expected to remain an important challenge for India, it should witness a downward trajectory during the major part of FY15
- The worst seems to be over for the Indian banking industry, as there will be increased clarity on macroeconomic and political fronts during FY15. On the positive side, liquidity remains steady, inflation is expected to move downwards for the major part of FY15 and the RBI is in full control to manage any volatility. Macroeconomic improvements and potential for post-election reforms should see a gradual reduction in stressed loans on lower slippages and higher recoveries. Recovery in macroeconomic environment and expected revival in economic growth will help to mitigate risks and resolve problems of asset quality.
- Not just that, the banking industry may see more participants and greater healthy competition. Two new banks have already received licences from the RBI i.e. IDFC and Bandhan Group, which apart from providing impetus to financial inclusion, is expected to intensify competition in the banking sector in the medium term. In addition, by postponing the implementation of Basel III capital norm by one year, RBI has given some breathing

space to banks struggling with stressed margins and lower profitability on account of increase in NPAs. The RBI's new norms will further encourage banks to identify potential bad loans and take corrective actions.

- The overall credit growth may revive marginally at 14-15% in FY15; private sector banks may continue to outpace PSBs in credit growth. Overall (PSBs + private banks) gross NPAs could remain at 4-4.2% by FY15 as against 3.9% in FY14.
- Banks need to raise capital of Rs. 1.8-2 trillion over the next two years (FY15-FY16); of which 45-50% may be issued in the form of additional Tier 1, 35-40 % through Tier II and balance through common equity. However, if there are no seekers for additional Tier 1 capital instruments, Indian banks may need to mop up Rs. 1-1.3 trillion common equity capital over the next two years as mentioned by a rating agency report.

SUGGESTIONS AND CONCLUSION

With growing number of foreign players, distribution of new banking licenses and the growing popularity of social networking sites like facebook and twitter, seems to be the future of banking. Banks can start maintaining their own blogs, create financial forums, provide video tutorial and video calling and engage in community banking. Banks actually need to provide a platform for interaction among its customers. This will increase the operational efficiency of banks manifold, as customers can directly interact with bank officials or with other customers over the web. There will be no need for customers to visit bank branches. Bank's cost for employing special advisory officers will also be reduced as customers will act as advisers to one another and also to the bank. We can say, virtual banking is the future of banking industry.

The intervention of information technology in banks has transformed the life of human civilization, and has improved not just the operational efficiency of banks but has also made the life of a customer easier. The human civilization which was earlier dependent on money lenders for money and were severely exploited by them can now make the optimum usage of their money. We can conclude, the use of information technology in banks is contributing immensely in the welfare of society as a whole

India's banking sector is set to witness a revolution. The Reserve Bank of India's decision to licence 11 new payments banks could mark the start of a new era of inclusive banking in India.

While the Prime Minister's Jan-Dhan scheme brought millions of people under the umbrella of banking, the primary objective of setting up of payments banks will be to boost financial inclusion by providing small savings accounts and payments & remittance services to migrant labour workforce, low-income households, small businesses, other unorganised sector entities and other users, by enabling high volume-low value transactions in a secured technology-driven environment.

Banks will have to revisit their strategies for attracting current account, savings account (CASA) and term-deposits. Most banks will need to start putting together strategic plans and identify teams to focus on deposit raising, and move from the model of servicing walk-in customers, to aggressively pursuing new customers through innovative bundling, promise of better returns, higher levels of customer service and attractive rewards programs.

REFERENCES

1. Radhe Shyam Rungta (1970). The Rise of Business Corporations in India, 1851-1900. CUP Archive. p. 221. GGKEY: NC1SA25Y2CB. Retrieved 12 January 2015.
2. H. K. Mishra (1991). Famines and Poverty in India. APH Publishing. p. 197. ISBN 978-81-7024-374-8. Retrieved 12 January 2015.
3. Muthiah S (2011). Madras Miscellany. Westland. p. 933. ISBN 978-93-80032-84-9. Retrieved 12 January 2015.
4. "The Advent of Modern Banking in India: 1720 to 1850s". Reserve Bank of India. Retrieved 12 January 2015.
5. "Evolution of SBI". State Bank of India. Retrieved 12 January 2015.
6. "Business Financing: Banks". Government of India. Retrieved 12 January 2015.
7. "Social Controls, the Nationalisation of Banks and the era of bank expansion - 1968 to 1985". Reserve Bank of India. Retrieved 12 January 2015.
8. D. Muraleedharan (2009). Modern Banking: Theory And Practice. PHI Learning Pvt. Ltd. p. 2. ISBN 978-81-203-3655-1. Retrieved 12 January 2015.
9. "Directory of Bank Offices: Certain Concepts". Reserve Bank of India. Retrieved12 January 2015.
10. Fred Gottheil (1 January 2013). Principles of Economics. Cengage Learning. p. 417.ISBN 1-133-96206-8. Retrieved 11 January 2015.
11. Santosh Kumar Das (1980). The economic history of ancient India. Cosmo Publications. pp. 229–. ISBN 978-81-307-0423-4.

Internet Sources:

1. http://economictimes.indiatimes.com/features/the-week-that-was/hdfc-bank-andcenturion-bank-of-punjab-to-merge/articleshow/2808784.cms
2. http://www.icicibank.com/aboutus/history.html
3. http://www.hindu.com/2004/07/27/stories/2004072707340100.htm
4. http://articles.economictimes.indiatimes.com/2010-05-19/news/27574194_1_tayal-bormd-private-sector-banks.

Mobile Banking A Catalyst for Improving Bank Performance

L. V. Sandhya Bala
Assistant Professor, Aurora's PG College.

ABSTRACT

Technology shows an important relevance in banking sector. Banking is one of the largest financial institutions constantly explores the opportunity of technology enabled services to provide better customer experience and convenience. Mobile phone is a common technology device that became part of every individual in the information era. The enhanced prominence of mobile/cell phones provides exciting opportunities for the growth of mobile banking (m-banking).

Mobile Banking is an emerging alternate channel for providing banking services. India is the second largest telecom market in the world, which is having high potential for expanding banking services using mobile. However, mobile banking has not become the choice of millions of people. The main objective of this study is to identify the mindset and analyse the security issues in Mobile banking among the banking customers in India. This paper focuses on m-banking overview, Features & Benefits of Mobile Banking,, Mobile banking/payment practices in Indian and key opportunities of m-banking.

Keywords: *Banking and Mobile Services, Customer, Issues, Mobile Banking, India, M-Banking, Challenges of m-banking in India.*

HISTORY OF MOBILE PHONES IN INDIA

A report of the Cellular Operators Authority of India (CAOI), regarding the entry of cell phones into India, depicts that it was in the year 1992 that telecommunication Sector in India liberalized to bridge the gap through Government spending and to provide additional resources for the nation's telecom target and the private sector was allowed to participate. In the year 1994 India was licensed to provide cellular mobile services granted by the government of India for the Metropolitan cities of Delhi, Mumbai, Kolkata and Chennai. Kolkata became the first metro to have a cellular network in 1995. In 2003 CDMA network was launched. In 2004 Broadband policy was announced. Mobile phone subscribers had reached 100 Million by 2006. In 2008, RBI issued operative guidelines for banks for mobile banking transactions in India. By the year 2009, wireless subscriber base crossed 400 million. At present wireless mobile phone subscribers are 867 Million i.e. it has almost doubled in the last four years.

With the advancement in the operating systems of the mobile phones and mobile technology like 2G, 3G, 4G has brought a significant change in the way of working of mobile banking services providers. Since the introduction of 2G and the subsequently 3G, the demand for mobile phone has increased many folds.

Mobile Banking

Mobile Banking in India, Banks are constantly adopting technology to expand its business and to reach different level of customers. Apart from ATM, Internet banking and other technology enabled services, Mobile Banking is one of the services provided by banks to its customers.

Astonishing growth in telecommunication sector, its penetration including rural population and technology feasibility are the major factors for the introduction of Mobile banking services. Some banks in India are started providing the mobile banking service to their customers that include State Bank of India (SBI), Union Bank of India (UBI), Punjab National Bank (PNB), HDFC, ICICI, Axis Bank, etc.

Factors influencing Mobile Banking Acceptance

Rapid adoption of Smartphones

Over the past several years, consumers have made smartphones their preferred mobile devices. Smartphones allow users to make calls send and receive e-mail and text messages, browse the Web, and perform many other tasks by downloading free or low-cost software applications or "apps." According to published reports, the number of smartphones sold in the United States rose more than 60%, from 26 million in 2008 to 42 million in 2010. Another 25 million consumers are expected to purchase smartphones by 2012, bringing the total number of units in use to 67 million, or 50% of market share.

Shifts in Consumer Preferences

Like automated teller machines "ATMs" and online banking services, smartphones are giving consumers more options. By being able to access account information and perform transactions without requiring access to bank branches, ATMs, or computers, consumers are able to "bank" wherever and whenever they want — and they are learning to expect such convenience.

A Significant Capability Build-out

Most large banks have made substantial investments in mobile banking capabilities, and smaller financial institutions are not far behind. In addition, mobile network carriers, credit card processors, and online personal finance services that allow consumers to aggregate their accounts on a single Web site or app are among the many nonbanks jockeying for position in this fast-growing space.

Product and Service Innovation

The mobile channel allows banks to offer customers features they cannot find online, such as remote check deposit, person-to-person (P2P) payments, and real-time fraud notification. Such features make mobile banking a richer experience and will drive adoption over the next few years.

Features of Mobile Banking

A mobile payment service is acceptable in the market due to the following conditions:

(a) Simplicity and Usability: The m-payment application is friendly with little or no learning curve to the customer. The customer is be able to personalize the application to suit his or her convenience.

(b) Universality: M-payments service provide for transactions between one customer to another customer (C2C), or from a business to a customer (B2C) or between businesses (B2B). The coverage includes domestic, regional and global environments. Payments are possible in terms of both low value micro-payments and high value macro payments.

(c) Interoperability: Development is based on standards and open technologies that allow one implemented system to interact with other systems.

(d) Security, Privacy and Trust: A customer is able to trust a mobile payment application provider that his or her credit or debit card information may not be misused. Secondly, when these transactions become recorded customer's privacy is be lost in the sense that the credit histories and spending patterns of the customer are openly available for public scrutiny. Mobile payments are anonymous as cash transactions. Third, the system is foolproof, resistant to attacks from hackers and terrorists. This may be provided using public key infrastructure security, biometrics and passwords integrated into the mobile payment solution architectures.

(e) Cost: The m-payments are not costlier than existing payment mechanisms to the extent possible. A m-payment solution competes with other modes of payment in terms of cost and convenience.

(f) Speed: The speeds at which m-payments are executed are acceptable by customers and merchants.

(g) Cross border payments: To become widely accepted the m-payment application must be available globally, world-wide.

Pros of Mobile Banking

A very effective way of improving customer service could be to inform customers better. A bank could, through the use of mobile technology

- It utilizes the mobile connectivity of telecom operators and therefore does not require an internet connection.
- With mobile banking, users of mobile phones can perform several financial functions conveniently and securely from their mobile.
- You can check your account balance, review recent transaction, transfer funds, pay bills, locate ATMs, deposit cheques, manage investments, etc.
- Mobile banking is available round the clock 24/7/365, it is easy and convenient and an ideal choice for accessing financial services for most mobile phone owners in the rural areas.
- Mobile banking is said to be even more secure than online/internet banking.

Cons of Mobile Banking

Mobile banking users are at risk of receiving fake SMS messages and scams.

- The loss of a person's mobile device often means that criminals can gain access to your mobile banking PIN and other sensitive information.
- Modern mobile devices like Smartphone and tablets are better suited for mobile banking than old models of mobile phones and devices.
- Regular users of mobile banking over time can accumulate significant charges from their banks.
- In recent years, mobile banking has become quite popular and convenient for many people.

Opportunities for Revenue Growth

Banks can realize operational efficiencies by adopting an integrated channel strategy that includes mobile banking. The more transactions that banks can drive to mobile phones, the greater the possibility that they can close poorly performing branches and increase operating efficiencies by shifting the focus of branch employees from transactions to more advisory-type services that will lead to greater sales or cross-selling rates.

Mobile banking offers banks several opportunities for increasing revenues.

These include monetizing the value of customer analytics, delivering greater real-time access to products and services, and conducting targeted marketing campaigns based upon the knowledge of consumer preferences that banks collect.

Expanding distribution and coverage models: Mobile banking gives banks the potential to expand beyond their geographical footprint as well as ability to cross-sell and up-sell products to existing customers. Banks that harness these additional mobile financial services capabilities can see a profound impact on the nature of the banking relationship.

Monetizing the value of customer analytics unlike supermarkets, department stores, and other businesses that see only one dimension of consumers' spending habits, banks have a broader view of what their customers buy and where they like to shop. This puts banks in a specific position to develop a new line of business focused on bundling data analytics for retailers and other entities vying for customer intelligence — while maintaining the privacy of individual customers' information. Merchants could employ such aggregated information to target customers more effectively than they might through other means. In addition, banks could use this knowledge of their core customers to strengthen their own abilities to acquire new customers, cross-sell existing customers, improve decisioning capabilities, and provide better customer service — resulting in significant value streams for banks. Delivering greater real-time access to products and services Mobile banking could provide bank customers with the ability to compare options at time and place of purchase. At the same time, banks could offer these shoppers complementary services, such as financing or leasing options, insurance quotes (through partnerships), and more.

Offering discounts and purchasing incentives to bank customers By establishing relationships with manufacturers and retailers that could offer bank customers discounts while they research product options at the point of sale, banks can position their mobile channel as something more than just a convenient way to pay. $ Opportunities for revenue growth Mobile banking.

A catalyst for improving bank performance.

Conducting targeted marketing campaigns.

Similarly, banks could conduct a variety of targeted marketing campaigns to customers who use mobile banking. For example, banks could pinpoint shoppers' physical locations to make relevant offers to their customers, such as offering them temporary line increases. In addition, banks could leverage the mobile banking interface as a real-time, tailored advertising engine by using behavioral analytics they compile to develop campaigns tailored to customers' shopping preferences. Additionally, banks might be able to offer their customers "smart" coupons while customers are in stores shopping for a flat-screen television or digital camera. The coupons would come from alliances banks form with the products' manufacturers and/or retailers — and banks would receive a fee for each coupon used.

Key Challenges in Mobile Banking

Customer experience and awareness Despite the popularity of mobile banking among younger market segments, many customers are unaware of the powerful value proposition that mobile channel affords. Banks need to educate their customers to the benefits of mobile banking and make sure they differentiate themselves from other competiting solutions, such as account aggregation services by providing advanced features.

Platform scalability Banks and third-party developers need to create software applications that support multiple mobile operating systems (including iOS4, Android, BlackBerry OS, Windows Mobile, and Symbian), multiple form factors (smartphones, iPads, and tablet computers), multiple telecommunication standards, and can be easily upgraded to support new features and advancements.

Complex integration and partnership model: To achieve operational efficiencies and realize the full growth potential, banks will need to integrate their existing bank platforms — including core banking, customer relationship management, and payment hubs with mobile banking solutions. Banks will also need to manage a multitude of partners, such as telecommunication providers, social media outlets, data analytics providers, retailers, payment networks, mobile device manufacturers, and many other stakeholders. Banks will also need to foster retail relationships to push mobile payment solutions to merchants and educate them on the benefits of installing terminals at the point of sale to enable customers to pay with mobile phones equipped with near field communications chips.

Increasing pressure from competitors: Differentiating capabilities from other banks and service providers is increasingly difficult. However, early adopters of mobile banking may still gain a competitive advantage in attracting new customers. Moreover, banks will face growing competition in the coming years from telecommunications providers and other nonblank payment processors offering services that compete with mobile banking. Consequently, banks should take steps to differentiate mobile banking from alternative services so that consumers regard banks' offerings as superior.

CONCLUSION

Banks should create awareness about the mobile banking services through Advertisements, Pamphlets, Demo Fares, Campaigning etc. so that the customer feel informed and it may create interest among them. Footfalls at ATM centres is likely to be very high, the campaigns may be carried out at these locations to attract more customers towards these services.

- Trust is also an important point of concern. Trust between the customers and the service provider is very important, without security and privacy users will not use mobile for financial transactions.
- Perceived ease of use and perceived usefulness are found to be important factors to influence the consumer intention to adopt mobile banking. Hence, the main attention of

management should be focused on the development of usefulness of system, trust building and cost reduction.

- Perceived cost is also an important factor; therefore, this study suggests that the creative promotional and pricing strategies, including cost reduction should be implemented to attract more price-conscious customers.
- It is also found that customers will adopt mobile banking if they find it easy to use and understand.

REFERENCES

1. Challenges in Mobile Banking In India: A Customers' Perspective.
   www.bankrate.com/finance/banking/finding-best-mobilebanking.aspx
   http://www.thejakartapost.com/news/2012/05/11/commonwealthbank-tapping-growing-mobile-banking-market.
   html www.palgrave-journals.com/jbr/journal/v11/n2/abs/jbr2009 16a.
   html http://warse.org/pdfs/ijatcse03122012.pdf
   http://www.trai.gov.in
2. Banzal S. Mobile Banking & M–Commerce and Related issues.
   www. public.webfoundation.org/……. / 25, Mobile_banking_M-commerce_15.03.pdf, 2010.
3. Barnes, S. J., and Corbitt, B. Mobile Banking: Concept and Potential, International Journal of Mobile Communications, 1 (3), pp. 273-288, 2003.
   http://www.rbi.org.in
   http://www.sbi.co.in
   http://en.wikipedia.org
   www.iiste.org
   http://www.trai.gov.in/WriteReadData/WhatsNew/Documents/Mont
   hly_press_release_February_2013_16april2013.pdf
   http://www.newfreeppt.com/banking/mobile-banking-ppt-freedownload

Digital Challenges to Retail Banking

R. Sushma
Associate Professor, Aurora's PG College.

ABSTRACT

Digital banking is not just more hype about the next big thing in the market. It is a necessary part of every bank's agenda as a way to overcome outdated approaches and mismanaged client relationships However, the steps taken so far—a combination of testing new offerings and following other market leaders—are just the beginning. True transformation will require deep, extensive change and letting go of old habits such as offering complex products and requiring clients to go to branches. It will also mean cleaning up legacy processes and technologies within the organization. outdated structures will need to be dismantled to create a new, environment.Smartphone ownership has reached a tipping point in the India, and two-thirds of financial institution's banking customers now own some form of a Smartphone. Consequently, mobile banking has become popular. With the consequent convergence of the online and mobile banking channels under way, the era of digital banking, which includes the best of both channels, has arrived. Banking customers now have a wide variety of choices as to how, when, and where to bank, including ways to access their accounts via computer, mobile phone, or tablet. This paper Studies major issues & challenges in the growth of the Digital retail banking sector.

INTRODUCTION

Digital banking means more than just going paperless. Leading players are offering a new and improved customer experience and delivering faster and more efficient services. Digital banking has been around for years, with many experts calling it the cure for the shattered banking industry after the recent financial crisis. And they are probably right.

However, banks are not known for being fast movers. Customers are still waiting for this new banking experience, touted as a revolutionary transformation that will bring many new features, including anytime and anywhere banking, ultra-fast response times, and omnipresent advisors. So why don't banks just pick up the pace? Because it requires more fundamental changes than expected at first sight.

The industry has been in a comfortable position for decades with low customer turnover, almost no regional competition, good personal relationships and trust as selling points, and not much intervention from regulators. Staying ahead of the curve was easy, and there was no pressure to change.

Now, new competitors from adjacent industries and financial technology startups are flooding the market with innovative, technology-driven deviations from the traditional banking model. And to add insult to injury, customers' attitudes have fundamentally changed. They are making decisions much faster and have access to a plethora of offers, leaving financial institutions struggling for customer loyalty.

The challenges in this fast-moving, demanding digital world are tough. The issue is not finding new digital solutions; the issue is the industry's long-standing history of not keeping in shape. The best running shoes will not make up for poor fitness, and banks are just warming up for the road ahead.

Retail Banking Priorities to Focus on

- **Moving from paper to digital**. In many banks and regions, paper still dominates. Capgemini Consulting reminds us in the earlier mentioned paper that back-office operations are still overly reliant on paper and manual processes.
- **Making sure the customer experience is indeed looked upon as a connected journey**, taking into account the cost of NOT offering the connected conditions for an overall customer experience journey approach by identifying all back-office bottlenecks and removing them.
- **Reducing errors regarding data and information**. This goes hand in hand with the move from paper to digital. And it's not just about, for instance, loan applications. In several regions making payments still happens using paper too, to give just one example.
- **Creating the conditions to be more agile**, at the very least from a customer perspective, digitalization should not only offer a journey-based customer experience but enable customers to "do" things themselves, for instance regarding "their" data, too. Also look at the customer onboarding process.
- **Mapping and improving the processes, applications and functions that are closely connected with overall goals** such as cost reduction and customer experience optimization. No process stands alone, no optimization effort stands alone.
- **Moving from disconnected information silos, manual processes and (expensive) legacy IT systems to connected systems**, all the way from data capturing to intelligent information management, analysis, better customer service and beyond. This doesn't have to happen overnight as McKinsey reminds us in the mentioned article. Maximizing the use of existing technology, applying lightweight technology interventions and focusing on areas where the best gains can be made, are just a few examples of a more staged approach. Digital transformation is not a holy grail: it also enables retail banks to provide the personal touch consumers still want in the areas it makes most sense by automating and optimizing all the rest.
- **Doing more with the increasing volume of data** and better connect workflows, information input, information silos and processes. Putting the right data at work for the right reasons starts with capturing and combining them the right way.
- **Better aligning IT with the information aspect and the business goals**. Reducing manual labor and processes, for instance, by better and automated data capturing and usage, reduces costs and errors so there is more room for innovation and transformation (and personal interaction where it's desired).
- **Involving the offline dimension.** The role of the retail bank branch is changing. Digital technologies become increasingly important in the physical environment (and vice versa). Although many experiments have been conducted and several retail bank branches underwent changes, the real innovative changes are yet to come.
- **Preparing tomorrow today**. Finally, consumers have been increasingly executing tasks themselves that once were executed by banks (as is illustrated in the graphic and that trend

will continue as the so-called empowered consumer wants to have more control in specific areas (and a more personal approach in others). The question is whether the (back-office) foundations to respond to these shifts and even pro-spond by enabling execution by the customer, while maintaining a relationship and offering more choice and greater customer experiences, will be there once you need them. Information management is essential in that regard.

Five Trends in Retail Banking

Five major trends are redefining the way banks inform and interact, transfer money, advise and sell, and shape the competition.

Trend 1. Inform and Interact: Mobile Web meets Social Media

The Internet changed the way people and companies interact, but the omnipresent mobile Web is revolutionizing those interactions. Online communication is no longer a one-way - street where industries broadcast their products to customers who may or may not buy them. As more customers use online and mobile channels, the challenge for a broad range of industries, including banks, is to find clever ways to get in touch with their customers

The availability of mobile broadband Internet and smart devices and the broad use of Web applications can be used to incorporate customers deep into the value chain. Smartphones and tablets have merged computing power with mobile broadband data connections. Many more ideas and applications are emerging.

Successful companies offer customers access to information anywhere at any time. In addition, listening to the opinion of the crowd and inviting customers into product development and services is standard operating procedure. However, naively offering everything to everyone causes information overflow. Clever techniques to analyze information to offer the right product at the right time are the keys to success. More companies are using sentiment analysis to cross-sell products more effectively, to track customer opinions, and to monitor employee behaviors. However, companies must avoid a Big Brother image if they want to build or maintain a trusting relationship with their customers.

All in all, acceleration, digitization, and increased mobility have created a hyper-connected world on the move. Online communication and online content dominate other media, including television, and nearly every industry is affected.

A generation ago, the ability to broadcast a message to a large number of people was restricted to a few people communicating via radio or TV. The levers and hurdles to share experiences were easy to control. The rise of social media such as YouTube, Facebook, and Twitter changed this in two major ways: First, everybody today has the ability to broadcast a message to millions of people around the world. Second, the crowd can immediately respond. Even spontaneous annoyances shared on Twitter or Facebook are instantly available to hundreds or thousands of people. More than simple entertainment, social media is a powerful tool, as seen by the 2011 Arab Spring civil uprisings.

Social media augments communication between companies and their customers. The crowd can immediately research and compare products and exchange experiences with industries, companies, their employees, products, and services. Indeed, 65 percent of users access their preferred online social network daily, and the average time spent on a social network is three to four hours, according to TNS Infratest. Equally important, by readily sharing nearly everything about themselves in online chats and blogs, the crowd including current and future financial consumers—provides an enormous amount of personal information, offering deep insights into customer behaviors, sentiments, and needs, and opens up new possibilities for using customer intelligence.

Trend 2. Transfer Money: Payments Reloaded

Digitization, mobility, changing lifestyles, and e-commerce are the impetus for new approaches in payments and account management. The rise of new methods and the penetration of Internet connected mobile devices with innovative capabilities such as near field communication (NFC), which allow users to quickly exchange text, images, URLs or other data between devices, or quick response codes (QR code), which can store much more data than a standard barcode and can quickly transfer this information into a mobile device have set the basis for dramatic changes in online and offline payments. A variety of small companies demonstrated innovativeness and profitability with solutions that threaten an important aspect of retail banking: traditional money transfer. Quick and safe electronic and mobile payment methods, combined with electronic wallets and innovative account management tools, are challenging the role and dominance of cash, credit, and debit cards. A recent study by ECC finds that 35 percent of consumers would like to use their mobile device as an e-wallet.

One could argue that profit margins are likely to stay low despite the fact that some customers are willing to pay fees for convenience. Although competitors such as PayPal demonstrate that e- and m-payments when done right can be highly profitable, income is not the only thing at risk. Losing e- and m-payments means losing regular customer contact and a glimpse into spending behaviors. In particular with mobile payments, a dramatic increase in the amount of data revealing payment behavior for purchased products, favored locations, method, and frequency offers new possibilities. Maintaining open access to payment data, and intelligently distilling and using it, will be key challenges for the financial services industry.

Trend 3. Advise: Segregation of Customer Groups

New technology and social media have opened up new ways for people to get in touch, be it with another person, a digital assistant such as Apple's Siri, or a shop to buy everyday goods. From a company perspective, there is a need to provide online and, even more importantly, mobile channels to interact with customers. Unfortunately, there is even more to come. Customers can be separated into two major groups. First, there is Generation Facebook, which consists of heavy social media and mobile Web users (digital natives) and the so-called digital migrants, who are older but open-minded adopters. This group is relatively weak concerning their financial possibilities—for now. Second, there is the large, financially strong, and attractive group of elderly people with many digital deniers who require different approaches.

This picture is valid for today and, for demographic reasons, for the near future. However, for nearly every industry, the more powerful and much more interesting group in the longrun is Generation Facebook and the digital migrants. Digital deniers will diminish over time, while the tech-oriented digital natives are likely to challenge and influence a range of industries with their needs, wishes, expectations, and behaviors.

This will force banks to reconsider their customer relationship approaches and the ways to interact with customers. Because some new competitors are better prepared for this change, their approaches might heavily cross existing business models and challenge established players for customers.

Trend 4. Sell: the Point-of-sale (r)evolution

The question of where and how to sell products and services will be asked again and again triggered by customer mobility, new possibilities of customer interaction through Web 2.0 applications, the ever-increasing migration of transactions into the Web, peer-to-peer approaches, and the capabilities of mobile devices. For the retail banking industry, this threatens the attractiveness of the traditional branch and its value for customers and banks. Our findings suggest that nearly every service offered by a branch today could be dispensable tomorrow, replaced by innovative technology or made available online. For instance, today, 58 percent of customers visit a bank to withdraw money from the ATM, 24 percent to view their account, with the remaining visits for personal contact (7 percent), to perform transactions (9 percent), or for other reasons (2 percent).

Most industries, including retail banking, are under pressure to reinvent the point of sale regarding setup, form, appearance, location, and product range to attract customers to visit them and provide an adequate purpose.

The point-of-sale revolution will heavily affect customer relationship management, the integration of technological innovations into multi-channel management, and the role and arrangement of traditional retail banking branches.

Trend 5. Drive Competition: a Changing Playing Field

The last trend shifts the focus from the relationship between the consumer and the provider toward competition in the industry. Technological developments and changes in customer behavior and expectations along with failures and other priorities of traditional players set the ground for new approaches in many industries. An increasing number of new players, be it start-ups or established players from the non-banking field, bustle around in several aspects of retail banking. The days in which banks were the only provider for banking products are over.

In today's environment, even start-ups are trustworthy enough for customers to commit their money. A variety of new players now compete to become part of customers' financial habits. This is massively transforming the industry because new players are often more innovative and flexible. Announcements by large Internet companies such as Google, Amazon, and Facebook engaging in payment or account management will shake the financial services industry the customer-facing side. Very few players have fundamentally changed their internal organizations or governance principles. Most customers still belong to branches. Consolidated IT systems have helped to reduce cost but do not cater to fast time-to-market and processing.

In addition to this mismatch for banks, the pace of change is increasing: New technology-savvy companies are flooding the market with innovative offers for financial services, customers are becoming more confident in using the full range of e-commerce offerings, and even regulators are reshaping long-established procedures to adapt to new concepts. Some regions are more advanced than others, and the timing of change is hard to predict, but banks are well advised in already preparing today.

Digitization will become more disruptive as value chains break apart, especially around customer interaction, product configuration and transaction processing. Moving forward will require flexible processes, new revenue models armed with new products and services, and sweeping cultural changes.

Blockchain and the Future of Banking

Meher Pradeep[1] and Thandava Krishna[2]
[1]Vice President BNP Parishas.
[2]Knowledge Engineer, Founder of Startup Company.

INTRODUCTION

The top buzzword echoing around the finance world this year is the blockchain. It was originally dismissed as merely the foundation of yet another fad propagated by hobbyist nerds dabbling in cryptography. Later it was reviled for its inextricable association with infamous cryptocoin markets and the fallout of most of their implosions.

It has since grown out of its awkward initial growth phase and shaken off previous dubious associations to emerge as a serious technology that could potentially form the backbone of the entire financial sector. Trade pundits and technologists have gone on to speculate its possibilities comparing its disruptive power to what e-mail did to the postal system and VoIP did to the telephone companies.

The blockchain that people talk about today is serious enough about its aspirations and focused enough on its opportunities to have attracted over 300 firms to work on products and offerings for the financial sector, while drawing over 24 of the world's biggest banks to form a consortium to implement the technology into their operations. Many giant banks are even independent steps to internally rollout the technology in various parts of their operations.

It has got technology and consulting firms like IBM, PWC, Accenture rushing to advise clients on the potential and startups like R3 rounding up funding and participation from some of the world's biggest banks like JPMorgan, UBS, Barclays, Citibank, HSBC and Bank of America for its CEV platform. The banking industry wants to get a headstart over dozens of startups that have been eating into many consumer facing offerings of the industry like ecommerce, payments, settlements, deposits, loans, etc. The adoption of a blockchain platform industry wide gives them the best chance to get ahead of nimble startups that seem to be able to turn their offerings on a dime, while the financial behemoths play catchup and shed their archaic processes.

What is the Blockchain?

The blockchain in simple terms is a distributed ledger for transactions that allows for the maintenance of a common central ledger that can then be branched out into autonomous nodes each capable of existing as an independent network while simultaneously feeding into the overarching central ledger. The technology allows for multiple branches and forks.

All the participants in the network can have a copy of all the transactions within the network, and validation of every transaction is performed at a network-level by all the participants, ensuring no single party repudiates a transaction. It also allows for traceability of the flow of money in the entire chain.

This allows for the ability to conduct transactions between anonymous parties or participants in any branch/node of the network seamlessly with any other participant/node of the overall network without any mediation/middlemen while maintaining the secrecy and autonomous hierarchy of their respective nodes/branches. It also allows automatic conclusion of non-repudiable transactions without any manual intervention or oversight.

What are its Advantages?

The blockchain has advantages at many levels, since it is a backbone technology that allows for multiple layers within its architecture and the possibility for myriad interactions between the various layers and nodes on the platform. The most common way of looking at its benefits would be to look at its functions from a micro to macro level.

The lowest form of benefits are at an intra-bank level, wherein the benefits include inter-account settlements like funds transfer, cheque clearance, bill payments, e-commerce transactions, etc. without the intervention of bank staff. Establishment of a blockchain application programming interface (API) can help 3rd party app developers build services and offerings that leverage the blockchain and provide customer-friendly interfaces and experiences with extremely reduced settlement timelines.

These translate into benefits like account management, loan management, e-payments for the customer through an interface of their preference. It also translates into streamlining benefits for the bank through automated tie-ins of their various service lines like credit cards, loans, insurance, mutual funds into customer accounts, reducing turnaround time for money transfers between subsidiary and affiliate entities freeing up precious working capital.

The next level of benefits are at an inter-bank level, wherein the benefits include inter-bank settlements like funds transfer, cheque clearance, merchant interactions, all of which currently depend on complicated intermediary systems that conduct the clearance work. The establishment of an API will permit 3rd party app developers to deploy nationwide apps that allow seamless transactions irrespective of the underlying bank.

These translate into benefits for commerce through near-instantaneous settlements drastically reducing collection timelines and costs due to the redundancy of costly and time-intensive intermediary systems. It also reduces costs for banks due to the lack of intermediation costs and near real-time position awareness as opposed to current day-end position clearances that is the standard world over.

The next level of benefits are at an international level, wherein the benefits include cross-currency transactions, international trade, investment management, money market operations, all of which currently are very commission-heavy, and riddled with middlemen like Visa and Mastercard. The lack of middlemen for transaction and foreign exchange negotiation leaves the banks with billions of dollars in savings.

International transactions are conducted either through outdated standards like SWIFT or through costly middlemen like Visa/Mastercard causing inordinate delays or unnecessary commissions for a redundant task that can be technologically accomplished at almost no cost or time. The ability to auto-negotiate transactions in multiple currencies would open the gates for investment options in multiple markets in real time allowing the participation in global money markets of all kinds by banks improving not only their working capital, but also their return on capital employed, greatly increasing their profitability.

These benefits would also extend to their ability to seamlessly get access to world markets for deposits as well as for loans greatly enhancing their reach and risk dilution. Banks that are able to tailor products for international trade through the use of this platform will be the biggest beneficiaries in terms of portfolio diversification and consolidation of their international operations through the streamlining of overlapping functions and systems. This would also open the doors for consolidation of global financial systems through strategic partnerships between banks globally, allowing for the best allocation of capital.

What are the other Benefits?

The benefits also extend to stakeholders like the governments of most countries in the blockchain network. Countries can benefit from better foreign exchange controls and management, due to the permissions and restrictions options available for specific branches and nodes of the blockchain network. Sovereign governments would have a comprehensive picture of the forex reserves in near real-time along with historic trends allowing for better forex management and the implementation of necessary controls.

It also provides the government with transparency in terms of the flow of money in the economy. Governments would have access to the availability and distribution of money in the financial systems and their availability in the banking channels at a micro-level allowing for better regulation and easier deployment to needy areas through analytics-based policy implementation. This would also be one of the most effective tools of preventing tax evasion.

The transparency afforded by the blockchain technology also allows for the combating of counterfeiting of currency that is estimated to be a trillion dollar industry globally. The implementation of blockchain prevents the rampant spread of counterfeit currency through extremely stringent controls in and out of the organized money sector, greatly constricting the flow and spread of counterfeit money.

What are its Limitations?

One of the biggest concerns currently facing blockchain as a technology is the size of the blockchain itself. The record of a few million transactions currently take up many gigabytes of storage. The banking industry runs through millions of transactions every day, making it unfeasible in its current form to support the storage requirements given present hardware limits. Storage needs to be compacted to a factor of thousand from current standards in order to effectively handle transaction for even a decade.

Another huge constraint holding back immediate widespread commercial adoption of the blockchain as the financial backbone of the world is the current transaction confirmation timeline. It presently takes anywhere between a couple of minutes to around half-an-hour to confirm a transaction and propagate it through the network. This needs to be brought down to the millisecond level in order for the blockchain to have any chance of adoption in this day of high frequency trading.

Another stumbling block would be the lack of standards for the banking industry with regard to blockchain. There are currently over a dozen parallel attempts at rolling out a blockchain-based product for various products of banks, some developed by a consortium of leading banks, some developed by regional bank associations, many being developed by individual banks. This would lead to the same incompatibilities that disparate core banking solutions have currently wrought on the banking industry creating the need for burdensome middlemen to enable their financial systems to talk to each other. As with numerous format/platform wars common in the technology, if most major banks put their weight behind one common standard early in the day, it would go a long way in hastening the commercial adoption of blockchain as the next revolution in banking.

CONCLUSION

Banks are exploring ways to convert to a more.

REFERENCES

1. Blockchain: Blueprint for a New Economy, *Melanie Swan*, O'Reilly Media.
2. Mastering Bitcoin: Unlocking Digital Cryptocurrencies, *Andreas M. Antonopoulos*, O'Reilly Media.
3. The Age of Cryptocurrency: How Bitcoin and Digital Money Are Challenging the Global Economic Order, *Paul Vigna,* St. Martin's Press.
4. Bit by Bit: How P2P Is Freeing the World, *Jeffrey Tucker,* Liberty.
5. Decentralized Applications: Harnessing Bitcoin's Block chain Technology, *Siraj Raval,*O'Reilly Media.
6. Block chain Revolution: How the Technology Behind Bitcoin Is Changing Money, Business, and the World, *Don Tapscott, Alex Tapscott,* Portfolio.
7. Great Chain of Numbers: A Guide to Smart Contracts, Smart Property and Trustless Asset Management, *Tim Swanson,* Amazon Digital Services.

Expected Trends in the Indian Banking Sector

Prof. A. Sreeram[1] and G. Siva Krishna[2]
[1]Professor, Econometrics and Finance, GITAM University.
[2]Research Scholar, School of Economics University of Hyderabad.

ABSTRACT

At the beginning of the 21st century, the biggest banks in the industrial world have become complex financial organizations that offer a wide variety of services to international markets and control billions of dollars in cash and assets. With the advent of new technology, banks are working to identify new business niches, to develop customized services, to implement innovative strategies and to capture new market opportunities. Further, globalization, consolidation, deregulation and diversification of the financial industry, the banking sector became even more complex. Today, we are having a fairly well developed banking system with different classes of banks – public sector banks, foreign banks, private sector banks – both old and new generation, regional rural banks and co-operative banks with the Reserve Bank of India as the fountain Head of the system. The Indian Banking sector characterized with unprecedented growth and diversification is poised to see significant changes in the immediate future. Reserve Bank of India (RBI) & Government of India are taking several steps to strengthen and liberalise the Indian financial system. These steps are expected to transform and boost the Indian banking sector further. The present article seeks to analyse the past trends, current status of financial innovation, opportunists available with banking sector and also forecast future projections.

INDIAN BANKING SECTOR: SNAPSHOT

As per the Reserve Bank of India (RBI), India's banking sector is sufficiently capitalised and well-regulated. The financial and economic conditions in the country are far superior to any other country in the world. Credit, market and liquidity risk studies suggest that Indian banks are generally resilient and have withstood the global downturn well.

The Indian banking system consists of 157 domestic banks out of which 26 public sector banks, 20 private sector banks, 43 foreign banks, 64 regional rural banks, and 4 local area banks in addition to cooperative banks and credit institutions. Public-sector banks control nearly 80 percent of the market, thereby leaving comparatively much smaller shares for its private peers. Standard & Poor's estimates that credit growth in India's banking sector would improve to 12-13 per cent in FY16 from less than 10 per cent in the second half of FY14. Indian banking sector credit growth has grown at a healthy pace. Credit off-take has been surging ahead over the past decade, aided by strong economic growth, rising disposable incomes, increasing consumerism and easier access to credit.

Innovations in Banking Sector

Financial innovation is key to survival of banks in contemporary banking environment. The importance of financial innovation is widely recognized. Many leading scholars, including Miller (1986) and Merton (1992), have highlighted the importance of products and services in the financial arena. Right from the beginning stage of financial modernization innovations have been playing major roles in curtailing financial exclusions and improving the ways banking services are rendered to people. Financial innovation is one of the commonly used banking terminologies. It has been used to describe any change in the scale, scope and delivery of financial services. The various innovations in banking and financial sector are ECS, RTGS, EFT, NEFT, ATM, Retail Banking, Debit & Credit cards, free advisory services, payments of utility bills, fund transfers, internet banking, telephone banking, mobile banking, selling insurance products, issue of free cheque books, travel cheques and many more value added services. While banks are striving to strengthen customer relationship and move towards 'relationship banking,' customers are increasingly moving away from the confines of traditional branch banking and seeking the convenience of remote electronic banking. Information technology and the communications networking systems have revolutionaries the working of banks and financial entities all over the world.

Expected Future Trends

Increased Thrust on Financial Inclusion

Financial Inclusion implies bringing low income and disadvantaged groups under the coverage of banking by providing them access to banking services at affordable cost. Nationalisation has increased financial inclusion substantially. Liberalisation has further boosted the process. Regional Rural Banks (RRBs) are important institutions that extend rural credit to farmers, artisans & rural traders. In addition to RRBs, Non Banking Financial Companies (NBFCs) have also emerged as a key supplement. Though substantial ground has been covered, much more still needs to be done to further financial inclusion. As per a current estimate nearly 40% of our population has no access to financial services.

However the best part is that banks have started viewing financial inclusion more as a significant opportunity than as a mandatory obligation. They are now devising strategies to cater to these vast low income customers. These low income customers, by their sheer volumes, make up for the lower revenues per person. Hence they are popularly called as bottom of the pyramid customers. Bankers have now started thinking of low cost models that will serve the local needs of these customers. RBI also has recognised that inclusive growth is a top priority to ensure that the benefits trickle down to all the sections of the society. This is clear from the recently announced guidelines for additional licenses to private players. One of the important conditions is that the new banks should have at least 25% branches in unbanked rural centres. RBI has permitted the **use of Business Correspondents (BCs) to further increase financial inclusion.**

It needs to be noted that including vast sections of the population into the ambit of banking services will lead to various positive consequences and will provide a further fillip to the India growth story. It is further noted that as of November 11, 2015, 192.1 million accounts had been opened under Pradhan Mantri Jan Dhan Yojna (PMJDY) and 165.1 million RuPay debit cards were issued. These new accounts have mustered deposits worth Rs 26,819 crore (US$ 4 billion).

Increased use of Technology

Economic reforms have given a facelift to Indian banking. The banking culture itself has considerably changed. Technological evolution increased automation of banking operations which enabled off-site banking through ATMs, internet banking, payment of utilities through banks, travel reservation through banks, etc. Core Banking Solution (CBS) implemented in many banks has enabled anywhere, anytime banking. This trend is further expected to continue. Specifically mobiles are expected to be increasingly used. Though European banks started to offer mobile banking from 1999 onwards, in India it was only in 2008, 39 banks were permitted to introduce mobile banking. Over the past couple of years, there has been huge growth registered in the number of transactions done through mobile devices. As per RBI, there were 49 banks with a customer base of about 13 mn offering mobile banking services as at the end of Mar 2012. During FY12, around 25.6 mn mobile banking transactions valued at Rs. 18.2 bn were transacted, recording a growth of 198%. As per an estimate of Price Waterhouse Coopers (PWC) once RBI permits full mobile banking services, mobile banking transactions are expected to be over 340 million by 2015. Further PWC estimates that this will lead to a cost saving of Rs. 11 billion. In addition, use of biometric devices (the UID initiative) is expected to provide a further fillip to the Indian Banking sector. This rapid growth is driven by availability of 3G/4G network, increasing number of smart phones and several telecom companies offering economical data usage packages. In the near term, it is expected to emerge as one of the most preferred medium for banking transactions.

Increased Size of the Top Indian Banks due to Growth & Consolidation

India, one of the fastest emerging economies, is expected to continue to witness a very high demand potential fuelled by the increasing educated working class, as also the growing future income levels. In light of the same an efficient financial system is one of the key imperatives. Indian policy makers have recommended consolidation to increase efficiency. This is because it is felt that large banks will be able to exploit the economies of scale better than smaller banks. Large banks can also widen the scope of the financial services activity. Banks need a large and healthy balance sheet to fund large transactions.

Consistent high growth in the Indian economy during the last 4-5 years has led to quantum increase in capital requirements of various corporate. The Banking Sector is one of the primary sources of capital. As per the prudential norms set by RBI, banks can extend credit to various categories of borrowers up to a certain percentage on their net-owned funds. It poses constraints on the net credit that can be extended upon the size of capital. A higher capital base, which could be possible through consolidation, will thus allow higher lending to borrowers. Other perceived benefits from Consolidation are increased efficiency and profitability. As per economic theories, creation of large firms due to Mergers and Acquisitions (M & A) will lead to significant advantages from lower average production cost through economies of scale and scope etc. It is expected that the Indian Banking sector will witness consolidation through M & A to meet challenges and exploit synergistic benefits. Currently SBI is consolidating its subsidiaries with itself.

Increase Online Sales: There will be no bank in coming days that can ignore the online channel as a sales channel. The portal (and microsite network) is responsible for customer acquisitions, while internet banking and mobile banking are great channels for cross sales. Internet bank is the ideal channel for sales and communication purposes: customers are fully identified here, and they visit this channel on a regular basis. Selling online however, is not only an issue for the electronic channel: this affects all areas in the bank from the product development to the internal processes. Successful acquisition requires streamlined customer origination processes (including branchless account opening) while successful cross-sales depends on personal and pre-approved (if applicable) offerings.

Data Management: Both to increase efficiency and ensure regulatory compliance, banks need better methods of gathering and reporting data. Most banks struggle with multiple back-office systems and siloed information. To address these issues in earnest, there will be a large investment in new and improved business process management tools in the year ahead, experts say. Data integration will help banks obtain a more accurate view of their customers,. Marketers often talk about breaking through data silos to look at data holistically and gain a more complete view of consumers' habits, and now banks will look to do the same. These big trends, and the move for strategic cost reduction, map very clearly to bigger Business Process Management investment.

CONCLUSION

In the past few years, the Indian banking sector has completely transformed. The banks are facing many challenges and many opportunities are available with the banks. Many financial innovations like ATMs, credit cards, RTGS, debit cards, mobile banking etc. have completely changed the face of Indian banking. But still there is a need to have more innovative solutions so that the challenges can be solved and opportunities can be availed efficiently by the banks. Financial innovation will continue to play an important role in promoting global growth, especially in emerging markets and developing countries. For growth to be truly inclusive, banking must reach out to many more people than it reaches now. Technological changes in the form of Information Technology and mobile banking greatly expand the potential reach of the banking system. Developing and under-developed economies all over the globe are looking for new modes and means to cub poverty and include their citizens in the financial system. One of the important factors that would help achieve this vision is to ensure total financial inclusion. Where in the role of banks is crucial.

REFERENCES

1. Chavan, J. (2013). Internet banking- Benefits and challenges in an emerging economy. International Journal of Research in Business Management.
2. Dr. Kanhaiya Singh, Dr. U. S. Pandey, Priya Gupta," TECHNOLOGICAL INNOVATION IN INDIAN BANKING SECTOR – USE OF IT PRODUCTS" (IJMS) 2011, Vol. No.II, Issue II, January-June 2011.
3. Dr. K.C. Biswal, "Emerging Trends in the Indian Banking Sector- Challenges & Opportunities" International Journal of Advances in Arts, Sciences and Engineering Volume 3 Issue 6 jan 2015.
4. K.S.Venkateswara Kumar," Innovations in Modern Banking and Innovative Financial Inclusion – Issues and Challenges" CLEAR IJRCM- Vol-01: Issue: 02-Jul-Dec-2011.
5. Kulkarni R V (2000), "Changing Face of Banking from Brick and Mortar Banking to E - Banking".
6. Miss. Shraddha Deoda Indian Banking Industry: Challenges and Opportunities" (JBREM) Volume 1, Issue 1.
7. Shastri, R.V. (2003), "Recent Trends in Banking Industry: IT Emergence", Analyst,(March).

8. Shilpi Khandelwal. (2007). Megatrends 2010: E banking Innovations: Trends in India Volume 3, Issue 3, September- December (2012), pp. 200-215 © IAEME.
9. http://simplifiedfinance.net/home/index.php?option=com_content&view=article&id=214:future-trends-expected-in-the-banking-sector&catid=36:articles&Itemid=72.
10. https://www.iisd.org/business/banking/sus_trends.aspx
11. http://www.ibef.org/industry/banking-india.aspx#sthash.UPpoIKdo.dpuf
12. https://www.dnb.co.in/News_Press.asp?pid=1179

www.ingramcontent.com/pod-product-compliance
Lightning Source LLC
Chambersburg PA
CBHW080935240926
51849CB00004BA/465
9789352301294